CHINA–INDIA

PROCEEDINGS OF THE BRITISH ACADEMY • 193

CHINA–INDIA
Pathways of Economic and Social Development

Edited by

DELIA DAVIN

and BARBARA HARRISS-WHITE

Published for THE BRITISH ACADEMY
by OXFORD UNIVERSITY PRESS

Oxford University Press, Great Clarendon Street, Oxford OX2 6DP

© The British Academy 2014
Database right The British Academy (maker)

First edition published in 2014

British Library Cataloguing in Publication Data
Data available

Library of Congress Cataloging in Publication Data
Data available

Typeset by Ellipsis Digital Limited, Glasgow
Printed in Great Britain by
TJ International, Padstow, Cornwall

ISBN 978-0-19-726567-3
ISSN 0068-1202

Contents

List of Figures   vii

List of Tables   ix

Notes on the Contributors   xi

Acknowledgements   xv

Map of China   xvi

Map of India   xvii

Introduction   1
BARBARA HARRISS-WHITE

Part I: China and India: The Domestic Economy   25

1   China: Development, Inequality, and Imbalance   27
     CARL RISKIN

2   The Indian Economy in the Post-Reform Period:
     Growth without Structural Transformation   47
     KUNAL SEN

Part II: China, India, and the International Economy   63

3   The Challenges of China and the International Economy   65
     PETER J. BUCKLEY

4   India and the World Economy   77
     VIJAY JOSHI & DEVESH KAPUR

Part III: Changing Demographic Profiles   93

5   The Social Consequences of Demographic Change in China   95
     DELIA DAVIN

6   The Social Consequences of Demographic Change in India   115
     PATRICIA JEFFERY

Part IV: Migration and the Regimes of Labour 137

7   The Modalities of Geographical Mobility in China
and their Impacts, 1980–2010 139
       DOROTHY J. SOLINGER

8   'Lopsided', 'Failed', or 'Tortuous':
India's Problematic Transition and its Implications
for Labour 157
       STUART CORBRIDGE, JOHN HARRISS,
       & CRAIG JEFFREY

Part V: The Environment: Crises and Responses 173

9   China: Energy, Environment, and Limits to Growth 175
       MINQI LI

10   Environment and Development in India 193
       S. RAVI RAJAN

Index 213

List of Figures

1.1 Household Saving Rate in Disposable Income 28

1.2 National Saving and Investment Rate, 1978–2010 30

1.3 Changing Composition of GDP by Category of Final Demand 31

1.4 Falling Share of Consumption in GDP and Falling Ratio
of Rural to Urban Income 31

1.5 Ratio of Total Profits of Large Industrial Enterprises
to GDP, 1998–2009 32

2.1 Per Capita National Income (NI), India, 1950–2008 49

2.2 Sectoral Growth in the Indian Economy, 1950–2008 50

4.1 India: Inward and Outward FDI 84

5.1 Estimate of Population of China by Age and Sex, Mid-2010 100

9.1 China's Agriculture, Inputs, and Grain Yields (1980–2010) 181

9.2 China's CO_2 Emissions from Fossil Fuels Burning
(2000–2100, Historical and Projected, based on a

Twenty-First-Century Emission Budget of 400 Billion Tons) 187

List of Tables

1.1	Total Urban and Rural Employment (millions)	34
1.2	Expenditure Composition of Stimulus Package	38
1.3	Increase in Urban Safety Net (*Dibao*) Expenditures, March 2007–June 2010	40
1.4	Rural and Urban Income of Selected Provinces, 2007 (yuan)	40
2.1	Composition of GDP, India, 1955–2008 (% share)	51
4.1	India: Structure of Tariffs (unweighted averages, %)	79
4.2	India: Structure of the Balance of Payments (Current Account) (% GDP unless otherwise indicated)	79
4.3	India: Indicators of Openness (% GDP)	80
4.4	India, China, Korea: Shares of World Merchandise Exports (%)	81
4.5	India: Structure of the Balance of Payments (Capital Account) (% GDP unless otherwise indicated)	82
4.6	India, China: FDI Inflows and Outflows ($ billion)	82
4.7	India's Trade Agreements	89
5.1	China: Percentage of Population Never Married, by Educational Level and Sex for Selected Age Groups: Censuses of 1990 and 2000	104
8.1	Employment Structure in India—Daily Status (%)	158
8.2	Distribution of GDP and of Employment across Sectors in India and Comparator Countries	159
8.3	Employment by Type and Sector (millions)	160
8.4	Annual Rates of Employment Growth for Usual Status Workers (%)	161
8.5	Classification of Rural Households According to Major Earnings Source, 2004–05	162

Notes on the Contributors

Peter J. Buckley OBE, Professor of International Business and founder Director of the Centre for International Business, University of Leeds, was President of the Academy of International Business 2002–04. He is currently Chair of the European International Business Academy and Cheung Kong Scholar Chair in the University of International Business and Economics (UIBE), Beijing.

Stuart Corbridge is Professor of International Development at the London School of Economics and Political Science, where he is currently also Pro-Director for Research and External Relations. Corbridge has conducted extensive field research, mainly in eastern India, over many years, and is the author, with John Harriss, of *Reinventing India* (Polity Press, 2000), and, with John Harriss and Craig Jeffrey, of *India Today: Economy, Politics and Society* (Polity Press, 2012).

Delia Davin is Emeritus Professor of Chinese Studies at the University of Leeds. She lived and worked in China for several years, and has published extensively on gender, migration, and population policy in China. Davin is the author of *Internal Migration in Contemporary China* (Macmillan, 1999) and *A Very Short Introduction to Mao Zedong* (Oxford University Press, 2013).

John Harriss, a social anthropologist, is Professor and Director, School for International Studies, Simon Fraser University, Vancouver, and a former Director of the Development Studies Institute at the London School of Economics. Harriss has conducted extensive field research, mainly in south India, over many years, and is the author, with Stuart Corbridge, of *Reinventing India* (Polity Press, 2000), and, with Stuart Corbridge and Craig Jeffrey, of *India Today: Economy, Politics and Society* (Polity Press, 2012).

Barbara Harriss-White is Emeritus Professor of Development Studies and Senior Research Fellow at Oxford University, former Director of Queen Elizabeth House, and founder director of Oxford's Contemporary South Asian Studies Programme. In 45 years of research, she has published widely on rural development and aspects of deprivation in India, notably *India Working* (Cambridge University Press, 2003), *Rural Commercial Capital* (Oxford University Press, 2008; Edgar Graham Prize), *Trade Liberalization and India's*

Informal Economy (Oxford University Press, 2007), and *The Comparative Political Economy of Development: Africa and South Asia* (Routledge, 2012; edited with Judith Heyer).

Patricia Jeffery is Professor of Sociology at University of Edinburgh. She has conducted long-term research in north India, and has published widely on gender issues, especially childbearing, social demography and health care, education, women's empowerment and intra-household politics, and the links between gender politics and communal politics. In 2009–10 she held a British Academy/Leverhulme Trust Senior Research Fellowship and Leverhulme Research Fellowship. She is co-investigator on 'Rural change and anthropological knowledge in post-colonial India: a comparative "restudy" of F. G. Bailey, Adrian C. Mayer and David F. Pocock' (funded by ESRC, 2011–14) and is on the Council of the British Association for South Asian Studies.

Craig Jeffrey is Professor of Development Geography at the School of Geography and the Environment, Oxford University, and a Fellow of St John's College, Oxford. Professor Jeffrey's work focuses on youth, politics, and globalization, and he has conducted extensive fieldwork on these issues in Uttar Pradesh and Uttarakhand, north India. His recent publications include *Timepass: Youth, Class and Politics in India* (Stanford University Press, 2010) and *India Today: Economy, Politics and Society* (Polity Press, 2012; with Stuart Corbridge and John Harriss).

Vijay Joshi is an Emeritus Fellow of Merton College, Oxford. His main areas of interest are macroeconomics, international economics and development economics, and he has published widely in these fields in scholarly journals and elsewhere. He has written (jointly with I. M. D. Little) two major books on India: *India's Economic Reforms 1991–2001* (Oxford University Press, 1996); and *India—Macroeconomics and Political Economy 1964–1991*, (World Bank and Oxford University Press, 1994). He is currently writing a book with T. N. Ninan on India in the coming decades. During his varied career, he has served as Economic Adviser, Ministry of Finance, Government of India, and Special Adviser to the Governor, Reserve Bank of India.

Devesh Kapur is Madan Lal Sobti Associate Professor for the Study of Contemporary India, and Director, Center for Advanced Study of India, University of Pennsylvania. He is the co-author of *The World Bank: Its First Half Century* (Brookings Institutions, 1997); *Give us your Best and Brightest: The Global Hunt for Talent and its Impact on the Developing World* (Center for Global Development, 2005); *Public Institutions in India: Performance and Design* (Oxford University Press, 2006); and, most recently, *Diaspora,*

Democracy and Development: The Impact of International Migration from India on India (Princeton University Press, 2010). He has a BTech and MS in chemical engineering and a PhD in Public Policy from Princeton University.

Minqi Li received his PhD in economics from University of Massachusetts Amherst in 2002 and taught political science at York University, Canada, from 2003 to 2006. He is currently Associate Professor of Economics at University of Utah. He has published many articles on the Chinese and the global economy, and his book *The Rise of China and the Demise of the Capitalist World Economy* was published by Pluto Press in 2009.

S. Ravi Rajan is Senior Research Fellow at the Asia Research Institute at the National University of Singapore, on sabbatical from the University of California, Santa Cruz. He is also a Visiting Senior Fellow at The Energy and Resources Institute (TERI), New Delhi, and Visiting Professor at TERI University. He is the author of *Modernizing Nature: Forestry and Imperial Eco-Development 1800–1950* (Oxford, 2006; Orient Blackswan, 2007); editor of five other books or journal special issues, and author of several scholarly papers in environmental history and related fields. Rajan made significant contributions to higher education administration as Provost of College Eight at UC Santa Cruz from 2006 to 2012, where he built a novel 'green' curriculum aimed at nurturing environmental entrepreneurs. He has also served in leadership positions in several national and international academic institutions and non-profit boards.

Carl Riskin is Distinguished Professor of Economics at Queens College, City University of New York, and Senior Research Scholar at Columbia University's Weatherhead East Asian Institute. He is the author of *China's Political Economy: The Quest for Development since 1949* (Oxford University Press, 1987, 1991); *Inequality and Poverty in China in the Age of Globalisation* (with A. R. Khan) (Oxford University Press, 2001); and editor of China's Retreat from Equality (M. E. Sharpe, 2001). He produced the first two China Human Development Reports for the United Nations Development Programme in 1999–2000. His recent research has focused upon the human development dimensions of China's modernization.

Kunal Sen is Professor of Development Economics in the Institute of Development Policy and Management (IDPM), and an Associate Director of the Brooks World Poverty Institute (BWPI), University of Manchester, UK. His current research examines the determinants of female labour force participation, the informal sector in developing economies, the political economy determinants of inclusive growth, and the dynamics of poverty and social exclusion. He was awarded the Sanjaya Lall Prize in 2006 and Dudley Seers Prize in 2003 for his publications.

Dorothy J. Solinger, Professor of Political Science at the University of California, Irvine, has published, edited, and co-edited numerous books; the most recent are *Contesting Citizenship in Urban China: Peasant Migrants, the State and the Logic of the Market* (California, 1999) (winner of the 2001 Joseph R. Levenson Prize of the Association for Asian Studies for best book on post-1900 China published in 1999); *States' Gains, Labor's Losses: China, France and Mexico Choose Global Liaisons* (Cornell, 2009); and the co-edited *Socialism Vanquished, Socialism Challenged: Eastern Europe and China, 1989–2009* (Oxford, 2012). She has also written nearly 100 articles and book chapters. Her current work is on China's urban poor.

Acknowledgements

The editors wish to thank the British Academy and especially Professor Duncan Gallie and Ms Jane Lyddon for the opportunity and privilege of helping to organize the conference and edit this book. They also wish to express their gratitude to all who took part in the conference and to the contributors to this volume, Professor Patricia Uberoi for her careful reading of the entire manuscript, and Ms Lucy Davin and Elizabeth Stone for their editorial help.

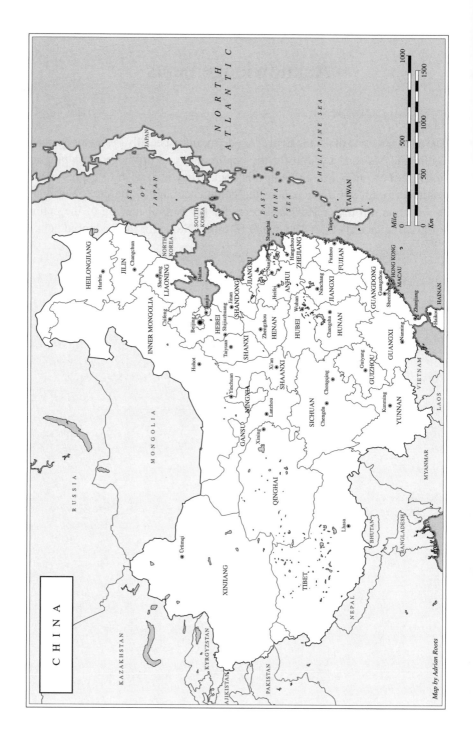

CHINA

Map by Adrian Roots

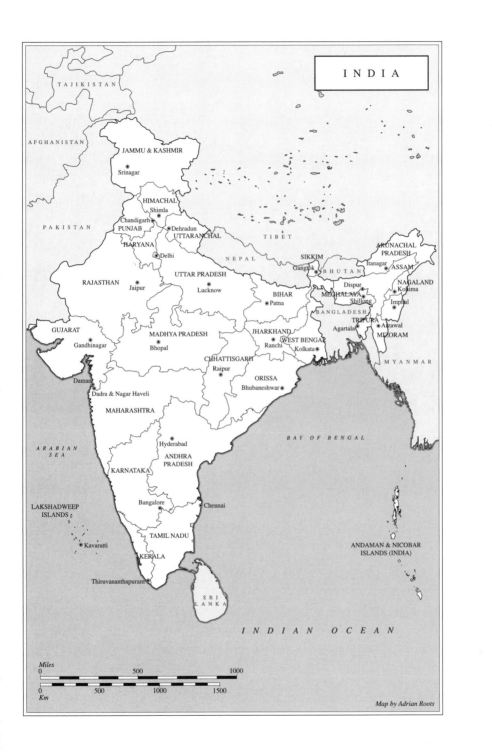

INDIA

TAJIKISTAN

AFGHANISTAN

JAMMU & KASHMIR

Srinagar

HIMACHAL

Shimla

PAKISTAN

Chandigarh

PUNJAB

Dehradun

UTTARANCHAL

TIBET

HARYANA

Delhi

NEPAL

SIKKIM

ARUNACHAL
PRADESH

Gangtok

Itanagar

ASSAM

RAJASTHAN

Jaipur

UTTAR PRADESH

Lucknow

BIHAR

Patna

BHUTAN

MEGHALAYA

Dispur

Shillong

NAGALAND

Kohima

Imphal

GUJARAT

Gandhinagar

MADHYA PRADESH

Bhopal

JHARKHAND

Ranchi

BANGLADESH

WEST BENGAL

Kolkata

TRIPURA

Agartala

MIZORAM

Aizawl

MYANMAR

Daman

Dadra & Nagar Haveli

CHHATTISGARH

Raipur

ORISSA

Bhubaneshwar

MAHARASHTRA

ARABIAN
SEA

Hyderabad

ANDHRA
PRADESH

BAY OF BENGAL

KARNATAKA

LAKSHADWEEP
ISLANDS

Bangalore

Chennai

Kavaratti

TAMIL NADU

ANDAMAN & NICOBAR
ISLANDS (INDIA)

KERALA

Thiruvananthapuram

SRI
LANKA

INDIAN OCEAN

Miles
0   500   1000

0   500   1000   1500
Km

Map by Adrian Roots

Introduction

CHINA AND INDIA have been intertwined in scholarship from the time of the great university of Nalanda, have engaged in trade for as long as the Silk and Sea Routes have existed, and have had tense stand-offs since the catastrophe of the Opium Wars. But since the middle of the twentieth century they have followed such different development paths that the two great nations are invariably seen in terms of lagged outcomes and contrasted trajectories. The aim of this book is to get behind the popular shorthand in which these 'population giants' and 'economic powerhouses' are typically described, and see more clearly what they have in common, as well as where they do indeed differ.

In the 1940s, their economic and demographic endowments were very similar. But subsequently, according to the prevailing narrative, independent India, with its electoral democracy, pursued a policy of socialist planned development until the 1991 crisis opened the country up incrementally to capitalism. Meanwhile, in a series of dramatic policy reforms after 1978, China, under the control of an authoritarian communist party, had opened up its socialist economy to state-managed capitalism (Bajpai and Jian, 1996). On closer inspection, however, the two political trajectories are not as dissimilar as these narratives imply. Indian state support for capitalism (in the form of the Foreign Exchange Regulation Act, the Monopolies and Trade Restrictive Practices Act, and the Companies Act) was put in place as early as the 1960s and 1970s. India's massive petty-capitalist informal economy has always been outside any kind of direct state control. And the quality of India's electoral democracy has been severely questioned inside India itself (Nandy, 1989; Guha, 2007). Conversely, in China the participation of women in local and city government has been impressive compared with that of India,[1] the seeds of democracy are now seen as germinating in civil society, and expressions of economic and political dissent are rapidly becoming more frequent and widespread (White, Howell, and Zhang, 1996; Freeman, 2010). On the other hand, in spite of the notorious corruption in both systems,[2] as long as Chinese Communist Party (CCP) rule is accepted for its material achievements, and Indian electoral democracy is accepted for its political potential (Anderson, 2012), the deep structures of difference will remain.

---

[1] Notwithstanding the reservations for women in the Panchayati Raj system of local government (Drage, 2001).

[2] Anderson (2012: 33) quoting Pratap Bhanu Mehta (2003).

Proceedings of the British Academy, **193**, 1–24, © The British Academy 2014

In late 2010, the British Academy hosted an international conference of experts on the two countries in order to examine not the politics of these two immensely potent players on the twenty-first-century world stage but what their politics have meant for their economies and societies. The result was the five pairs of essays in this book, covering domestic and international development, the social consequences of demographic change, the labour force, and the impact of both economy and society on the environment. It cannot be exhaustive. In particular, stratified by caste, religion, and ethnicity, India's distinctive cultural and political plurality take a back seat here, having no exact Chinese equivalent (Blum, 2002). The distinctively different politics and economics of Chinese and Indian federalism is also outside the scope of this book.[3] And while income inequality receives some comparative attention, the formation of social classes or economic groups and their mapping onto other elements of the social structure proved outside the scope of this project. The two middle classes in particular differ in size, in the point at which they surged, in their cultures of consumption, and in their political leverage (Jaffrelot and van der Veer, 2008; *The Economist*, 2009). Probing behind the obvious contrasts, however, the essays disclose important ways in which the two countries are alike—to a degree not anticipated when the conference began.[4]

But at the outset the essential contrasts between the two countries' modern development paths do need to be accurately recognized. To begin with, they are very different in both the size of their economies and in their respective rates of transformation. Both were overwhelmingly rural and had similar GDPs per capita in the early 1980s, but China's GDP has grown from $1.2 trillion in 2000 to $6 trillion in 2010, while India's has risen from $0.5 trillion to only $1.7 trillion. China's unprecedented growth rate has weakened from an average of 11 per cent (in the first decade of the twenty-first century) as it makes the transition into an upper-middle income country, while India's equally

---

[3] See Singh (2007) for comparative analysis of Chinese and Indian federalism. The nub of the differences lies in India's linguistic states and decentralized parliamentary politics, in which states have bargaining power with the centre, contrasted with China's centralized unitary bureaucratic and political authority. China's provinces are economic agents of the centre, planning is top down, and fiscal autonomy has been hard to devolve. While taxsharing has long been formalized in India, the constituent states have been slower to have economic controls devolved to them. Then, while both countries have several tiers of government below ('local') provinces and constituent states, India's local regulative powers are severely circumscribed, while China's have long been incentivized. Chinese and Indian 'market-preserving' federalism shares problems of revenue authority and clarity in the assignment of expenditure, exacerbated by the significant impact on both of public enterprises, the 'overawing' of local government by provincial/state power, and increased regional inequalities.

[4] That the chapters are non-identical twins speaks volumes about the social production. classification, and quality of data and other evidence, the state of theories, the focuses of scholarly debate, and previous attempts at formulating comparisons—as well as the scholarly expertise of the writers.

unprecedented growth rate has weakened from a more modest 8 per cent, and the country is thought unlikely to graduate from lower-middle income status without further reforms (World Bank, 2012a). China's phenomenally rapid growth has resulted from incentivizing foreign direct investment (FDI) and town and village enterprises in export-led industrialization, combined with the rebalancing of the structure of ownership between the state-owned enterprises and the growing private sector, cutting the number of state sector workers, and massively increasing the productivity of labour. In India's economy, which also has a labour surplus, the share in production and employment of the most labour-intensive sectors of manufacturing declined from the mid-1970s to the 1990s; and their recovery has been due not to state-led investment but to trade liberalization and private investment. India's growth is powered by knowledge- and capital-intensive sectors; whereas, as Riskin argues in Chapter 1, China has relied on manufacturing industry with low labour costs to drive economic growth and mop up agricultural labour surpluses. India's service economy is a combination of dynamic IT, business process, and telecom sectors at one extreme, and a vast range of low-productivity services provided by an explosion of self-employed mini-enterprises in the informal economy at the other (Harriss-White, 2012).

China is now reducing the leading role of exports, which stood at 31 per cent of GDP in 2011–12 (World Bank, 2013), in order to develop the domestic economy, whereas India is expanding the export-led sectors of her economy. Currently accounting for 22 per cent of GDP (up from 7 per cent in 1990), a sizable export role is now played by 'invisibles' such as IT. Still, China's share of world exports is ten times larger than India's.

While both economies are integrated into the global economy, the extent of their global engagement differs. India had annual inward FDI of $25 billion, and outward FDI of $15 billion in 2010. The corresponding figures for China in 2011–12 were $116 billion and $53 billion (*Business Mirror*, 2012). China's inward investments have also been strongly associated with the transfer of cutting-edge technology, but the spillover of this technology from foreign to local firms has been weak, and the balance between the need to build innovation capabilities and the need of the state to retain economic control is still thought to be tilted towards the latter (Fu, Fu, and Li, 2008). With a strong local industrial sector of its own, India has depended less on FDI for technological innovation and has less of the latter. In the first decade of this century, the outward investments of Chinese state-owned enterprises (SOEs) with access to state finance and sovereign wealth institutions—the so-called 'Asian Drivers'—have expanded tenfold to a total of nearly $300 billion. That their activity tends to be extractive has been exaggerated—it is but 14 per cent of total outward FDI; but it does tend to be sited in sectors and regions without strong local competition (as in parts of Africa), or where competition has been barred (e.g., Burma/Myanmar), or where markets can be developed.[5] Of late, the preferred destinations have been South East Asia, island tax havens, and Europe. Indian multinationals have lately embarked on dramatic mergers and acquisitions throughout the world, and have focused on energy and natural resources, but involve more private capital than from China. Though India has graduated from being a major aid receiver to being an aid donor, its aid is mainly tied to exports and technical cooperation, and directed towards African countries and strategic pearls such as Afghanistan and Burma.

In the end, what most distinguishes the two countries' economies is scale. India is altering its external economic and political relations, especially with the USA and the UK, and is increasingly a force to be reckoned with. But its global economic impact lags and is far less than China's. China's activity as the workshop of the world is capable of raising world commodity prices and hitting both raw materials importers and manufacturers in high wage economies. This is reflected in the dramatic contrast between the two countries' reserves. Whereas China's dollar reserves ('exported savings') amount to $3.2 trillion, India's foreign currency reserves, considered healthy, stand at $289 billion (Reserve Bank of India, 2013).

The two giants differ in their supply-side structures—the sectors of the economy—particularly in terms of their productivity. Excepting services, productivity is greater in China than in India. India's cultivable land area is half as big again as China's, yet China's yields per hectare are half as big again as India's. Chinese agriculture has shed more labour than India's, and shed it faster. There is a similar gap between the two countries' levels of labour productivity in most other sectors. Across the entire manufacturing sector, China's productivity exceeds India's by a median rate of 50 per cent (Pandey and Dong, 2009). On the other hand, the productivity of services compared with that of manufacturing is growing faster in India than in China (Ghani, 2011). India's informal economy has always been the larger part of the economy, currently accounting for nine out of every ten jobs,[6] and some 60 per cent of GDP, with no sign of declining, whereas China's has always been much smaller. China's informal sector did grow rapidly after the restructuring of the late 1970s, however, and now accounts for an estimated half of all urban jobs (or, by some reckonings, half the workforce) and roughly 30 per cent of GDP (Harriss-White and Sinha, 2007; Jutting and Xenogiani, 2007; Huang, 2009). The two countries' workforces are huge, but again, the Chinese

---

[5] The result of an Oxford research project: see Fu (2013). Fu's research suggests that Chinese overseas FDI has negative short-term effects—including enclave dualism, the crowding out of local firms, and environmental damage—but positive long-term ones—especially local employment. It concludes that, though hard to calculate and dependent on local contingencies, Chinese FDI is no different from other FDI in its effects.

[6] Many of the tiny minority in the formal economy being in government (Bardhan, 2010).

workforce is far larger: 796 million compared with India's 487 million, part of the difference caused by the greater labour-market participation of Chinese women (Nagaraj, 2007).

Both countries illustrate Karl Polanyi's dictum that 'laissez-faire was planned', but in different ways (Polanyi, 1957; Sternberg, 1993). With a total public debt equal to 26 per cent of GDP, China has far greater room for economic manoeuvre in policy than India, which has a debt equal to 68 per cent of GDP (IMF, 2012). India's level of economic protection is much higher than China's, yet despite inducements and privileges, India's capitalists invest in their homeland far less than China's do in theirs (Bardhan, 2010; Anderson, 2012). In an era said to be one of neoliberalism and the triumph of markets, both countries retain significant state monopolies: the Chinese state controls oil and banking,[7] chemicals, transport, telecommunications, and most health care provision. A different way of putting this is that all of the Chinese firms in China's top 300 are state-owned. Meanwhile, even in India, 16 key sectors including coal, many aspects of power, transport, and aviation (but not health care) are under state monopoly control (Huang, 2009), and six out of India's own top ten companies are state-owned.

The two countries also differ markedly in their demand-side structure.[8] This has several components—consumption, savings, and investment. The Indian economy consumes 59 per cent of GDP (57 per cent of this consumption is that of households, the rest being that of government).[9] By contrast, China 'under-consumes': consumption is only 48 per cent of GDP, of which just 35 per cent is by households. China has suppressed rural consumption, in part thanks to the state being able to keep wages low, even when productivity has grown, because of the availability of a huge surplus of agricultural labour.[10] Next, China's savings rate (53 per cent in 2008) is unusually high in all three components (corporate, household, and government), whereas India's is but 34 per cent, par for the course for lower-middle income countries. Chinese households save not only as a result of a history of frugality but also because of exiguous social protection. And with 'financial repression', negative real interest rates, and state control of finance and banking, their savings are a channel through which resources are transferred to state banks and thence to state-owned enterprises (SOEs) and private small and medium enterprises (SMEs) (Ma and Yi, 2010). Effectively, Chinese households are taxed, and state and private corporates can then retain earnings for their own savings and investment. Like China, India has also developed with a nationalized

---

[7] Announcing opening up in April 2012: <http://topsy.com/business-standard.com/india/news/china-to-end-monopolystate-owned-banks/470345/?utm_source=otter>.

[8] The proportion of Chinese government consumption is very similar to India's.

[9] Central Statistics Office data for India, see GOI (2013).

[10] This is not to argue that India does not have a labour surplus in agriculture.

banking sector but, unlike China, it directed loans towards 'priority sectors', notably agriculture and smaller private firms—what are called SMEs in China. Liberalization and privatization led to a retreat in both kinds of lending, one only recently being countered. Finally, investment in plant and machinery amounts to 29 per cent in India, but is significantly greater—at 48 per cent GDP—in China. And a lot of the subsidies for household savings and incentives for corporate investment in India have been clawed back recently.

The net account for external trade (exports minus imports) turns out negative (-3 per cent GDP) for India but positive (4 per cent) for China. China's undervalued exchange rate raises the profits of exporting firms. India differs from China in not manipulating the exchange rate to subsidize exports. In fact, the incentive on the part of Indian policymakers is to let the rupee appreciate to tame the inflation rate, a political problem growing from 2012 (Kunal Sen, personal communication, 2012).

So while both countries display a record of growing investment and stagnant ratios of consumption to GDP, China's liberalization has been more closely planned than India's, and Chinese growth has been driven by investment in a way that India's has not.

The results of these different trajectories are different economic and social outcomes. China's per capita income is four times that of India. Despite inroads of investment, a recent tightening of the agricultural labour market, and rises in rural household incomes, regional inequalities persist, and rural–urban gaps in incomes are growing wider. Despite a surprising similarity in the structure of inequality—China's top 20 per cent of households corner 49 per cent of total income and the bottom 20 per cent obtain 6 per cent, while the corresponding figures for India are 46 per cent and 8 per cent—India's top-end inequality exceeds China's. India's billionaires are fewer but richer (Bardhan, 2010). Sixty-six of them control more than 20 per cent GDP. And India's poverty is wide, deep, and tenacious: in 2005, 37 per cent of Indians were living on less than $1.25 per day, compared with 13 per cent in China.[11] Yet, according to the CIA, India's Gini coefficient was 0.37 in 2009 contrasted with China's at 0.48.[12] The UN predicts that in 2015 India's poverty figure will be 22 per cent, and China's 5 per cent. Each of the two countries has 'lifted more boats' than at any other time in its history. On the other hand, reducing poverty is not a prime policy initiative. India's military expenditure, for example, is greater than its anti-poverty allocations, and in

[11] World Bank (2011: 71). Even in the World Bank, India's figure is much contested (59–60). Meanwhile, the National Commission for Enterprise in the Unorganized Sector estimated that in 2007, 70 per cent were living on under 20 rupees a day (approx. $0.44).
[12] Distribution of family income—Gini index 2009 Country Ranks:<http://www.photius.com/rankings/economy/distribution_of_family_income_gini_index_2009_0.html> (CIA, 2009).

2011 exceeded the proportion of GDP allocated to military expenditure in China (2.5 per cent against 2 per cent), although in absolute terms China's military budget far exceeds India's military budget ($106 billion versus $47 billion) (Berteau et al., 2012).

In terms of social welfare, India's growth trajectory leaves much to be desired, not least when compared with China's. Performance in relation to the Millennium Development Goals (fraught as they are with arbitrariness, measurement problems, obfuscating aggregations, and untransparent analytical methods)[13] is suggestive of India's manysided lag behind China. India's infant and child mortality rates (respectively 48 and 63 per 1,000 in 2010) are three times worse than China's, and India's achievements in primary education are also less impressive. While only about 5 per cent of children aged 5–14 are not in school—a huge advance since 2000, when the figure stood at 20 per cent (World Bank, 2009)—putting India on a convergence path with China and moving towards gender parity, Indian education is of such poor quality that 85 per cent of children with five years' schooling are said not to be able to perform a simple arithmetic division (Dholakia, 2011). China has taken education far more seriously. India's malnutrition is also a source of national shame (Singh, 2013) and puzzlement; shame because it is worse than rates in sub-Saharan Africa (IFPRI, 2011) and because 42 per cent of under-fives are underweight (in contrast with 3 per cent who are malnourished in China), and puzzlement because malnutrition exists even the very top of the distribution of income in India—a fact that isn't well explained. India's total expenditure on health per capita is under half of China's, and whereas both infectious and non-communicable diseases are declining in China, their incidence is rising in India (WHO, 2011). Indian women's incomes are rising only 12 per cent, as fast as men's, whereas in China the rate is 87 per cent of men's (ActionAid, 2008). And last, let us not peer too closely at sanitation. Whereas in China just 5 per cent of the population is without access to latrines, in India half the population defecates in the open (UN, 2011).

Indeed, such are the dimensions of the contrasts between China and India that, in a project of comparison, China might be more fruitfully matched with the USA, given how closely their economic destinies are now intertwined (Prasad, 2010).

However, the unexpected finding of the British Academy conference was that China and India were, in many respects, more alike than is generally realized. While, paraphrasing Patricia Jeffery (Chapter 6), neither country readily lends itself to grand narratives, the rest of this Introduction attempts to sketch the substance of these similarities.

---

[13] I.e. 8 goals, 21 targets, and 60 indicators (Manning, 2009).

China and India: the domestic economy

Carl Riskin's account of China (Chapter 1) is structured around the recent history of demand-side macroeconomic outcomes, in particular incomes, which he concludes have been uniquely taxed. By contrast, Kunal Sen's treatment of Indian economic development (Chapter 2) examines the supply-side transformation of the structure of production, and builds to the conclusion that India's growth pathway is completely atypical for an Asian country. The contrasts in their development pathways are so significant that the registering of any economic similarities is unexpected.

In both countries, agriculture has steadily declined since the 1960s as a proportion of GDP—more so in China (now down to 10 per cent) than in India (20 per cent); and while the contrast is drawn between Chinese manufacturing and India's services as engines of growth, in fact services currently account for slightly more of China's GDP (43 per cent) than of India's (41 per cent) (Ghani, 2011; World Bank, 2011b; Liu, Yang, and Fang, 2013). Some of these services are in fact internal parts of China's vertically integrated manufacturing systems. A dualism between high tech–high productivity and the exact opposite pervades these sectors in both countries, though it is thought to constrain poverty reduction more powerfully in India. The rural non-farm economy has also attracted labour: in China, 39 per cent of rural income now comes from outside farming, and almost all the young work there. In India, it's estimated at 25–35 per cent (Coppard, 2001). And in both countries, while the non-agricultural sectors that absorb surplus rural unskilled labour (trade, travel services, urban services, and construction) may service the export sector, as non-tradables they are not thought capable of driving GDP growth.

Another similarity is that neither country has suffered from recession after the financial crisis of 2008—but the fall-out is developing for different reasons. China's post-2008 stimulus package (to avert the threat to over 40 million jobs) was larger even than that of the USA, in relation to GDP; the Chinese state had already revitalized the raising of revenue and was able to direct income transfers so as to increase living standards and consumption in disadvantaged regions (investing in housing, health, and education, in the welfare state, and the prices of food and basic wage goods). In a spending spree on high-speed railways, airports, energy projects, and R&D, the package also incentivized investment to create jobs in the interior provinces. The Indian government, for its part, stimulated consumption through, among other things, excise rate cuts, increases in public sector pay, and a rural employment programme. With a 2 per cent rise in consumption, the effects of a drop in investment were neutralized (Damodaran, 2011). These efforts seem to have borne fruit; even in agriculture, evidence is emerging of rising wages in both China and parts of India.

If growth in Chinese wage levels exceeds growth in productivity, the model will have to change, and the market will, in an ironical twist of history, finally accomplish what the Chinese state has been unable to complete, shifting from the kinds of export goods that are luxuries for Chinese workers to the production of commodities they want and could afford as incomes rise.

China, India, and the international economy

The historical trajectories of the two countries' engagement with the wider world since the 1940s are more similar than is often imagined. India's 'Licence Raj' (state-managed 'socialist' development strategy) ended some ten years later than China's reforms began, but although the latter are usually seen as starting in 1978, in Chapter 3 Peter J. Buckley argues that their external effects did not become really significant until after China's accession to the World Trade Organization (WTO) in 2001. For both countries, then, it is the twenty-first century that has witnessed the greatest dynamism in international economic relations, trade flows, and investments.

There are further similarities in the extent of the dependence of both on productive activity in the outside world. Half of China's exports are 'processing trade', exporting goods that are 'Created in China' rather than 'Made in China'—having been assembled from imported components with exemptions from tariffs. There is a close parallel here with India's services, and some of India's manufactures, in the form of cross-border outsourcing, notable examples of which are IT services and the polishing of diamonds.

But both China and India still present obstacles to FDI. The transactions costs of greenfield sites are high. Regulations, local laws, patent regimes, licences, state control over essential commodities, and the material requirements of national security, plus the only incremental and still incomplete liberalization of capital accounts, are all seen as constraints on flows of investment. In both countries, the reforms that have been made are far from being 'mindlessly laissez faire', as Vijay Joshi and Devesh Kapur rightly observe in Chapter 4.

Engagement in the international economy also has a human resource dimension to it. China is preparing new cadres of skilled managers for this international engagement, and highly qualified workers are now migrating abroad: between 250,000 and 500,000 a year—plus 250,000 students.[14] India has more differentiated migration streams—for example, a working-class outflow to the Middle East, in the wake of an earlier one to the UK.

---

[14] Skilled and unskilled labour is also migrating in order to manage the outward FDI, but we have been unable to discover in what numbers (Liu, Buck, and Shu, 2005).

Skilled migrants are also now flowing from both China and India to the USA, Europe, countries of the former Soviet Union, and Africa.[15] Their remittances are reckoned to be similar in magnitude—India's at $53 billion and China's $51 billion (World Bank, 2012a), but have a greater impact on India, constituting 3 per cent of GDP in 2010. Remittances have transformed the income distributions of states like Kerala, Punjab, and Goa, where they form significant components of both local consumption and local investment.

Changing demographic profiles

In 2011–12, China and India had similar populations—1.34 billion and 1.22 billion respectively. In both cases, the demographic transition—the long march from being societies with high birth and death rates to ones with low rates of both kinds—has been accompanied by two other transitions, those of nutrition and of disease. In the nutrition transition, calorie contents have risen and diets have been enriched in protein, vitamins, and minerals. Diets have diversified into animal products (China) and dairy products (India), and into fish, fats, sugar, and alcohol. Food has become increasingly produced using energy from fossil fuel. A food industry now preserves food and prepares new combinations of it, forming a giant economic superstructure on top of agriculture. The balance between human energy intake and effort in food production has also shifted, because in each country mechanization has reduced the need for physical activity. Obesity trails in the wake of these changes (Popkin et al., 2001), and in this China leads India. The disease transition sees the infectious and parasitic diseases of poverty give way to the non-communicable diseases of affluence. But as the three transitions follow their own social and geographic courses, seemingly anomalous effects are common. For example in both China and India malnutrition and obesity may be found inside a single family, or be experienced in a single lifetime (Popkin, 2001).

Since 1960, both China and India have experienced rapid increases in life expectancy—from 48 to 73 years in China, and from 40 to 65 in India (World Bank, 2012b)—and declines in fertility. Households are now quite small: the average Chinese family/household has 3.1 members and even

---

[15] UN (2007); and 'From Angola to Uzbekistan, Iran to Indonesia, some 740,000 Chinese workers were abroad at the end of 2008, with 58 per cent sent out last year alone, the Commerce Ministry said. The number going abroad this year is on track to roughly match that rate. The workers are hired in China, either directly by Chinese enterprises or by Chinese labor agencies that place the workers; there are 500 operational licensed agencies and many illegal ones' (Wong, 2009).

India's has only 4.7.[16] State enforcement played a role in cutting birth rates in both countries: in the 1970s and '80s in China, and during the Indian Emergency in the 1970s. The 'one-child' policy, however, now applies to jurisdictions covering only about 40 per cent of the Chinese population. The other causes of these falls are a mix of declining infant mortality, the rising costs of having children, and aspirations for the next generation, mediated, however, by the abiding desire for a boy—for both economic and cultural reasons in both countries. China's population growth rate is now 0.7 per cent, India's is 1.7 per cent. China's total fertility rate of 1.7 is now below the replacement level of 2.1, while India's average fertility rate is still much higher at 2.5.[17] Geographic differences in life expectancy within the two countries reflect relative failures and successes in rural development: in Tibet life expectancy is 64, in Shanghai municipality it reached 82 in 2010; the central tribal states of India have a life expectancy of 58, while Kerala's is 74 (*China Daily*, 2011; Saikia et al., 2011).

In both countries, the poor, wherever they live, lag behind in all three transitions and live the shortest lives. There is also a massive and increasing discrimination against girl children, in which China, in the post-Mao years, has come to hold the lead (Attané and Guilmoto, 2007). In China there are around 120 boys per 100 girls at birth, in India 111. In India, adverse sex ratios were crawling towards improvement throughout the twentieth century, but have deteriorated dramatically since the advent of the reforms. Experts associate these disasters with the economic reforms. Girls are in double jeopardy: while post-natal family planning methods such as active infanticide and killing by neglect were once rife, now sex-selective abortion is becoming widespread, even though in both countries it is illegal (Harriss-White, 2008). The desire, if not the necessity, for small families to have at least one son—to work, to import a bride, to support parents in old age—and in China to keep the family name, and in India to light the funeral pyre—motivates sex-selective abortion for those able to afford it, and post-natal culling of girls for those who cannot

---

[16] Family and household need distinguishing if only because of the significance of long-term-absent migrants. The two terms are often used interchangeably but refer to different principles of social organization. While 'family' may be an aspatialized concept involving kinship, household generally invokes 'common residence'. There are longstanding debates about the heart of the family relationship: at one extreme the mother and child; at the other—and relevant to both China and India—male rights in property. There is also fierce disagreement about the heart of the household: common residence includes servants, apprentices, and migrant boarders; the domestic activity of common residence, food, and children may involve non-residence and a porous, contingent relationship with the public sphere and income flows. Yanagisako (1979) offers a fine review of these issues.

[17] States in the south, the mountain states of the far north, and the relatively developed states of Punjab and Maharashtra together with West Bengal are already at below the replacement rate and are driving the aggregate fertility decline.

(Cai and Lavely, 2007).[18] Very few women do not marry. The increasingly scarce status of Chinese women combines with high levels of workforce participation to raise the age at marriage. In India, except at the extremes of the social hierarchy, adult female work participation is much lower, yet the marriage age has also increased, aided in some states by state incentives and laws about the age threshold for marriage. In both countries, marriage migration means social as well as physical mobility for women. In China, the skewed sex ratio and the desire for women to achieve upward mobility through marriage means that long-distance marriage migration is more commonplace, with brides learning to negotiate new dialects and food cultures as well as adapting to married life. In India, marriages are still arranged through a vast diversity of caste-fragmented markets. If brides are scarce, the problem is solved by brides marrying into socially higher families. In both countries, it is poor men who are most in surplus and least likely to marry. The relative scarcity of women, on the other hand, leads to their being subjected to more intense personal control, and violence against women is reportedly on the increase. Both countries also report a growing incidence of female trafficking and of prostitution.

As a result of these socio-demographic changes, a 'demographic dividend' is claimed for both countries in which there are fewer non-working dependents to support than before. But India's window of low dependency ratios is smaller (at 0.54) than China's (at 0.38). In fact, both depend on good-quality employment, the aspiration of all educated youth; whereas the reality is long waits, fierce competition, and casual work (Nagaraj, 2007; Jeffrey, 2010). In both countries, agriculture is being feminized as women are increasingly left on the land to feed the cities.

The so-called intergenerational contract—the obligation in both societies for parents to invest in their children and for adult children in turn to care for their parents—is already changing (Croll, 2006; Vera-Sanso, 2012; Davin, Chapter 5, this volume). In both societies, where different generations live in the same house, or close by, elderly women care for grandchildren, while men work until incapacitated (which, among the poor, long precedes the age when they become entitled to the minimal state pension entitlements). Old age is largely defined by becoming disabled. The contract between generations is stressed by the conflict between social obligations and limited income, and between the costs of meeting old people's health care needs and the costs of

---

[18]In China, son preference is strongest round the developed coast, in the rural east, and in a patchy spine running from Guangdong north-east to Shandong. In India, from an epicentre in the developed north-west, anti-female-biased culling practices are spreading southwards and outwards through society. China's male–female sex ratios are now higher than those of Muslim countries. Chinese Muslims, like Indian Muslims, have much lower sex ratios than Han Chinese (Cai and Lavely, 2007: 269). Chinese Muslims have the advantage of often being allowed more than one child.

meeting the educational and marriage-settlement needs of the young. Since few old people have either adequate pensions or access to state health care, they are vulnerable to a looming crisis of filial piety in both countries. The most vulnerable are assetless widows and poor, unmarried men.

Migration and regimes of labour

While capital can migrate, labour is, for the most part, stuck within national boundaries. In both countries, despite the pace of the economic transformation, and despite the large labour productivity gap between agriculture and the non-farm economy,[19] agriculture is still the great labour-absorber. While between the 1970s and 2008 India's agricultural labour force declined from about 70 per cent of the total to around 60 or perhaps even as low as 55 per cent, China's declined from 56 to 39 per cent, or possibly even 28 per cent (see Riskin, Chapter 1). Women's labour force participation in agriculture is said to be 8 per cent higher than men's (World Bank, 2006). In both countries landholding sizes are so small that they threaten viability. In India, 70 per cent are below 1 hectare and in China an estimated 93 per cent, (APCAS, 2010: 13); there is consequently a debate over whether it is accurate to call agricultural workers 'peasants' rather than 'disguised wage labour'. And while the differences between the structures of the two countries' non-farm economies are well established (most notably labour-intensive manufacturing in China as opposed to services in India), it is less often appreciated that both kinds of non-farm economy pose similar barriers to women, and that non-farm informal activity, already important in India, is increasingly significant in China too.

Major debates continue in both countries over the relation between growth and employment; but although the preoccupations are similar, the content is different. For China, Riskin emphasizes (Chapter 1) that capital-biased growth restricts formal employment (creating a state of 'employment aversity'), while lack of finance for SMEs restricts informal employment; and the combined effect keeps informal wages lower than they might otherwise be. In China, therefore, it is high growth alone that powers employment growth. India's debate is about so-called 'jobless growth'. In reality, despite rises in labour productivity, India's growth has not failed to create jobs; the question is whether the new jobs offer what the International Labour Organization (ILO) calls 'decent work', or only jobs in the informal sector. The engine of growth

---

[19] 1:6 in China and 1:4 in India—though both figures are contested: see Cook (1999) and Kuijjs and Wang (2005) for China and Binswanger-Mhkize (2012) for India. The income gap between agricultural and non-agricultural households is also large—though in fact these categories are blurred and estimated from surveys which vary. Urban incomes are approximately three to four times rural ones in China, while they are reckoned to be two to three times higher in India.

in livelihoods has been above all in self-employment. The question, then, is whether self-employment in the informal economy is 'good-quality work'. Those arguing that growth is 'jobless' think it is not, and there are schools of thought pushing the argument even further, arguing that India's informal economy is 'excluded labour', 'non-capitalist space', or the fall-out from ongoing 'primitive accumulation'.[20] Though there is evidence both ways, the majority view is that the bulk of self-employment is more likely to be due to distress (i.e., the lack of any other means of survival) than to 'growth' (with which 'distress' is conventionally contrasted). Over the years, India's Economic Census shows that the vast mass of self-employed (accounting for 64 per cent of all non-agricultural 'enterprises', compared with only 6.5 per cent of the non-agricultural workforce in China) has grown through the multiplication of tiny firms. Indeed, under Indian labour legislation they are classed as 'labour', not 'enterprises', which incidentally deprives them of the recognition and rights accorded in law to both labour and businesses (Sankaran, 2006; Harriss-White, 2012).

Another shared preoccupation concerns internal labour migration, though within very different parameters: China's level of urbanization is 51.3 per cent, as against India's 28 per cent, and while China's cities continue to grow, India's urban growth rates are slowing down. So the literature on Chinese labour is all about migration—whereas 'migration' is still a small but growing subfield of labour studies in India. 'Migration' is also the term under which 'informality' and 'rural–urban' differences tend to be discussed in China. The statistics are neither exact nor comparable. Estimates for China suggest that by 2010, 149 million had migrated to the east and the coast, while a further 84 million had migrated to towns in the interior, nearer where the migrants come from. In India 100 million are thought to have migrated permanently, with some 30 million more moving seasonally to find work. The trends in internal migration are thought to be diverging, accelerating in China and decelerating in India (Nagaraj, 2007).

In this book (Chapter 7), Dorothy J. Solinger argues that whereas Chinese cities used to be deliberately designed to be labour fortresses, with superior stocks and flows of essential public goods for those allowed to work in them, over the last three decades the reasons for remaining beleaguered fortresses against migrant labour have changed. Now, cities lack the financial resources to fulfil civic obligations and provide services and welfare benefits to all their workforces.

The *hukou*, or household registration system, has been deployed so as to greatly reduce the cost to the local state of providing welfare, health, and

---

[20] See the discussion and references in Stuart Corbridge, John Harriss, and Craig Jeffrey here (Chapter 8); and a critique by Jan (2012).

services to the workforce. In the Maoist era, the *hukou* was used to prevent or to limit population mobility. People only had the right to live in the place where they were registered, which meant the places where they were born, or, in the case of married women, the place of their husband's registration. The result was that rural residents were rarely permitted to move to the cities, where economic opportunities, food rations, health care, welfare, and educational provision were all more generous. After the economic reforms, the *hukou* system was modified but did not disappear. The demand for labour that arose with economic growth brought an end to the rigid suppression of rural to urban migration, but, even now, rural residents are allowed to live in the cities only on sufferance. They are supposed to obtain temporary residence permits, which may be cancelled if they become unemployed, and they do not have the rights to health, welfare, or even education enjoyed by those with an urban *hukou*. Migrants suffer social discrimination, victimization, and poor returns from labour markets. The better paid jobs are often only open to those with an urban *hukou*. Migrants report difficulties in getting redress for delays in pay, intimidation and extortion, and work without contracts. Their children lack access to schools. At best, only a fifth have access to public health facilities, let alone social security. A few towns are experimenting gingerly with relaxing the *hukou*. In rather the same way, India's migrant workers have been shown to be highly vulnerable both at work and in access to state benefits, the main difference from China being that the condition of India's migrant workers resembles that of all workers in India's informal economy.

It is no doubt true, as the *State of the World's Cities 2010/2011* reports, that the 'two countries have together lifted at least 125 million people out of slum conditions between 1990 and 2011' (UN-Habitat, 2010). Nonetheless (and despite differences in the basis of estimations), as of 2007, roughly a third of the urban population of both countries were still living in settlements regarded as slums.

The calculation and comparison of average wages is fraught with difficulties, but China's average wages are thought to have been consistently somewhere between three and five times higher than India's. This suggests that the cheapness of India's informal, un-unionized labour force is not a sufficient lure to induce Chinese investors to overcome other obstacles to investment in India—even when millions of Chinese workers, in spite of having neither independent unions nor the right to strike, are nonetheless organizing and protesting about pay and conditions on an exponentially rising scale (Riskin, Chapter 1);[21] and when a few collective contracts are being negotiated by Chinese workers with foreign investors who are under pressure from their

---

[21] A trend Riskin (Chapter 1) attributes to the safety net of rising rural incomes. As the labour surplus shrinks and the stimulus package takes root, the opportunity cost of migration rises.

shareholders at home. In contrast, the incidence of industrial disputes in India is declining. However, given competing theories and inconclusive evidence (Joshi and Kapur, Chapter 4), it cannot be said with confidence that India's labour laws and unions have an adverse effect on industrial development (Bardhan, 2010). And actual conditions in the two countries are really more similar than their different legal frameworks would suggest. Only 2–3 per cent of the Indian workforce is organized—through party-politicized unions— and union membership has been declining. Some celebrated successes in organizing self-employed workers are exceptions that prove the rule, and their goal is more likely to be to demand welfare rights outside work than pay and conditions at work. Labour activism is not coherent, is said to have no class character, and is far from being a single All-India movement.

The environment: crises and responses

It is labour exploited with capital, machinery, and fossil fuels that has generated the new historical era, the Anthropocene, in which man is an agent of geological and planetary-atmospheric change (Steffen et al., 2011). The final set of paired essays reflect on the clashing priorities of development and environment, conceiving the socially constructed environment both as global and as local.

The first few years of the twenty-first century are thought to have already used up a third of the entire century's global ration of CO_2, if global temperature rise is to be contained below 2 degrees from pre-industrial levels. Since the environmental crisis is global, in the two essays on the environmental correlates of the economic and social changes we have compared, the general problems of environment are introduced before situating the specificities of China and India. The physicality of economic growth and social change can then be explored through local case studies of the use and multi-level governance of resources critical to human well-being: forests, food, water, energy, and their cause–effect relations with climate change—extrapolating them into seriously dire forecasts for the future. The essays also examine industrial environments, environmental threats, and disasters due to technology, as well as the role of science in environmental governance. These in turn, expose for the Indian case, the lack of political, legal, and expert capacities needed to respond flexibly, creatively, and authoritatively to new and multiscaled environmental risks.

China and India now rank first and third respectively in the world's league table of greenhouse gas emitters. But the contrast between China's heavy manufacturing economy and India's relatively light agrarian and service economy is clearly reflected in their CO_2 accounts. In gross terms,

China emits 9,980 million tons a year, compared with India's 2,000 million (though exports to the rest of the world account for a third of China's). That is 7 tons of CO_2 per capita, compared with just under 2 for India. While both economies are progressively reducing the CO_2 released in production, China emitted 2.3 kg CO_2 per $ unit of GDP in 2008 (halved since 1990), against India's 1.7 (a lower level of pollution, which is moving much more slowly towards decarbonification) (IEA, 2012). Clearly, China's environmental hubris is in a different league to India's—absolute or per capita, gross or net of the emissions content of trade.

Yet in the biophysical cycles of extraction, regeneration, and the absorption of pollution, by the millennium even India had already passed the threshold of unsustainability (Wackernagel et al., 1997). Both countries' resource footprints are around double their biophysical capacities.[22] China has the dubious distinction of having 16 of the world's 20 most polluted cities, but in both countries, cities harbour serious epidemics due to air pollution (Mannucci, 2013). Both countries' remarkable achievements in agriculture have also been bought at a heavy price in water table depletion and contamination, species extinction, soil degradation, and dependence on fossil fuels. It is highly unlikely that phosphorus will keep pace with demand for fertilizer. Nor is it likely that oil production will increase by 26 per cent over the years 2011 to 2030 to keep pace with the combined projected demand of the two countries, or that biodiversity conservation and progress with afforestation will be able to halt the rate of biodiversity loss.

China and India are relative newcomers to the ranks of mega-polluters and have so far encountered little serious concern from those already there. What global agreements have been forged have not reduced the rate of greenhouse gas emission increases or biodiversity losses (Steffen et al., 2011). As a result of climate change, changes in rainfall, in water resources, in the chemical composition of the atmosphere, and in the incidence of extreme weather events are all affecting and will further affect crops and livestock, diseases and pests, in ways that are already quite well known in both countries, but as yet are not precisely enough measured and understood (Piao et al., 2010). Biodiversity loss will threaten agriculture and food supplies, agro-industrial raw materials, and water quality, and will have complex effects on health in both countries.

Both China and India are growing at rates that far outstrip those of the Organisation for Economic Co-operation and Development (OECD) countries,

---

[22] Wright, Kemp, and Williams (2011), write of biophysical capacity that it is a 'measure of the total amount of carbon dioxide (CO_2) and methane (CH_4) emissions of a defined population, system or activity, considering all relevant sources, sinks and storage within the spatial and temporal boundary of the population, system or activity of interest. Calculated as carbon dioxide equivalent (CO_2e) using the relevant 100-year global warming potential (GWP1000).' For the concept of the ecological footprint, see Confederation of Indian Industry (CII, 2008).

but neither has a resource base that would enable it to complete the earlier industrialization trajectory of any OECD country. While policy documents include rhetorical flourishes, there is little sign from the competition for resources in either country that the implications of this are recognized sufficiently to move towards a low carbon transition.[23] And as Joshi and Kapur rightly note, the fact that this is equally true of the OECD heartland is not lost on the political and industrial elites of China and India.

Despite reports that China is embarking on a drive to move towards solar photo voltaic as an energy source, and despite the rhetorical claims by the Indian Ministry of Environment and Forests, the regulative capacity of both countries' central and local states has so far proved weak and their bureaucratic organization dysfunctionally fractured (Harriss-White, Rohra, and Singh, 2009; Ma, forthcoming). Chinese NGOs are muzzled, and the media contend with censorship, though both are beginning to have some impact on the public's awareness (Li, Chapter 9). India has better data transparency, more active NGOs, and an attentive and critical media[24]— yet the bridge from public awareness to bipartisan, consistent, and effective policymaking is as shaky as the bridge from policymaking to policy implementation. Like China, India is unable even to harvest much of the 'low-hanging fruit' from achieving greater energy efficiency (Harrison and Kostka, 2013), and the state is unable to mediate against extractive industries and in favour of the legally protected citizen (Ravi Rajan, Chapter 10). Responses to the 2008 financial crisis confirmed that in both countries decarbonification takes second place to growth (Scrugs et al., 2012). As in the OECD heartland, in neither China nor India is there a significant political constituency with both a vision of the new low carbon industrial revolution that will be needed and the political power and economic muscle to advance it. For India, Rajan argues that pervasive corruption, waste, rent-seeking, and predation prevail instead.

In this respect, China and India, because of their economic and social weight, may surely be taken as symbols of global society's physical boundaries—greenhouse gases, biodiversity, ocean acidification, ozone depletion, the phosphorus and nitrogen cycles, water and land use—that we threaten to trespass over, or have already perilously crossed (Rockström et al., 2009). There is no sign of the institutional, economic, and political

---

[23] Prof. X. Fu, pers. comm. (2013).

[24] Amartya Sen has argued influentially that the differences in media control have far-reaching consequences, including the capacity of India's free media to intervene in ways which prevent famine deaths (Sen, 1981). Ram (1995) responded that this did not stop the media from ignoring chronic malnutrition and other developmental pathologies, and Banik (2007) showed that, while famine continues to be a political label, the free media in India's democracy does not protect all citizens from starvation deaths.

preconditions for 'steady state growth' that are so urgently needed, as Minqi Li persuasively argues in this book (Chapter 9).

Development pathways can be similar, but lagged or different in objective and means. In terms of lag, there are few indicators in which India does not lag China. In terms of trajectory, there is much in common, though China's has required developing an educated skilled workforce together with capabilities for adaptive innovation and productivity enhancement. In terms of transformative capacity, as C. P. Bhambhri (2012) has put it, India 'muddles through'. It will take far longer for India to spread decent work conditions, let alone a decent mass standard of living, let alone a biophysically sustainable economy.

Let Joshi and Kapur (Chapter 4) have the last word: 'The optimistic vision for the future is of a world in which the great powers, old and new, cooperate to supply global public goods. The pessimistic vision is one of disharmony and conflict between the major powers.' This book is offered in a spirit of optimism, to help inform everyone who wants to understand the way China and India are shaping their destinies and, through their immense importance, the destiny of the whole twenty-first-century world.

Acknowledgements

I have put my head on the block in writing this multidisciplinary comparison in memory of Professor Gordon White, scholar of Chinese politics and society. I am very grateful to Yuge Ma and Professor Kunal Sen for discussions during the writing of this Introduction, to Professors Patricia Uberoi and Xiaolan Fu for comments on the first draft, and to Professors Delia Davin and Colin Leys for improving it. None of them are responsible for errors that remain.

References

ActionAid (2008) Women's rights and the millennium development goals <http://www.actionaid.org.uk/doc_lib/pdfaam> (accessed 20 January 2013).

Anderson, P. (2012) After Nehru. *London Review of Books*, 2 August 2012, pp. 21–37.

APCAS (Asia and Pacific Commission on Agricultural Statistics) (2010) Characterisation of small farmers in Asia and the Pacific (Food and Agriculture Organization). <http://www.fao.org/fileadmin/templates/ess/documents/meetings_and_workshops/APCAS23/documents_OCT10/APCAS-10-28_-Small_farmers.pdf> (accessed 20 January 2013).

Attané, I. and Guilmoto, C. Z. (eds) (2007) *Watering the Neighbour's Garden; The Growing Demographic Female Deficit in Asia* (Paris: Committee for International Cooperation in National Research in Demography).

Bajpai, Nirupam and Jian, Tianlun (1996) *Reform Strategies of China and India: Suggestions for Future Actions* (Cambridge, MA: Harvard Institute for International Development, Harvard University).

Banik, D. (2007) *Starvation and India's Democracy* (London: Routledge).

Bardhan, P. (2010) *Awakening Giants, Feet of Clay: Assessing the Economic Rise of China and India* (Princeton, NJ: Princeton University Press).

Berteau, D., Ben Ari, G., Hoffbauer, J., Herman, P. and Raghavan, S. (2012) *Asian Defence Spending* (Washington: Centre for Strategic International Studies).

Bhambhri, C. P. (2012) *The Indian Transition* (New Delhi: Jawaharlal Nehru University).

Binswanger-Mkhize, H. (2012) *India 1960–2010: Structural Change, the Rural Nonfarm Sector, and the Prospects for Agriculture* (Berkeley: Department of Agricultural and Resource Economics, University of California). <http://are.berkeley.edu/documents/seminar/Binswanger.pdf> (accessed 20 January 2013).

Blum, S. D. (2002) Margins and centers: a decade of publishing on China's ethnic minorities. *The Journal of Asian Studies*, 61(4), pp. 1287–1310.

Business Mirror (2012) China FDI drops amid slowing growth. *Business Mirror*, 20 October. <http://businessmirror.com.ph/index.php/news/world/821-china-fdi-drops-amid-slowing-economic-growth> (accessed 20 January 2013).

Cai, Yong and Lavely, W. (2007). Child sex ratios and their regional variation, in Zhao Zhongwei and Fei Guo (eds) *Transition and Challenge: China's Population at the Beginning of the 21st Century* (Oxford: Oxford University Press), pp. 1–17.

China Daily (2011) Shanghai residents live longer, healthier lives. *China Daily*, 4 March, p. 7.

CIA (Central Intelligence Agency) (2009) *World Factbook* (Washington: Directorate of Intelligence).

CII (Confederation of Indian Industry) (2008) *India's Ecological Footprint* (New Delhi: CII, WWF).

Cook, S. (1999) Surplus labour and productivity in Chinese agriculture: evidence from household survey data. *Journal of Development Studies*, 35(3), pp. 16–44.

Coppard, D. (2001) The rural non-farm, economy in India: a review of the literature, *Natural Resources Institute Report, no. 2662*, Chatham, UK. <http://www.dfid.gov.uk/r4d/Output/189327/Default.aspx> (accessed 30 September 2012).

Croll, E. (2006) The intergenerational contract in the changing Asian family. *Oxford Development Studies*, 34(4), pp. 473–491.

Damodaran, H. (2011) How India's growth differs from China's. *The Hindu Business Line*, 4 June. <http://www.thehindubusinessline.com/features/investment-world/article2077037.ece> (accessed 20 January 2013).

Dholakia, Viral (2011) Enrollments in Indian schools surge, but performance drops! *Trak-in: The Indian Biz-Tech Buzz*, 12 February. <http://trak.in/tags/business/2011/02/12/india-school-enrollment-performance-low/>.

Drage, J. (2001) Women in local government in Asia and the Pacific (ESCAP). <http://www.unescap.org/huset/women/summit/substantive_overview/jean_drage_speech_text.htm> (accessed 20 January 2013).

Economist, The (2009). The middle class in emerging markets: two billion more bourgeois. *The Economist*, 12 February, p. 15.

Freeman, Will (2010) The accuracy of China's 'mass incidents'. *Financial Times*, 2 March. <http://www.ft.com/cms/s/0/9ee6fa64-25b5-11df-9bd3-00144feab49a.html#axzz2aumLns9Z> (accessed 30 September 2012).

Fu, M., Fu, X., and Li, T. (2008). International and intra-national technology spillovers and technology development paths in developing countries: the case of China, Working Paper RP2008/96, World Institute for Development Economic Research UNU-WIDER.

Fu, Xiaolan (2013) Does FDI provide spoils, or does it just spoil? *China Daily*, 28 January. <http://www.chinadaily.com.cn/business/2013-01/28/content_16180216.htm> (accessed 20 January 2013).

Ghani, E. (2011) The service revolution (Geneva: ILO). <http://natlex.ilo.ch/wcmsp5/ groups/public/---ed_emp/---emp_policy/documents/presentation/wcms_175061.pdf> (accessed 20 January 2013).

GOI (Government of India) (2013) First revised estimates of national income, consumption expenditure, saving and capital formation, 2011–12 (New Delhi: Press Information Bureau). <http://mospi.nic.in/Mospi_New/upload/nad_press_release_31jan13.pdf> (accessed 30 September 2012).

Guha, R. (2007) Adivasis, Naxalites and Indian democracy. *Economic and Political Weekly*, 42(32), 11–17 August, pp. 3305–3312.

Harrison, T. and Kostka, G. (2013) Balancing priorities, aligning interests: developing mitigation capacity in China and India. *Comparative Political Studies*, 19 November. DOI: 10.1177/0010414013509577 (accessed 20 January 2013).

Harriss-White, B. (2008) Girls as disposable commodities, in L. Panitch and C. Leys (eds) *Violence Today: Actually Existing Barbarism*, Socialist Register 45, pp. 128–140.

Harriss-White, B. (2012) Capitalism and the common man. *Agrarian South: Journal of Political Economy* 1(2), pp. 109–160.

Harriss-White, B. and Sinha, A. (eds) (2007) *Trade Liberalization and India's Informal Economy* (New Delhi: Oxford University Press).

Harriss-White, B., Rohra, S., and Singh, N. (2009) Political architecture of India's technology system for solar energy. *Economic and Political Weekly*, 44(47), pp. 49–60.

Huang, P. (2009) China's neglected informal economy reality and theory. *Modern China*, 35(4), pp. 405–438.

IFPRI (International Food Policy Research Institute) (2011) Global hunger index report (Washington: IFPRI). <http://www.ifpri.org/tools/2011-ghi-map> (accessed 30 September 2012).

IMF (International Monetary Fund) (2012) *World Economic Outlook: Database: Government Gross Debt* (Washington: IMF).

Jaffrelot, C. and van der Veer, P. (eds) (2008) *Patterns of Middle Class Consumption in India and China* (New Delhi: Sage).

Jan, M. A. (2012) Ideal types and the diversity of capital: a review of Sanyal (South Asian Studies, University of Oxford). <http://www.southasia.ox.ac.uk/sites/sias/files/ documents/ali%20jan%20sanyal-review-final.pdf> (accessed 30 September 2012).

Jeffrey, C. (2010) *Timepass Youth, Class, and the Politics of Waiting in India* (Stanford, CA: Stanford University Press).

Jutting, J. and Xenogiani, T. (2007) *Informal Employment and Internal Migration: The Case of China* (Beijing: Organisation de Coopération et de Développement Economiques).

Kuijs, L. and Wang, T. (2005) China's pattern of growth: moving to sustainability and reducing inequality. World Bank Policy Research Paper No. 3767 (Washington: World Bank).

Liu, D., Yang, L., and Fang, Y. (2013) China makes headway in transforming growth model. Xinhuanet English News, 28 February 2013. <http://news.xinhuanet.com/ english/china/2013-02/28/c_132197789.htm> (accessed 3 July 2013).

Liu, Xiaohui, Buck, T., and Shu, Chang (2005) Chinese economic development, the next stage: outward FDI? *International Business Review* 14(1), pp. 97–115.

Ma, Guonan and Yi, Wang (2010) China's high saving rate: myth and reality, Bank for

International Settlements, Working Paper No. 312, Basle <http://www.bis.org/publ/work312.htm> (accessed 20 January 2013).

Ma, Yuge (forthcoming) Regulation and low carbon development in reform era: power politics of China and India in comparison. DPhil thesis in Geography and Environment, Oxford University.

Manning, R. (2009) Using indicators to encourage development lessons from the millennium development goals, DIIS Report 2009_01, Copenhagen. <http://www.econstor.eu/bitstream/10419/59842/1/591898950.pdf> (accessed 30 September 2012)

Mannucci, P. (2013) Airborne pollution and cardiovascular disease: burden and causes of an epidemic. *European Heart Journal*, 19 February, pp. 1–3. <http://eurheartj.oxfordjournals.org/content/early/2013/02/18/eurheartj.eht045.full.pdf+html> (accessed 17 July 2013).

Mehta, P. B. (2003) *The Burden of Democracy* (Harmondsworth: Penguin).

Nagaraj, R. (2007) *Labour Markets in China and India* (Mumbai: Indira Gandhi Institute of Development Research and Harvard, Women in Informal Employment, Globalizing and Organizing). <http://wiego.org/sites/wiego.org/files/resources/files/Nagaraj-labour_markets_china_india.pdf> (accessed 20 January 2013).

Nandy, A. (1989) The political culture of the Indian state. *Daedalus*, 118(4), pp. 1–26.

Pandey, M. and Dong, X. (2009) Manufacturing productivity in China and India: the role of institutional changes. *China Economic Review*, 20, pp. 754–766.

Piao, Shilong, Ciais, Philippe, Huang, Yao, Shen, Zehao, Peng, Shushi, Li, Junsheng, and Zhou, Liping (2010). The impacts of climate change on water resources and agriculture in China. *Nature*, 467(7311), pp. 43–51. <http://www.readcube.com/articles/10.1038/nature09364> (accessed 20 January 2013).

Polanyi, K. (1957) *The Great Transformation* (Boston: Beacon Press).

Popkin, B. M. (2001) The nutrition transition and obesity in the developing world. *Journal of Nutrition*, 131(3), pp. 871S–873S.

Popkin, B. M., Horton, S., Kim, S., Mahal, A., and Jin, Shuigao (2001), Trends in diet, nutritional status, and diet-related noncommunicable diseases in China and India: the economic costs of the nutrition transition. *Nutrition Reviews*, 59(12), pp. 379–390.

Prasad, E. (2010) The U.S.–China economic relationship: shifts and twists in the balance of power, Brookings (Testimony), 25 February. <http://www.brookings.edu/research/testimony/2010/02/25-us-china-debt-prasad> (accessed 30 September 2012).

Ram, N. (1995) An independent press and anti-hunger strategies: the Indian experience, in A. K. Sen and J. Drèze (eds) *The Political Economy of Hunger* (New York: Oxford University Press).

Reserve Bank of India (2013) Database on Indian economy. <http://www.rbi.org.in/scripts/wssviewdetail.aspx?type=section&param1=2> (accessed 26 June 2013).

Rockström, J., Steffen, W., Noone, K., Persson, Å., Chapin III, F. S., Lambin, E. F., Lenton, T. M., Scheffer, M., Folke, C., Schellnhuber, H. J., Nykvist, B., de Wit, C. A., Hughes, T., van der Leeuw, S., Rodhe, H., Sörlin, S., Snyder, P. K., Costanza, R., Svedin, U., Falkenmark, M., Karlberg, L., Corell, R. W., Fabry, V. J., Hansen, J., Walker, B., Liverman, D., Richardson, K., Crutzen, P., and Foley, J. A. (2009) A safe operating space for humanity. *Nature*, 461, pp. 472–475. <http://pubs.giss.nasa.gov/abs/ro02010z.html> (accessed 20 January 2013).

Saikia, N., Jasilionis, D., Ram, F., and Shkolnikov, V. M. (2011) Trends and geographic differentials in mortality under age 60 in India. *Population Studies*, 65(1), pp. 73–89.

Sankaran, K. (2006) Protecting the worker in the informal economy: the role of labour law, in G. Davidov and B. Langille (eds) *Boundaries and Frontiers of Labour Law: Goals and Means in the Regulation of Work* (Oxford: Hart).

Scruggs, L. and Benegal, S. (2012) Declining public concern about climate change: can we blame the great recession? *Global Environmental Change*. <http://www.sciencedirect.com/science/article/pii/S0959378012000143> (accessed 20 January 2013).

Sen, A. (1981) *Poverty and Famines: An Essay on Entitlements and Deprivation* (Oxford: Oxford University Press).

Singh, Manmohan (Indian Prime Minister) (2013) Problem of malnutrition a matter of national shame. *The Indian Express*, 21 February. <http://www.indianexpress.com/news/problem-of-malnutrition-a-matter-of-national-shame-prime-minister/898024> (accessed 26 June 2013).

Singh, N. (2007) Fiscal decentralisation in China and India: competitive, co-operative or market preserving federalism? (Santa Cruz Department of Economics, University of California). <http://ssrn.com/abstract=1282264> (accessed 20 January 2013).

Steffen, W., Grinevald, J., Crutzen, P., and McNeill, J. (2011) The Anthropocene: conceptual and historical perspectives. *Philosophical Transactions of the Royal Society*, A369, 842–867.

Sternberg, E. (1993) Justifying public intervention without market externalities: Karl Polanyi's theory of planning in capitalism. *Public Administration Review*, 53(2), pp. 100–109.

UN (n.d./2007) International migration and development regional factsheet, Asia. <http://www.un.org/migration/presskit/factsheet_asia.pdf> (accessed 30 September 2012).

UN (2011) Millennium development goals report, 2011. <http://www.un.org/millennium goals/11_MDG%20Report_EN.pdf> (accessed 30 September 2012).

UN-Habitat (2010) *State of the World's Cities 2010/2011 – Cities for All: Bridging the Urban Divide*. <http://www.unhabitat.org/pmss/listItemDetails.aspx?publicationID=2917> (accessed 20 January 2013).

Vera-Sanso, P. (2012) Gender, poverty and old-age livelihoods in urban south India in an era of globalisation. *Oxford Development Studies*, 40(3), pp. 324–340.

Wackernagel, M., Onisto, L., Callejas Linares, A., López Falfán, I. S., Méndez García, J., Suárez Guerrero, A. I., and Suárez Guerrero, M. G. (1997) *Ecological Footprints of Nations: How Much Nature Do They Use? How Much Nature Do They Have?* Commissioned by the Earth Council for the Rio+5 Forum (Toronto: International Council for Local Environmental Initiatives).

White, Gordon, Howell, J., and Zhang, Xiaoyuan (1996) *In Search of Civil Society: Market Reform and Social Change in Contemporary China* (Oxford: Clarendon Press).

WHO (World Health Organization) (2011) World health statistics. <http://www.who.int/whosis/whostat/2011/en/index.html> (accessed 20 January 2013).

Wong, E. (2009) Chinese export of labour faces scorn, *New York Times*, 20 December 2009. <http://www.nytimes.com/2009/12/21/world/asia/21china.html?pagewanted=all&_r=0> (accessed 30 September 2012).

World Bank (2006) Gender gaps in China: facts and figures. <http://siteresources.worldbank.org/INTEAPREGTOPGENDER/Resources/Gender-Gaps-Figures&Facts.pdf> (accessed 20 January 2012).

World Bank (2009) Making elementary education universal. <http://web.worldbank.org/WBSITE/EXTERNAL/NEWS/0,,contentMDK:21388039~menuPK:141310~pagePK:34370~piPK:34424~theSitePK:4607,00.html> (accessed 30 September 2012).

World Bank (2011a) *Perspectives on Poverty in India* (Washington: World Bank).

World Bank (2011b) *World Development Indicators* (Washington: World Bank). <http://data.worldbank.org/data-catalog/world-development-indicators/wdi-2011> (accessed 5 August 2013).

World Bank. (2012a) World Bank indicators. <http://chartsbin.com/view/2438> (accessed 20 January 2013).

World Bank (2012b) Life expectancy at birth. <http://data.worldbank.org/indicator/SP.DYN.LE00.IN> (accessed 20 January 2013).

World Bank (2013) World Bank exports of goods and services (% of GDP). <http://data.worldbank.org/indicator/NE.EXP.GNFS.ZS (accessed 20 January 2013).

Wright, Laurence A., Kemp, Simon, and Williams, Ian (2011) 'Carbon footprinting': towards a universally accepted definition. *Carbon Management*, 2(1), pp. 61–72.

Yanagisako, S. J. (1979) Family and household: the analysis of domestic groups. *Annual Review of Anthropology*, 8, pp. 161–205.

Part I

China and India:
The Domestic Economy

1

China: Development, Inequality, and Imbalance

CARL RISKIN

CHINA PRESENTS A CASE of growth with increasing income inequality,[1] a pattern that has been exacerbated by a number of serious structural imbalances. These include excessive dependence on demand from investment and exports for economic growth, and, conversely, an extraordinarily low rate of consumption in gross domestic product (GDP); underdevelopment of services relative to manufacturing; and a very heavy reliance on natural resources and energy in producing GDP. It is clear that China's problems of growing inequality—especially the urban–rural gap and inequality among regions—are closely linked to its structural imbalances.[2] The forces that have produced imbalance also produced inequality. To reduce inequality will require rebalancing, and vice versa.

Although China is a still quite low income country with a large poor population, it consumes only 35 per cent of its GDP. This is only in part because its people are very frugal, saving a large fraction of household income.[3] There are many reasons for households to save, even from very low personal incomes. Most Chinese still lack an effective safety net, although this has begun to change, so are largely dependent upon their own resources to pay for education, medical emergencies, and their livelihood in old age. Moreover, China's undervalued currency has raised consumer prices and discouraged consumption. An additional factor promoting personal saving may be the large

---

[1] See Wan (2008) and Wan (2007) for a recent battery of studies of inequality in China. For India, see Deaton and Dreze (2002) and Pal and Ghosh (2007).

[2] China's large urban–rural income gap stems in large part from the population registration (*hukou*) system imposed in the late 1950s. This policy, combined with the rationing of food, put a formidable wall between urban and rural Chinese, and ensured that income gains produced by urban-biased policies accrued mainly to urban residents.

[3] In 2008, urban households saved 28.8 per cent of their disposable income and rural households saved 23.1 per cent of their net income. See World Bank (2009). An alternative series by Calla Wiemer is shown in Figure 1.1.

imbalance in sex ratio of the population (around 120 boys born for every 100 girls), which is stimulating increased saving behaviour in regions where the imbalance is most pronounced, because 'hoarding cash is one way to triumph in a competitive marriage market'.[4] This phenomenon, which is much less prevalent in developed urban regions, is also, in part, a byproduct of urban–rural inequality and the lack of social insurance for the rural population.

For the past decade, household saving rates have risen to well above their already high long-term average (see Figure 1.1). This increase corresponds to a period of very low real interest rates. As Lardy (2012) states, Chinese households behave like 'target savers', who respond to a fall in earnings of their saving by saving even more to accomplish their goals. The increase in saving also corresponds to a marked decline in the dependency ratio, as the age structure of China's ageing population entered a sweet spot in which the proportion of young dependents dipped more sharply than that of old dependents rose. A lower total dependency rate led to a higher rate of saving.[5]

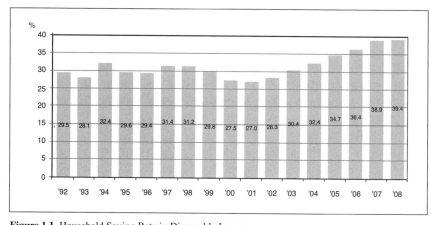

Figure 1.1. Household Saving Rate in Disposable Income
Source: Bonham and Wiemer (2012), based upon flow of funds data from China's National Bureau of Statistics.

The above factors help to explain high personal savings rates out of income. However, they are not the only explanations of the low share of household consumption in GDP. The primary cause of this is the very low share of household income in GDP. Recently, this share has fallen to only about 50 per cent, 'one of the lowest shares ever recorded' (Pettis, 2011). One reason that the growth of personal incomes lagged behind that of GDP is the large

---

[4] This idea is proposed by Shang-jin Wei and Xiaobo Zhang (Wei, 2010).
[5] Bonham and Wiemer (2012). In addition to the falling dependency ratio, these authors also attribute the rise in personal savings rate to the very high growth rates of the period in question.

labour surplus in both urban and rural areas that existed when China started its transition to a market-based economy in about 1980. Surplus labour depressed basic wages and kept them tied to the average income in the rural areas, which rose over time but much more slowly than GDP.[6] Moreover, the transition to a market economy required abandoning the policy of keeping redundant labour in urban jobs as a de facto policy of income maintenance. When millions of state enterprise workers were laid off in the late 1990s and early 2000s, their wages were replaced either by smaller transfers (subsistence payments, unemployment insurance, 'minimum livelihood guarantee' payments, or—if they were near retirement age—pensions), or by lower earnings in the informal sector.

In addition to the role of surplus labour in repressing the household share of GDP, various government policies have also contributed to this result. First, government's share of GDP, after falling to very low levels in the early 1990s, began to rise again because of tax reform and related policies designed to raise the state's fiscal capacity. Before the period of transition to a market economy began, state-owned enterprises (SOEs) simply turned over their profits to the state, which then reallocated capital to them according to the current plan. This was an efficient, low-cost method of revenue collection, but provided no incentive to increase revenue or profits. Moreover, it progressively failed to generate revenue once the economy opened up and foreign, private, and township and village enterprises were allowed into markets previously monopolized by SOEs. The tax reform of 1994 reversed this trend, and the share of government revenue in GDP doubled from only 10.3 per cent in 1995 to 20.4 per cent in 2008 (He, 2009).

Second, market liberalization in China has focused on goods markets, while leaving most resource markets constrained by substantial government intervention (Huang, 2010). In practice, this has meant very low capital costs, low prices of natural resources (fuel, water, etc.), as well as the official discouragement of independent labour unions that might have exercised some upward pressure on wages. Low capital costs have led to the adoption of capital-intensive technologies that have restricted the expansion of employment in the formal sector of the economy, and thus prolonged the survival of the labour surplus and kept wages lower than they would otherwise have been. Small and medium enterprises, which could create jobs and income, have been held back by lack of access to capital. Large capital-intensive enterprises, fed by artificially cheap credit, have generated profits, but few jobs and little wage income.

---

[6] Rural income increased very rapidly over the half-decade following decollectivization of agriculture, roughly 1979–1985. Between 1985 and 1998, however, wages in the collective sector rose at a rate of only 2.3 per cent a year; real wages in collective construction and in wholesale/retail trade grew at rates of 2.5 and 3.2 per cent a year respectively; and real rural incomes per capita grew by only 1.9 per cent a year (Perkins, 2012).

Indeed, the practice of keeping interest rates on bank deposits below the rate of inflation (negative real interest rates) has imposed a de facto tax on the population, transferring wealth from households to banks and the manufacturing enterprises that borrow from banks. In addition, the maintenance of an undervalued exchange rate for China's currency has further suppressed household real income by raising prices of goods in the marketplace. This combination of market forces (wages rising more slowly than GDP) and government policies (increasing tax revenues relative to GDP, financial repression, and an undervalued exchange rate) has ensured that household incomes—and, with them, household consumption—have lagged behind GDP growth.

Because of the low ratio of personal income to GDP, household saving has recently contributed only a quarter to a half of total saving, the remainder coming from government and enterprises (Kraay, 2000; Bonham and Wiemer, 2012), which financed the extremely high investment rate (see Figure 1.2) largely with swollen retained earnings.

Figure 1.3, taken from RIETI (2009), shows the changing composition of gross domestic expenditures in the years leading up to the global downturn. Most remarkable is the decline, after 2003, in the share of private consumption (also shown in Figure 1.4) and the increase in the shares of capital formation and net exports.

SOEs that survived the restructuring of the 1990s have seen profits rise very substantially, as have profits of other ownership forms. Figure 1.5 shows that the profits of very large industrial enterprises increased rapidly in the early 2000s to exceed 10 per cent of GDP by 2007. Although large, centrally

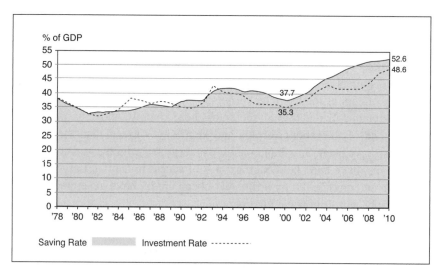

Figure 1.2. National Saving and Investment Rate, 1978–2010
Source: Bonham and Wiemer (2012: 2) used with permission.

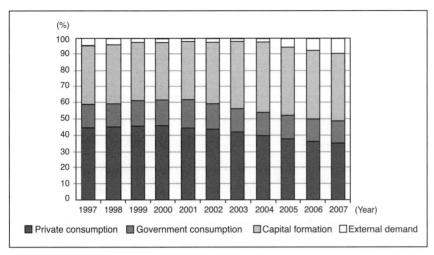

Figure 1.3. Changing Composition of GDP by Category of Final Demand
Sources: RIETI (2009); China Statistical Abstract (2008).

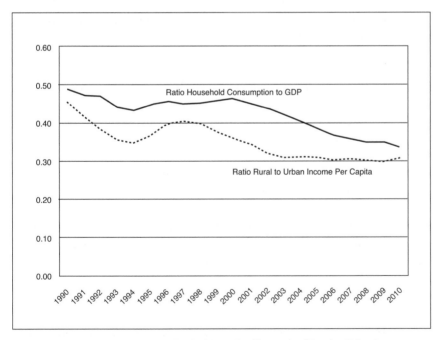

Figure 1.4. Falling Share of Consumption in GDP and Falling Ratio of Rural to Urban Income.
Source: *Statistical Yearbook of China*, 2011.
Note: Urban income is per capita disposable income; rural income is per capita net income. The close correlation between the decline in the ratio of consumption to GDP and the increase in the urban-rural income gap shows one aspect of the link between inequality and imbalance.

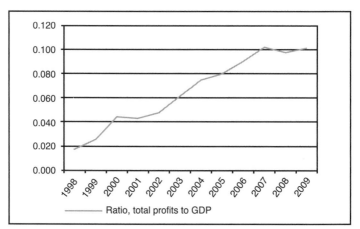

Figure 1.5. Ratio of Total Profits of Large Industrial Enterprises to GDP, 1998–2009
Source: SSB, (2010).
Note: Profits are those of large industrial enterprises, that is, with annual revenue from principal business of over 5 million yuan.

controlled SOEs were required to pay to the government either 5 per cent or 10 per cent of their profits (according to industry type) in 2008, most enterprise earnings have been retained as undistributed corporate profits, a growing source of national saving.

A rising profit share of GDP (Figure 1.5) has contributed to the increase in income inequality, as it has benefited the wealthy industrial sector relative to the much poorer rural economy, as well as those whose incomes derive from profits at the expense of those dependent upon wages. Similarly, the regimen of negative real interest rates on deposits, by subsidizing capital at the expense of labour, has contributed to China's extremely low elasticity of employment with respect to GDP. A crude calculation of the gross GDP elasticity of employment for the period 2000 to 2008 yields a value vanishingly close to zero.[7] A 1 per cent increase in GDP is associated with a 0.0003 per cent increase in employment.[8] Employment here includes agriculture, in which employment has been declining. If the same calculation is performed for value added of the secondary (manufacturing and construction) and tertiary sectors separately—the most rapidly growing parts of the economy—the output elasticity of employment works out to 0.14 in both cases, still very low.[9] Yet

---

[7] 0.00037; i.e., a 1 per cent increase in GDP is associated with a 0.0004 per cent increase in total employment.
[8] Hu and Sheng (2007) give the total employment-output elasticity in 1995–2003 as 0.13, and that of urban employment as 0.4 (p. 45).
[9] A good discussion of the problems of China's labour and employment statistics can be found in Banister (2005).

the generation of employment is a sine qua non for maintaining social stability, which is the leadership's first objective. Under such circumstances, to generate the necessary growth in employment requires the hypergrowth that China has experienced in recent years, albeit at the cost of an increasingly unbalanced economy, rising income inequality, and environmental destruction. In sum, China has been bound to a growth model that taxes household income, under-consumes, over-saves, subsidizes capital formation and exports, magnifies economic inequality, and chews up the environment, but through all of this generates fast enough growth to contain a growing reservoir of social and economic grievances, while the central government uses part of the growth premium to address these.

One gauge of the sustainability of this model is the objective need to absorb China's famously large reserve of surplus labour. Until the mid-1990s, when the reform of state enterprises produced a large surplus of urban workers, the visible labour surplus was entirely rural, taking the form of too many farmers on the limited amount of cultivated land. At the beginning of the reform era in the 1980s, the usual estimate was that some 250 million rural workers were redundant, in the basic sense that they could be released from production without reducing farm output. As the household registration (*hukou*) system was relaxed and the rationing of urban food was discontinued, rural–urban migration became possible, and was soon characterized by very large flows. If an economy grows at a rate of close to 10 per cent a year for long enough, even a very large labour surplus will eventually be absorbed. In China's case, this has been happening for more than 30 years, as China has become the twenty-first century's 'workshop of the world'.

There is reason to believe that the impact of the massive migration that has occurred during more than three decades has made great inroads into the rural labour surplus. This stands to reason: a simple hypothetical calculation tells us that if the net rural–urban migration averaged, say, 10 million people per year from 1985 to 2010, then the total number of persons leaving the countryside to work in towns and cities over that period would amount to 250 million. Most migrants remained 'rural' by official designation, while some were granted temporary or permanent urban registration. In fact, the officially defined rural population peaked in 1995 at 859.5 million, and between that year and 2009 fell by some 137 million. Over that same period, total rural employment also decreased (Table 1.1).

Moreover, many workers who remained in rural areas shifted out of agriculture to off-farm employment. Information about the rural labour force is consistent with this picture. While primary sector (overwhelmingly agricultural) incomes rose by only 3.9 per cent per year during 1999–2008, real rural incomes per capita grew at 11.3 per cent a year, an indication that rural incomes were increasingly dominated by non-agricultural wage-earning jobs,

Table 1.1. Total Urban and Rural Employment (millions)

	1978	1998	2005	2009
Urban employed persons	95	216	273	311
Rural employed persons	306	490	485	469

Source: SSB (2010).

which, by 2008, were generating 39 per cent of total rural income (Perkins, 2012). In 1980, full-time off-farm work was done by only 4 per cent of the rural workforce, but this fraction had, by 2007, soared to 55 per cent of all rural workers and to 80 per cent of young (16–25 years) workers (Li et al., 2010). From around 2004, a majority of the rural labour force, and an overwhelming majority of younger workers, were, for the first time, working in non-agricultural jobs (Li, Huang, and Liu, 2013). As one recent study concludes, 'It is safe to say that China's labour transition from the agricultural sector to the non-agricultural sector is nearly complete for the younger generation' (Li et al., 2010; see also Li et al., 2013), which is the generation that comprises the most mobile and best educated component of the rural labour force. Older workers in the countryside, who maintain control of family farms and look after small children, are less mobile and less inclined to take off-farm jobs, whether locally or through migration. In sum, whether rural workers migrated to towns and cities or took advantage of increasing nearby off-farm employment opportunities, after three decades of extraordinarily rapid industrial growth China has begun to exhaust the large reserve of surplus rural labour whose absorption into urban industries has made possible the implementation of the Lewis model of development up to the present (Lewis, 1954).

Survey evidence on wages is also consistent with this picture. While wages of unskilled rural workers remained stagnant from the 1980s to the early 2000s, in about 2003 they began to rise perceptibly (Liu et al., 2009; Park, Cai, and Du, 2010). Rural wages in the first quarter of 2010 were 16.4 per cent above a year earlier. Moreover, a tightening labour market appears to characterize not only the eastern coastal export zones but large parts of the interior as well.[10]

This conclusion is not universally shared. Yiping Huang suggests that labour-intensive infrastructure construction projects resulting from the stimulus may have led to a temporary labour shortage, which will subside when the projects come to an end (Huang, 2010). Lardy (2012) argues that there is no compelling evidence that labour shortages are producing faster

---

[10] Xinhua News Agency.

wage growth than before (see also Bradsher, 2012). Kuijs (2009) of the World Bank has argued that there still exists a relatively large labour surplus in agriculture, which will stave off the Lewis turning point for some time to come: 'The official employment statistics suggest that over 40 per cent of China's employees are still employed in agriculture, where labour productivity is 1/6th of that in the rest of the economy. Even after adjustment for possible overstatement of agricultural employment following Brandt, Hsieh, and Zhu (2008) by as much as 10 percentage points … agricultural employment is relatively high.'[11]

In fact, if 55 per cent of the rural labour force is working in non-agricultural jobs, as Li et al. (2010) conclude, and if the rural labour force constitutes 63 per cent of the total labour force (2009), as shown in Table 1.1, then agricultural workers make up only about 28 per cent of total employment. This is still high by the standard of industrialized countries. However, a previously flat labour supply curve is now likely to move gradually upward to reflect the progressive exhaustion of the most mobile portion of the rural labour surplus and the rising social and cultural costs of recruiting labour, as the surplus declines relative to total labour demand. The changing market conditions are likely to be reflected in a reduced willingness of migrant workers to tolerate very low wages and poor working conditions, which is exactly what qualitative accounts of worker attitudes suggest is happening.[12] Moreover, demographic change, namely the rapidly impending ageing of the population, is likely to accelerate what remains of the process of surplus absorption. To some degree, this debate is about a distinction without a difference, as both sides agree that wages are likely to continue rising, and an environment of buoyant wages favours rebalancing.[13] Moreover, just before and again immediately after the global downturn, wage growth in China began to exceed growth of labour productivity, causing unit labour costs to rise.

When the global recession hit China in 2008, the labour surplus absorption problem looked quite different. According to the Chinese Academy of Social Sciences (CASS), some 41 million workers lost their jobs as a result of the downturn. Academic studies projected huge job losses among migrant workers, not counting existing unemployment of formal sector workers.

[11] Kuijs (2009: 16).

[12] See Ranis (2003) for a discussion of the continuing relevance of the dual economy model of development.

[13] Thus Kuijs writes: 'Our medium term outlook on the domestic economy, urbanization, and the urban labour market suggests continued robust wage and employment growth' (2009: 8). Huang is an exception to this consensus, believing that the end of the stimulus could bring renewed weakening of labour markets. The last time a government policy transformed labour conditions from surplus to shortage over night, as it were, was the great leap forward of 1958. As big as the 2008–09 stimulus was, it was no great leap forward. If tight labour market conditions were caused by the stimulus, this would seem further evidence that the historical labour surplus is petering out.

As one observed, 'Jobless migrant workers on this mass scale implies a severe political and social problem. Any minor mishandling may trigger a strong backlash and could even result in social turbulence.'[14] The problem of unemployment quite suddenly took on great urgency and the restoration of employment became a high-priority objective. The $586 billion stimulus package that China adopted in late 2008 was larger relative to GDP than that of the USA, and far more stimulatory in nature. Moreover, the extraordinary surge in bank credit in early 2009 greatly magnified the impact of the stimulus. Since China's mode of economic growth is employment averse, as we have seen, it would take large increases in GDP to restore lost jobs.

Several components of the stimulus were also aimed at reducing both economic imbalances and inequality, for example: investment in public housing focusing on urban low-rent units and renovation of rural housing; investment in rural infrastructure, such as water supply, conservation, irrigation, roads, and the power grid; increased spending for health and education, including improved local clinics and renovation of schools in the interior; increased spending on public transport systems (11 Chinese cities already have underground rapid transit systems, and many more are under construction); increases in the extremely meagre payment standards for China's urban anti-poverty programme, the 'Minimum Living Allowance' scheme;[15] increased grain procurement prices for farmers and farm subsidies. Subsidies for rural purchases of home appliances, farm machinery, and vehicles have stimulated rural consumption, and steep cuts in sales taxes on energy efficient cars boosted sales. In a September 2009 speech to the World Economic Forum (Davos) meeting in Dalian,[16] the then premier, Wen Jiabao labelled the view that China's stimulus package was only about investment spending 'simplistic' and a 'total misunderstanding', and argued that the stimulus package was aimed at expanding both consumption and investment.

In fact, the stimulus underwent several mutations that substantially changed its character. Its original composition featured a list of familiar large-scale industrial beneficiaries: steel, auto, machinery, shipbuilding, textiles, electronics, and petrochemicals. This brought a rebuke from Cai Fang, a distinguished demographer and economist and a member of the NPC standing committee, who complained that 'The central government's incentives seem more attentive to big companies than small ones, which are the mainstay of employment' and warned against the danger of a 'jobless recovery'.[17] The stimulus was also criticized for focusing on capital-intensive industries with

---

[14] Yu Qiao, in van Ark et al. (2009).

[15] The payment standards are discussed in Gao and Riskin (2009).

[16] See <http://news.xinhuanet.com/english/2009-09/11/content_12032065.htm>.

[17] See *China Daily Online* at <http://www.chinadaily.com.cn/bizchina/2009npc/2009-03/09/content_7553041.htm>.

close connections to the CCP leadership, for ignoring small businesses and the jobs they could create (Divjak, 2009), and for focusing only on GDP and not on employment. As we have seen, however, that has been China's approach to job creation all along: very rapid growth to overcome the employment-averse nature of the growth model. Indeed, the surge in investment spending ran ahead of any increase in consumption. By the end of 2008, excess capacity in China's steel industry was already approximately equal to Europe's entire output, yet 58 million tons of new capacity were under construction. Capacity utilization rates were running low in aluminium, wind power, cement, and chemicals, among others, yet 'vast additional capacity is on the way' (FT.com, 29 November 2009).

Similarly, environmental protection, a key component of the leaders' plan to rebalance the economy and build a more 'harmonious' society, got shoved aside in the fervour to approve stimulus projects: 'In the rush to invest $585 billion in stimulus spending and revive flagging industrial production, China has at least temporarily back pedalled on some environmental restraints …'[18]

With a system that is resistant to job creation in the core industrial sector, it takes very high investment rates—the antithesis of rebalancing—to have an impact on employment. If restoring employment was the most important short-run objective, then perhaps rebalancing would have to wait. Employment levels in China in fact did recover from the middle of 2009 as a result of the extraordinary expansion of bank lending and heavy public investment. Recovery was not jobless, as Cai Fang feared. Researchers at the Chinese Academy of Social Sciences reported that, of the 41 million Chinese workers who lost their jobs as a result of the crisis, some 18 million had regained employment as of early September 2009,[19] and by February 2010 there were widespread reports of labour shortages in the coastal export zones.

China's previous major stimulus package, the one adopted in the late 1990s to combat the impact of the Asian crisis, did have a regionally equalizing effect, as much of it was aimed at less developed areas of the centre and west. The redistributive impact of the earlier programme was picked up by the 2002 China Household Income Project (see Khan and Riskin, 2005), which found improved intrarural distribution owing largely to the increase in off-farm employment in poorer provinces, which was probably due to the huge increase in interior infrastructural spending (Riskin, 2007). What about the 2008–09 stimulus?

[18] *New York Times*, 18 April 2009. The *Times* reported that environmental impact assessments were being cut back from 60 days to as little as 5.
[19] This was the analysis of the Chinese Academy of Social Sciences' *China Population and Labour Yearbook*, 2009, as reported by China Labour Net, at <http://www.worldlabour.org/eng/node/253>. The *Yearbook*'s editor is Cai Fang.

As the stimulus programme was amended in response to criticism, it changed character. The categories of expenditure, as broken down by Barry Naughton, are shown in Table 1.2. Naughton observes that the character of spending changed from the original emphasis on transport and power infrastructure to a greater emphasis on affordable housing, rural village infrastructure, and health and education, all categories with a more direct impact on living standards. In the February 2009 round, these three categories comprised almost 60 per cent of total spending. Moreover, infrastructure spending was focused on the less developed interior provinces, as during the Asian crisis. In the first half of 2009, fixed asset investment grew by 42 per cent in the western provinces, compared with 24 per cent in the east. Output growth in 12 western provinces outpaced that in 11 eastern ones by 8 per cent to 7 per cent (FT.com, 13 September 2009).

Stimulus-produced growth quickly restored employment, while the government continued its earlier announced policy of increased transfers to rural and low-income residents. Income maintenance transfers (*dibao*) going to around 70 million poor urban residents rose by a third or RMB20 billion in 2009, accelerating a trend of several years. Monthly pension payments for enterprise retirees increased by RMB120 or 10 per cent in January 2009, almost double the 5.9 per cent increase in consumer prices in 2008. This raised payments to retirees by about RMB75 billion. Thus, the stimulus had evolved into something that was intended to increase consumption, especially of low income groups, even if the huge spurt of investment worsened imbalance, at least in the short run.

Table 1.2. Expenditure Composition of Stimulus Package

	Per cent of total spending in plan	First spending round (RMB 100 billion), Dec. 2008	Second spending round (RMB 130 billion), Feb. 2009
Transport and power infrastructure (roads, railways, airports, power grid)	50	25	21
Rural village infrastructure	12	34	24
Environmental investment; natural areas	7	12	8
Affordable housing	13	10	22
Technological innovation and structural adjustment	12	6	12
Health and education	5	13	13

Source: Naughton (2009).

China's Minimum Livelihood Guarantee (*dibao*) programme for assisting poor families and individuals in urban areas is administered locally.[20] The income poverty line used to determine eligibility for assistance depends on local conditions, including cost of living and the budgetary situation of the local government. Thus, there is wide variability in '*dibao* line' throughout the country. For instance, in June 2010, among 36 large cities, the line ranged from a high of 450 yuan per month in Shanghai to a low of 156 yuan in Urumqi, a range of almost three times. The range would be even greater if small cities, whose *dibao* lines are generally lower, were considered.

Table 1.3 shows the average of these *dibao* lines among 36 large cities from March 2007 to June 2010, the period covering the sharp downturn of 2008 and the recovery from it. During the course of these months, the average urban poverty line used to identify an individual's eligibility for *dibao* assistance in China's cities rose by 35.6 per cent from 174 yuan per month in March 2007 to 236 in June of 2010. The average amounts of such assistance per capita rose even faster, by 76 per cent. Because the total number of beneficiaries increased by almost 3 per cent, overall spending on the *dibao* programme rose by 81 per cent to over 3.7 billion yuan in June 2010. In rural areas in the middle of 2010, there were about 51 million people designated as rural *dibao* eligible and 5.5 million traditional 'Five Guarantee' individuals, totalling over 56 million rural recipients of assistance. Thus, about 79 million very poor people, urban and rural, were receiving assistance. Transfer payments to these poor people rose by about a third in 2009 (Lardy, 2012). Pension payments to retirees also increased by 10 per cent, well above the rate of inflation. As Lardy summarizes, 'The increases in employment, transfer payments, and pension income contributed to a 9.8 per cent increase in the disposable income of urban residents and an increase of 8.5 per cent in the net income of rural residents in 2009.'[21] For the first time in eight years, consumption grew faster than GDP, at least temporarily halting the long-term decline in the rate of consumption, if not the continuing growth of the urban–rural income gap.

Table 1.4 presents basic information on per capita income of seven provinces, three of them relatively well off and four quite poor. The provinces are sorted by income. Note that the correlation between the urban and rural rankings is perfect, and that the range between high and low income province is much greater for rural income than for urban.

It has long been evident that China's labour and capital markets are both segmented. Full-status urban residents do not generally build skyscrapers, wash windows, or fill export processing factories. State enterprises' borrowing rates are kept below the market cost of capital and their technologies are

---

[20] See Hussain (2005) for a discussion of urban poverty and poverty policy in China.
[21] Lardy (2012: 8).

Table 1.3. Increase in Urban Safety Net (*Dibao*) Expenditures, March 2007–June 2010

Month/Year	National average urban *dibao* line (yuan/month/person)	National average amount of assistance (yuan/month/person)	Total number of beneficiaries (persons)	Total *dibao* spending (bills of yuan)
Jun 10	236	162	23,050,105	37.34
Mar 10	232	n/a	n/a	n/a
Dec 09	228	n/a	n/a	n/a
Sep 09	224	n/a	n/a	n/a
Jun 09	221	n/a	n/a	n/a
Mar 09		n/a	n/a	n/a
Dec 08	208	n/a	n/a	n/a
Sep 08	208	n/a	n/a	n/a
Jun 08	208	n/a	n/a	n/a
Mar 08	186	n/a	n/a	n/a
Dec 07	182	n/a	n/a	n/a
Sep 07	179	n/a	n/a	n/a
Jun 07	177	n/a	n/a	n/a
Mar 07	174	92	22,427,000	20.63
Increase Mar 07 to Jun 10 (%)	35.6%	76.1%	2.8%	81.0%

Source: <www.dibao.org>. I thank Qin Gao for compiling these data.

Table 1.4. Rural and Urban Income of Selected Provinces, 2007 (yuan)

Province	Per Capita Net Income of Rural Households	Per Capita Disposable Income of Urban Households
Shanghai	10,145	23,663
Zhejiang	8,265	20,574
Jiangsu	6,561	16,378
Sichuan	3,547	11,098
Shaanxi	2,645	10,678
Guizhou	2,374	10,763
Gansu	2,329	10,012

Source: China Data Center Online (University of Michigan) at <http://141.211.142.26/>.

excessively capital-intensive, creating few new jobs. Export industries and urban construction, on the other hand, are filled with migrant workers, their production is more labour-intensive and employment grows along with output. These sectors, then, are exceptions to the employment-averse nature of recent industrial growth discussed above. There, labour-intensive techniques have taken advantage of China's formerly large pool of surplus workers. And for that reason, after some 30 years of very rapid growth based upon tapping this pool, it has begun to shows signs of exhaustion.

Conclusion: rebalancing and the end of the Lewis model

By early 2010, with exports recovering, there were widespread reports of labour shortages and sharply rising wages in much of the export-oriented south-east coastal region where migrant labour is predominant. It is unclear as yet whether this is principally a phenomenon of friction from the lag between the extraordinarily fast recovery of labour demand prompted by China's massive stimulus and credit expansion on the one hand, and the migrant labour response on the other; or whether it is a return to the growing labour market tightness that had been experienced just before the 2008 downturn and that had already begun to push unit labour costs up in the export zones. We have seen that reported labour shortages may not be merely frictional. First, a large part of stimulus spending was aimed at interior, less-developed regions, as was the case during the Asian crisis of the late 1990s. The jobs thus created in the interior, along with improved conditions for farmers as the government cut taxes and raised purchasing prices for agricultural goods, and construction booms in inland cities such as Chongqing and Wuhan, have all combined to raise the opportunity cost of migration to eastern export enclaves far from home (*Wall Street Journal*, <wsj.com>, 22 Feb. 2010).[22] Labour productivity, whose rapid increase has heretofore offset rising wages and kept unit labour cost low, shows signs of flattening out.[23] The same Cai Fang, who criticized the stimulus at the National People's Congress in 2009, said in March 2010 that 'It's certain that the migrant worker shortage is here to stay in China.' Cai reported that wages for China's migrant workers increased 19 per cent in 2008 and 16 per cent in 2009, despite the downturn; that companies were shifting production to the interior to take advantage of lower labour costs; and that

---

[22] Enrolment in colleges and universities has also been growing very rapidly, quadrupling from 5.6 million in 2000 to 21.5 million in 2009. Although only a minor influence on the supply of migrant labour, this must have influenced the labour supply offered by full-status urban residents.

[23] See Perkins (2012). Much of this rise in labour productivity derived from the offloading of millions of state sector workers by restructuring SOEs from the mid-1990s on.

local governments would have to abandon their 'pro-capital' postures for
'pro-labour' ones, raising minimum wages and easing living conditions for
migrants and their families in their new urban homes.[24]

To the degree that gains in labour productivity match those in wages, unit
labour costs remain stable. Part of the explanation for China's hypergrowth
of the last few decades is its huge supply of labour and the advantages of
extensive growth—that is, shifting very low productivity farmers into newly
built factories, where their productivity is immediately multiplied.

But even *within* industry, labour productivity has risen very rapidly since
the mid-1990s—by 15–20 per cent per year from 1997 to 2003 and 10–12
per cent per year from 2005 to 2009. Reasons include the restructuring of
SOEs, which saw them shed some 40 per cent of state enterprise jobs (43
million workers) between 1997 and 2004 (World Bank, 2010), as well
as the productivity gains from China's accession to WTO in 2001. These
increases more than offset wage growth between 1995 and 2003, when
SOE restructuring had been completed, reducing unit labour costs steadily.[25]
However, unit labour costs stopped falling in about 2003 and, most recently,
began rising. They increased significantly in 2008, fell in 2009 (owing to
the sharp downturn), and rose again in 2010 (World Bank, 2010). If China's
large pool of surplus labour is beginning to run out and wages rise faster than
productivity, then China's development model will be very different from the
one that it has followed for some three decades.

For instance, strong growth in exports in early 2010, after their collapse
a year earlier, raised the question whether China would quickly regain its
past peak (2008) level of exports (*NY Times*, 10 Mar. 2010). As long as China
remains burdened with a large pool of surplus labour whose employment
depends on expanding exports, the temptation to continue the addiction to
export promotion remains strong. But the shrinkage of that pool and consequent
increases in labour costs will threaten that addiction, as will sluggish world
growth and the reluctance of China's trading partners to countenance
continuous large trade imbalances. As the Lewis model of unlimited labour
is left behind, development will continue shifting to the lower-cost interior.
Rising wages and falling profits relative to GDP could produce increasing rates
of consumption and falling rates of investment, helped along by strong social
welfare spending by the central government. Growth could moderate without
reducing consumption. China's economy could thus begin to rebalance along
the lines its central government has been advocating fruitlessly for years. Its

---

[24] See 'China wages to rise as labour shortages grow', Reuters, <http://www.reuters.com/article/id
USTRE62I14B20100319> (accessed 25 March 2010).
[25] Van Ark et al. (2009) find that labour cost per unit in manufacturing fell 38 per cent from 1995 to
2004.

vigorous expansion of spending to improve and extend rural education and health care (World Bank, 2009), build up transport and energy infrastructure in the underdeveloped interior, and even initiate a rural pension system will facilitate market-driven change by making interior regions more attractive to investors escaping from high coastal labour and real estate costs. At that point, both market forces and state policy would cooperate to rebalance China's growth model and make it work better in combining growth with equity.

The state could encourage this transformation by spending more on safety net and social insurance programmes; changing the bureaucratic incentive structure at the local level to one that no longer favours only growth and investment; and, by allowing interest rates to rise to market levels, thus reverse the policy of shifting wealth from households and consumption in order to subsidize banks and investment. Successful promotion of rebalancing in this manner would reverse the steady growth of inequality. Without such rebalancing, however, that trend is very likely to continue.

References

Banister, Judith (2005) Manufacturing employment in China, *Monthly Labor Review*, July, pp. 11–29.

Bonham, Carl and Wiemer, Calla (2012) Chinese saving dynamics: the impact of GDP growth and the dependent share. UHERO Working Paper No. 2010–11R.

Bradsher, Keith (2012) In China, sobering signs of slower growth. *New York Times*, 5 March.

Brandt, Loren, Hsieh, C., and Zhu, X. (2008) Growth and structural transformation in China, in Loren Brandt and Thomas G. Rawski (eds), *China's Great Economic Transformation* (New York: Cambridge University Press).

Deaton, Angus and Dreze, Jean (2002). Poverty and inequality in India: a re-examination. Working Paper No. 107, from Centre for Development Economics, Delhi School of Economics.

Divjak, Carol (2009) Millions of job losses threaten to trigger social unrest in China. (Montreal: Centre for Research on Globalization). <http://www.globalresearch.ca/index.php?context=va&aid=12246> (accessed 8 October 2012).

Gao, Qin and Riskin, Carl (2009) Explaining China's changing income inequality: market vs. social benefits, in Deborah Davis and Wang Feng (eds) *Creating Wealth and Poverty in Post-Socialist China* (Berkeley: University of California Press).

He, Qinglian (2009) The relationship between Chinese peasants' right to subsistence and China's social stability. *China Rights Forum*, 1.

Hu, Angang and Sheng, Xin, Urban Unemployment in China, a Background Analysis (1995–2003), in Grace Lee and Malcolm Warner, eds, *Economy, Human Resources and Labour Markets*, Oxford and New York: Routledge, 2007.

Huang, Yiping (2010) Five predictions for the Chinese economy in 2010. *East Asia Forum*, 10 January.

Hussain, Athar (2005) *Urban Poverty in China: Measurement, Patterns and Policies*. (Geneva: International Labour Office).

Khan, Azizur Rahman and Riskin, Carl (2005) Household income and its distribution in China, 1995 and 2002. *China Quarterly*, 182, June.

Kraay, Aart (2000) Household saving in China. *The World Bank Economic Review*, 14(3), pp. 545–570.

Kuijs, Louis (2009) China through 2020 — a macroeconomic scenario. World Bank, China Office Research Working Paper No. 9.

Lardy, Nicholas R. (2012) *Sustaining China's Economic Growth after the Global Financial Crisis* (Washington, DC: Peterson Institute for International Economics).

Lewis, W. Arthur (1954), Economic development with unlimited supplies of labour. *Manchester School of Economic and Social Studies*, 22(2), pp. 139–191.

Li, Qiang, Huang Jikun and Liu Chengfang, (2013). China's labor transition and the future of China's rural wages and employment. *China and World Economy*, 21(3), pp. 4–24.

Li, Xiaofei, Liu, Chengfang, Luo, Renfu, Zhang, Linxiu, and Rozelle, Scott (2010) The challenges facing young workers during rural labor transition. *China Agricultural Economics Review*, 2(2), 185–186.

Liu, C., Luo, R., Rozelle, S., Sharbonom, B., and Shi, Y. (2009) *Development Challenges, Tuition Barriers and High School Education in China* (Beijing: Centre for Chinese Agricultural Policy, Chinese Academy of Sciences).

National Bureau of Statistics (2008) China Statistical Abstract 2008. Beijing, China Statistics Press.

Naughton, Barry (2009) Understanding the Chinese stimulus package. *China Leadership Monitor*, 28, 8 May.

Pal, Parthapratim and Ghosh, Jayati (2007) Inequality in India: a survey of recent trends. UN/DESA Working Paper No. 45, July. <http://www.un.org/esa/desa/papers/2007/wp45_2007.pdf> (accessed 8 October 2012).

Park, Albert, Cai, Fang, and Du, Ying (2010) Can China meet her employment challenges? in Jean Oi, Scott Rozelle, and Xuegang Zhou (eds) *Growing Pains: Tensions and Opportunities in China's Transformation* (Stanford, CA: Stanford Asia-Pacific Research Center), pp. 27–55.

Perkins, Dwight H. (2012) Rapid growth and changing economic structure: the expenditure side story and its implications for China. *China Economic Review*, 23(3), September, pp. 501–511.

Pettis, Michael (2011) The contentious debate over China's economic transition. (Policy Outlook: Carnegie Endowment for International Peace). <http://carnegieendowment.org/2011/03/25/contentious-debate-over-china-s-economic-transition/37hy> (accessed 8 October 2012).

Ranis, Gustav (2003) Is dualism worth revisiting? Yale University Economic Growth Center Discussion Paper No. 870.

RIETI (Research Institute of Economy Trade and Industry) (2009) China exploring measures to boost consumption. <http://www.rieti.go.jp/en/china/09012901.html> (accessed 8 October 2012).

Riskin, Carl (2007) Has China reached the top of the Kuznets curve? in Vivienne Shue and Christine Wong (eds) *Paying for Poverty Reduction in China* (Stanford, CA: Stanford University Press), pp. 29–45.

SSB (State Statistical Bureau) (2010, 2011) *China Statistical Yearbook* (Beijing: China Statistics Press).

Van Ark, B., Erumban, A. A., Chen, V., and Kumar, U. (2009) The cost competitiveness of the manufacturing sector in China and India, an industry and regional perspective, Economics Program Working Paper Series 9-02, The Conference Board and Growth and Development Center of the University of Groningen. <http://www.conference-board.org/pdf_free/workingpapers/E-0042-09-WP.pdf> (accessed 8 October 2012).

Wan, Guanghua (2007) Understanding regional poverty and inequality trends in China: methodological issues and empirical findings. *Review of Income and Wealth*, special issue, 53(1), 28 February, pp. 23–34.

Wan, Guanghua (ed.) (2008) *Understanding Inequality and Poverty in China: Methods and Applications* (Basingstoke: Palgrave Macmillan).

Wei, Shang-jin (2010) 'Why do the Chinese save so much?' Forbes.com. <http://www.forbes.com/2010/02/02/china-saving-marriage-markets-economy-trade.html> (accessed 12 March 2012).

World Bank (2009) From poor areas to poor people: China's evolving poverty reduction agenda: an assessment of poverty and inequality in China (Washington: The World Bank). <http://siteresources.worldbank.org/CHINAEXTN/Resources/318949-12390 96143906/China_PA_Report_March_2009_eng.pdf> (accessed 8 October 2012).

World Bank (2010) Beijing office quarterly update, November.

2

The Indian Economy in the Post-Reform Period: Growth without Structural Transformation

KUNAL SEN

Introduction

AT THE TIME OF INDEPENDENCE, India was primarily an agrarian economy, with three-fifths of output originating from agriculture. In the 60 years since independence, there has been a significant transformation of economic activity away from agriculture, with less than a fifth of output now originating from agriculture and the rest from manufacturing and services. Since the 1980s, along with structural change, there has been strong economic growth, with a growth rate that has been among the highest in the world. The service sector has been the engine of this growth. During the 1980s and early 1990s, significant economic reforms were initiated: India effectively abandoned the import—substituting the industrialization strategy that it had followed since independence under a partial command and control economic regime—and started to pursue a more market-oriented economic system.

In this chapter, we provide an overview of the key analytical issues and debates relating to India's domestic economy. We begin by setting out the important features of the growth process and that of structural change since independence. Although the economy has observed sustained economic growth for well over three decades, the process of structural change has been uneven, with a significantly dualist structure as well as slow growth in the manufacturing sector, and low productivity growth in the agricultural sector. India's pattern of structural change has been atypical in the Asian context—in contrast to other high-growth Asian economies, the service sector, not the export-oriented manufacturing sector, has been the engine of growth. We then examine the changes that have occurred in the three

Proceedings of the British Academy, **193**, 47–62, © The British Academy 2014

main economic sectors—agriculture, manufacturing, and services—since the onset of the economic reforms. Another feature of structural change in developing economies is the rapid rate of urbanization: we look at the process of urbanization, and note that, contrary to what has been observed in other fast-growing countries, the rate of urbanization in India seems to have slowed down. We then discuss the causes of India's growth acceleration, and argue that they suggest a more complex causal story than has been commonly portrayed in scholarly writings on India: both the state and the market are important in India's trajectory, though the precise roles of the state and the market in India's growth experience differ over time. We conclude with some reflections on India's possible development trajectory.

Growth and structural change in the Indian economy

In this section, we set out the 'stylized facts' of India's economic development, focusing in particular on the more recent period. We begin with an overview of India's record in economic growth, and then move on to a description of the process of structural change in the economy.

Economic growth

After a long period of stagnation, especially from the mid-1960s to the late 1970s, GDP per capita started rising in the late 1970s, and has kept on steadily increasing over the last two decades of the twentieth century and into the first decade of the twenty-first century. In Figure 2.1, we plot per capita national income for India from 1950 to 2008, indexing 1950 to 100. The rising growth rate can be clearly seen, though the acceleration is gradual, beginning from the late 1970s. Introducing a trend line for per capita national income based on the actual observations from 1950 to 1980 in Figure 2.1, we can see a clear deviation upwards of actual per capita national income from the trend line, from 1980 onwards. By the time we reach 2008, actual per capita income is double what it would have been if the Indian economy had followed the average growth rate of the first three decades since independence. This is a remarkable achievement in terms of increases in average standards of living, and one paralleled by few other countries in the same period, except for China.

However, the process of economic growth has not been balanced, at least across the major sectors of the economy—agriculture, manufacturing, and services. The average annual rate of economic growth accelerated from 2.9 per cent in 1965–79 to 5.8 per cent in 1980–90 (Figure 2.2). This was mostly

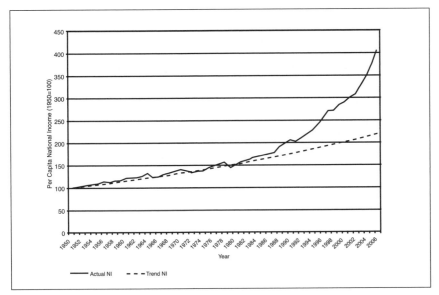

Figure 2.1. Per Capita National Income (NI), India, 1950–2008
Source: *National Accounts Statistics*, Central Statistical Organization, my calculations.

due to an increase in the rates of growth of the service sector (which rose from an annual average of 4.3 per cent in 1965–79 to 6.5 per cent in 1980–90), and the manufacturing sector (which grew from an annual average of 4.1 per cent in 1965–79 to 6.9 per cent in 1980–90). In the most recent period, 2001–08, the annual average rate of economic growth has been 7.3 per cent, the highest since independence and in large measure due to very strong growth in the service sector (8.7 per cent annually over this period). By contrast, the annual average rate of growth of the agricultural sector has been around 3 per cent over 1991–2008. Since the early 1980s, agriculture has been the laggard in economic growth in India.

How does India's pattern of economic growth compare to that of China? China's rate of output growth in 1978–2004 was 9.3 per cent per year— almost 4 percentage points higher than that of India, which was 5.4 per cent a year during the same period (Bosworth and Collins, 2008). This superior performance is attributable either to a higher rate of growth of employment or to a higher rate of growth of labour productivity (output per capita). But between 1978 and 2004, employment grew at exactly the same rate in both China and India: 2 per cent a year. So the higher rate of growth of output in China relative to India was almost completely due to a higher rate of growth of labour productivity. Indeed, over the last quarter century it stood at 7.3 per cent a year in China as compared with 3.3 per cent a year in India. This, in turn, was due to a higher rate of capital accumulation—3.2 per cent a year

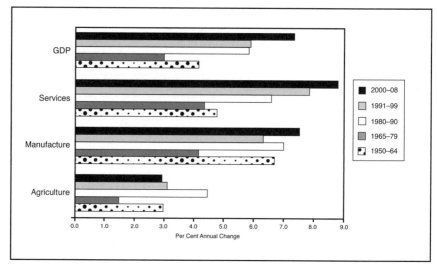

Figure 2.2. Sectoral Growth in the Indian Economy, 1950–2008
Source: *National Accounts Statistics*, Central Statistical Organisation, my calculations.

in China as compared with 1.3 in India—and higher total factor productivity growth—3.6 per cent a year in China as compared with 1.6 in India. While India's performance in labour productivity compares favourably with those achieved by East Asia in its peak growth period, it has been dwarfed by the remarkable performance of China, both in capital accumulation and productivity growth.

Structural change

There has been significant change in the structure of the Indian economy in the six decades since independence. Whereas in 1955 agriculture comprised 57 per cent of output, in 2008 it comprised a mere 19.8 per cent (Table 2.1). While in 1955 manufacturing comprised 9.9 per cent of output, in 2008 it was 15.6 per cent. This was mostly due to the growth in the output of the organized or formal manufacturing sector, from 4.9 per cent in 1955 to 10.6 per cent in 2008. Perhaps the most remarkable feature of the Indian economy's structural change has been the increase in the share of the service sector—from 19 per cent of GDP in 1955 to 40.7 per cent in 2008 (Table 2.1). It is well known that India's pattern of economic development has been atypical, in that the service sector has comprised a far higher share of economic activity than should have been the case, given India's level of per capita income.

Table 2.1. Composition of GDP, India, 1955–2008 (% share)

Year	Agriculture and Mining	Man	Of which:		Cons	THR	TSC	FIEBS	Miscell
			Formal Man	Informal Man					
1955	57.0	9.9	4.9	5.0	4.6	9.1	3.4	6.5	9.5
1960	54.5	10.9	5.9	5.0	5.1	9.8	3.9	6.1	9.7
1970	48.0	12.6	7.6	5.0	6.1	10.9	4.6	5.9	11.8
1980	41.8	13.8	8.1	5.8	6.1	12.2	6.2	6.5	13.3
1990	34.9	16.6	10.5	6.1	5.5	12.5	6.2	9.7	14.5
2000	25.7	15.6	10.4	5.3	5.8	14.6	7.7	13.2	17.3
2008	19.8	15.6	10.6	5.0	8.6	16.7	7.9	16.1	15.4

Source: *National Accounts Statistics*, Central Statistical Organization—India, author's calculations.

Notes: Man = Manufacturing; Formal Man = Registered or Organized Manufacturing; Informal Man = Unregistered or Unorganized Manufacturing; Cons = Construction; THR = Trade, Hotel, and Restaurants; TSC = Transportation, Storage, and Communication; FIEBS = Finance, Insurance, Real Estate, and Business Services; Miscell = Miscellaneous (includes Community, Social, and Personal Service, and Public Administration and Defence).

With respect to manufacturing, a distinctive feature of this sector has been its dualism—the existence of a relatively small number of formal sector firms, which have a largely protected workforce, along with a large number of firms in the informal sector, where workers have no access to social security, employment protection, and other benefits. Formal sector firms are very different from informal sector firms both in labour productivity and wages paid to their employees—in 2005–06, labour productivity in formal sector firms was 28 times higher than that in informal sector firms, and wages five times higher (Mazumdar and Sarkar, 2012). More strikingly, productivity differences have been widening over time—labour productivity in formal sector firms was only five times that of informal sector firms in 1984–85. We have already observed in Table 2.1 that the share of organized manufacturing in GDP has increased, especially since 1980, while the share of unorganized manufacturing in GDP has remained remarkably constant over the 60 years since independence, at around 5 per cent of GDP. The persistence of dualism in Indian manufacturing and the presence of a large low productivity (and low wage) informal sector in the face of significant and rapid economic change remains a matter of policy concern, and may have played a contributing role in the relatively weak effect of economic growth on poverty reduction in India (Sen, 2008).

Another distinctive feature of India's pattern of economic development has been the slow movement of labour from the agricultural to the higher productivity manufacturing and service sectors. The reallocation of labour from agriculture to manufacturing and services has been slower in India than China. While in 1980 the employment share of agriculture in China was very similar to India—at 68 per cent—by 2000 the share of employment in agriculture had fallen to 50 per cent in China, while it remained at 59.3 per cent for India (Kochhar et al., 2006). The shift in employment away from agriculture has been mostly towards the services sector, total employment in which grew from 20 per cent in 1983, to 29 per cent in 2004. In contrast, the share of manufacturing in total employment has hardly changed—with a small increase from 10.6 per cent in 1983 to 11.7 per cent in 2004.

India's pattern of structural change during the process of economic growth in the past three decades has been different from other Asian economies during their own growth phases. All the major Asian economies, starting with Japan, then Korea, Singapore, and Taiwan, and more recently China and Vietnam, have moved from the import-substituting phases of their economic development to an export-oriented development strategy that involved a strong growth in the labour-intensive segment of the manufacturing sector in the initial years (Riedel, 1988; Haggard, 1996; Krueger, 1997). In all these countries, as their economies integrated more closely with world markets, economic growth and structural transformation (that is, a shift of employment from agriculture to manufacturing) went hand in hand, and surplus labour was pulled from less productive agriculture to the more productive manufacturing sector. This has not happened in India, where the share of the labour-intensive textile, clothing, and footwear industries actually contracted from the mid-1970s to the late 1990s in organized manufacturing production and employment, in spite of India's apparent comparative advantage in labour-intensive industries (Wood and Calandrino, 2000; Sen, 2008). At the same time, the lack of growth in the formal segments of labour-intensive industries was not accompanied by an increase in the share of the informal/unorganized sector in output and employment in the same industries (Raj and Sen, 2010). The lack of growth in export-oriented labour-intensive manufacturing along with the emergence of a highly skill-intensive export-oriented segment of the services explains in great part the atypical pattern of structural change in India.

Agriculture: the lagging sector

After a period of slow growth in the 1950s, the new Borlaug seed-fertilizer technology introduced in the mid-1960s had a significant impact on raising yields and output levels of some crops, and ushered in the Green Revolution and a rise in India's aggregate agricultural production. In the beginning, the new technology was initiated for wheat in the irrigated north-western region of India, but, by the 1970s, the Green Revolution had covered rice and other crops, had spread to many other parts of the country and to small producers (Farmer, 1977; Bhalla and Singh, 2009). The growth rate of agricultural output at the All-India level accelerated from 2.24 per cent a year in 1962–83 to 3.37 per cent a year between 1980 and 1993. Most of the output growth was owing to increased productivity, with yields accounting for 85.2 per cent of output growth. In the 1980–93 period, agricultural growth kicked off in the previously stagnant states of eastern India (Rogaly, Harriss-White, and Bose, 1999). By 1992–93, the diffusion of high-yielding varieties of seeds which formed the basis of the Green Revolution was more or less complete, with about 90 per cent of wheat area and 70 per cent of rice area occupied by them (Kotwal, Ramaswami, and Wadhwa, 2011). There was a strong association between agricultural growth and rural poverty decline in this period (Palmer-Jones and Sen, 2003).

However, since 1993 output growth has decelerated to 1.74 per cent a year, a slowdown observed in most states of India (Palmer-Jones and Sen, 2003). At the same time, there was a shift in cropping pattern changes towards high-value crops compared with the period 1980–93 before the agricultural reforms. In addition, the labour/land ratio has increased in most regions in India, in part owing to the weak demand for labour from the non-farm sector and in part owing to the decline in agricultural productivity in the post-reform period, which implied a falling productivity-induced demand for labour from the farm sector. The exhaustion of the possibility of an increase in the gross cropped area of most parts of India meant that agricultural development relied heavily on intensive growth. It is not clear what led to the decline in agricultural productivity in the post-reform period—a decline in public investment in agriculture may have been a contributing factor, though input subsidies to agriculture increased during the 'reforms' (Harriss-White and Janakarajan, 2004). In addition, expenditures on the public-sector agricultural research system for agriculture faltered, as did the productivity of the research system (Kotwal, Ramaswami, and Wadhwa, 2011).

The economic reforms themselves were not directly targeted to the agricultural sector, though there were indirect effects working through changes in the credit system for agriculture, with a weakening of the mandatory requirements for commercial banks to open rural and semi-urban branches, as well as an improvement in the terms of trade for agriculture in the 1990s as protection for industry was removed (along with higher minimum support prices for rice and wheat), leading to a fall in industrial prices (Balakrishnan, Golait, and Kumar, 2008). While the decrease in bank density in rural areas may have had an adverse effect on the financing of private agricultural investment, rising real prices for agricultural commodities in the post-reform period seemed to have a positive effect on output growth in the agricultural sector (Joshi, Birthal, and Minot, 2006).

Industry: the partial success of economic reforms

For the first four decades since independence, the government intervened in almost all aspects of the activities of formal manufacturing firms. Industry in India was subject to rather formidable legal barriers to entry. Investment, both in terms of the expansion of capacity of existing firms and of the creation of new firms, was controlled by the government through its licensing policies. These were in turn determined according to plan priorities. Though the purported objective of the licensing regime was balanced growth, it effectively led to a more monopolistic structure and significantly encouraged rent-seeking by corporations entrenched with public powers (Aghion et al., 2008). Following an initial attempt in 1975–76, the liberalization of industrial controls gathered momentum in 1985–86, when some industries and small-sized firms were taken out of the purview of industrial licensing, and the modernization of equipment along with an expansion of capacity were also allowed in a limited manner (Mookherjee, 1995).

On 24 July 1991, the Licence Raj effectively came to an end, when industrial licensing was abolished irrespective of the level of investment, except for 16 core industries. The number of industries reserved for the public sector was also significantly reduced. Under the new policy guidelines on foreign investment, automatic permission came to be granted for foreign equity participation up to 51 per cent in industries on a specified list of high technology and high investment priority.

What have been the effects of these major changes in industrial policy on productivity and innovation, on the ownership and management of industry? The available evidence suggests that domestic deregulation has had surprisingly little effect on productivity and innovation. Trade liberalization, especially in the form of access to imported intermediate goods, has been the dominant factor behind the increase in productivity growth in Indian manufacturing (Chand and Sen, 2002). But there has been little evidence of creative destruction or product churning since the reforms of 1991 (Goldberg et al., 2010). The industrial sector is still dominated by incumbents—state-owned firms and business groups—and there is limited new firm entry in the formal manufacturing sector (Alfaro and Chari, 2009). The reasons for this appear to be, first, significant impediments to firm exit in the form of stringent bankruptcy laws, which still favour the restructuring of existing loss-making firms rather than their closure; and, second, the political connections that incumbents have which allow them to prevent the entry of new firms, especially in concentrated, profitable industries and in industries dominated by state-owned corporations (Walton, 2010).

Services: the leading sector?

As we noted earlier, the service sector had the fastest growth rate of all three sectors in the post-1991 period. Between 1993 and 2004, the two fastest growing service sectors were business services (an average growth rate of 24.3 per cent a year over the ten years) and communications (an average growth rate of 20.3 per cent a year). This was mostly owing to the advent of cellular technology, as the government opened telecommunications to the private sector by relinquishing its monopoly control over communication services (Kotwal et al., 2010). Economic reforms that relaxed the entry of foreign firms into the services sector were also directly behind service sector growth, as the share of services in foreign direct investment increased from 10.5 per cent in the early 1990s to nearly 30 per cent in the second half of the decade (Chanda, 2007). As a consequence of the entry of outward-oriented foreign direct investment (FDI) into the information technology sector after 1992, software exports grew substantially—at nearly six times the rate for world exports of services.

It is often observed that the service sector in India is commonly skill-intensive, and that its growth has mostly required skilled labour. This is certainly true for export-oriented information technology-related sectors, for example, communications and business services. However, other fast-growing segments of the service sector are intensive in unskilled labour, the most important of which are the 'trade, hotel, and restaurants' sector. These services have rapidly increased their share in GDP from 9.1 per cent in 1955 to 16.7 per cent in 2008. Kotwal et al. (2010) show that the 'trade, hotel, and restaurant' sector grew rapidly in the 1990s, and was an important sector for the creation of unskilled labour-intensive jobs. The growth in the hospitality sector may be attributed in part to growth in domestic demand, and the increased practice of eating out by middle-class Indians. However, this sector is a non-tradable service sector (in that the services provided cannot be exported) and is therefore dependent on the growth of export sectors such as manufacturing and information technology-related services. So the trade, hotels, and restaurants sector will never be a leading sector of the economy in the way that information technology has been in the immediate post-reform period.

The puzzle of slowing urbanization

In most developing economies, a higher rate of economic growth and an expanding share of the secondary and tertiary sectors in economic activity are usually associated with greater urbanization. But another surprising feature of India's economic development in the recent past has been that the rate of growth of urbanization seems to be slowing down, even in the presence of high economic growth and the faster growth of the secondary and tertiary sectors over that of agriculture. While India's urban population was 31.1 per cent of total population in 2001, compared with 17.3 per cent in 1951, the rate of growth of urban population declined from 3.80 per cent in 1971–81 to 3.11 per cent in 1981–91, then to 2.74 per cent in 1991–2001, and finally to 2.76 per cent in 2001–11. In other words, India's rate of urbanization was fastest in the 1970s, when the economy grew slowly and when manufacturing and services were not expanding as rapidly as in the 1980s and 1990s.

Another feature of India's urbanization has been the increasing concentration of the urban population in the largest Indian cities. Data from the Indian censuses show that the share in total urban population of towns with a population of less than 0.1 million decreased from 55.4 per cent of the total urban population in 1951 to 29.8 per cent in 2011. Much of the increase in urban population has occurred in cities with a population of more than 5 million and between 1 to 5 million, with the percentage of urban population in these two city-size classes increasing from 15.6 per cent in 1981 to 22.6 per cent in 2011, and 12.1 per cent in 1981 to 20.0 per cent in 2011 respectively.

What explains the puzzle of slowing growth of the urban population in the post-1991 period, when overall economic growth and the growth of urban-biased activities has accelerated? There is no satisfactory answer. Kundu (2011) argues that this was primarily owing to lower employment opportunities in urban areas, with the slow growth of employment in manufacturing in the post-reform period. However, the faster growth of the labour-intensive and mostly urban 'trade, hotels, and restaurants' sector in the post-1991 period would have led to a high demand for minimally skilled labour. Moreover, while the possibilities of rural labour migrating to cities to work in most other swiftly growing urban-based sectors are fairly low (except in the case of the construction industry), there is a long tradition of rural migrants arriving in cities to work in hotels and restaurants of cities such as Bangalore and Mumbai (Iversen, 2002). Another possible explanation could be that stronger environmental regulations on the location of manufacturing firms within city boundaries, along with the higher cost of land in inner city areas, may be pushing these firms out of city limits and relocating their production activities in the rural hinterland of large cities.

The great growth debate

What has caused economic growth to accelerate in India since the late 1970s? The causes of India's growth acceleration have provoked a 'great growth debate' with two separate but overlapping dimensions. The first has concerned the role of the state versus the market. On the one hand, Virmani (2006) and Panagariya (2008) have argued that the piecemeal market-oriented reforms in industrial and trade policy introduced in the early 1980s, followed by the more comprehensive set of economic reforms enacted by the Congress-led minority government in 1991, were responsible for the increase in economic growth in India since the 1980s, and its most recent growth surge since the early 1990s. On the other hand, Kohli (2006) and Nayyar (2006) have highlighted the role of the state (or at least statist policies) in initiating India's economic growth. A variant of the state–market debate on the causes of India's growth acceleration has been provided by De Long (2003) and Rodrik and Subramanian (2004), who have argued that the acceleration in India's growth occurred primarily because of a change—under the prime ministership of Indira Gandhi in the 1980s—in attitude of the national government towards the private sector, from being anti-business to being pro-business and having less to do with economic reforms.

A second area of debate has been on the contributions to India's growth acceleration of capital accumulation versus trends in productivity. Many studies have suggested that the primary cause of India's growth acceleration has been the sharp and sustained rise in the investment rate from around 18 per cent in the 1970s to over 35 per cent over 2001–08, which have been driven by increases in private investment, mostly in machinery and equipment. In contrast, Bosworth, Collins, and Virmani (2007) and, more recently, Robertson (2010) argue that India's increase in economic growth has been mostly due to an increase in total factor productivity growth, with capital accumulation playing a less important role.

The two areas of debate overlap where those who argue that the state has been crucial to India's economic growth highlight the bank nationalization of 1969 and the significant increase in public investment that occurred in the 1980s, which both led to an increased flow of credit to private investors, especially small farmers and small and medium enterprises (Basu and Maertens (2007) and Sen (2007)). By contrast, those who argue that the market-oriented reforms of the 1980s and 1990s are behind India's growth acceleration stress the effect of deregulation on productivity growth. In this view, industrial deregulation leads to increased pro-competitive effects on productivity along with the ability of Indian firms to achieve economies of scale, and the beneficial effects of outward orientation (through 'learning by exporting') on the efficiency of domestic Indian firms. Trade reforms lead to increased access to specialized inputs that have strong positive effects on productivity (as indeed has been established by Goldberg et al., 2010).

The evidence for India's growth acceleration suggests a more complex causal story than has been commonly portrayed in scholarly writings on India. As I have argued elsewhere, both the state and the market have been important in India's growth acceleration, though their precise roles differed over time (Sen, 2009). In the early phase of growth, from the late 1970s to the mid-1980s, the increase in financial resources available to the private sector, by way of the nationalization of banks, and the mandatory requirement imposed by the Indian central bank on commercial banks to open branches in rural underbanked areas, along with an increase in public investment, were all triggers for accelerated economic growth. In the later phase, from the mid-1980s onwards, trade reforms played an important role in bringing about an increase in private investment, and, consequently, economic growth. Thus, India's growth acceleration can be attributed in its early phase to a classically statist model of development and, in its later phase, to market-oriented reforms.

The debate on whether capital accumulation or productivity was the main proximate cause of India's growth is far from over, as evident from Robertson's contribution to the *Economic and Political Weekly* (Robertson, 2010). Yet this debate is important to resolve as it has serious implications for policy. Should the government encourage further household saving and private investment by means of tax concessions and the rolling back of recent policies that have led banks to withdraw savings facilities to households in rural areas — or should it press ahead with further reforms, especially those that relate to labour regulations and infrastructural bottlenecks? The available evidence suggests that the relative contribution of total factor productivity growth to economic growth has been greater than that of capital accumulation — in fact, according to the estimates of Bosworth and Collins (2008), the contribution of total factor productivity growth to growth in output per worker was higher in India's case than in the case of China. One possible reason for this was the sharp increase in private corporate investment in machinery that occurred in the post-reform period in India. Machinery investment triggered an increase in productivity, first by 'learning by doing' as workers learned the skills necessary to operate the new machines, and, second, through the adoption of state-of-the-art technology embodied in new capital goods (Sen, 2007).

Conclusions, and reflections on India's way forward

This chapter has provided an overview of India's domestic economy, focusing on economic growth and structural change in recent decades, especially since the economic reforms of the 1980s. We highlight the atypical nature of structural change in the Indian economy, with the service sector being the engine of economic growth, in contrast to what has been observed in other Asian countries, and especially China, where manufacturing has led to economic growth. We also note the persistent dualism in the Indian manufacturing sector, with a large difference in productivity and earnings between very large and very small firms, and an absence of small to medium-sized firms in the size distribution. We discuss the possible causes of India's growth acceleration, noting that the debate on the role of capital accumulation and productivity growth has remained unresolved. Notwithstanding this debate, economic reforms have played a key role in both capital accumulation and productivity growth, and so have been central to India's recent growth experience.

Although the economic reforms were specifically targeted towards the industrial sector, the evidence suggests that there has been no discernible change in the ownership structure of Indian industry, and the productivity growth observed in the manufacturing sector can be mostly attributed to trade reforms, and less to the dismantling of the Licence Raj. Market reforms have not, evidently, led to 'creative destruction'. This has been an important failure where there needs to be significant policy attention, along with removing the barriers to labour-demanding growth in formal manufacturing.

What prospects are there for a more labour-absorbing growth path for the Indian economy than there has been in the past several decades since independence? At least in the short to medium term, the prospects are dim. As noted earlier, large Indian business groups who built up their capabilities in capital-intensive industries under the Licence Raj have remained entrenched in the manufacturing sector. The politics around the easing of constraints on the growth of the labour-intensive sector (better infrastructure, better schooling, and labour law reforms) belong to what the political scientist Ashutosh Varshney (1999) has termed 'mass politics reforms'—reforms that may be considered antipopulist and are therefore difficult to implement in India's current context of political coalitions. The export-oriented services sector is significantly skill-intensive, and will remain so for the foreseeable future. In agriculture, both the limited possibilities for intensive growth and the increasing labour/land ratios suggest that this sector cannot be the leading sector for productive employment creation. It seems likely, then, that India's pattern of growth will remain atypical in the Asian context. It will privilege the growth of the knowledge-intensive and capital-intensive sectors over the labour-intensive sectors for some time to come.

References

Aghion, P., Burgess, R., Redding, S. J., and Zilibotti, F. (2008) The unequal effects of liberalization: evidence from dismantling the License Raj in India. *American Economic Review*, 98(4), pp. 1397–1412.

Alfaro, L. and Chari, A. (2009) India transformed? Insights from the firm level 1988–2005, NBER Working Paper No. 15448. Cambridge, MA: National Bureau of Economic Research.

Balakrishnan, Pulapre, Golait, Ramesh, and Kumar, Pankaj (2008) Agricultural growth in India since 1991, Reserve Bank of India Department of Economic Analysis and Policy Study 27.

Basu, K. and Maertens, A. (2007) The pattern and causes of economic growth in India. *Oxford Review of Economic Policy*, 23(2), pp. 143–167.

Bhalla, G. S. and Singh, G. (2009) Economic liberalisation and Indian agriculture: a statewise analysis. *Economic and Political Weekly*, 14(52), pp. 34–44.

Bosworth, B. and Collins, S. (2008) Accounting for growth: comparing China and India. *Journal of Economic Perspectives*, 22(1), pp. 45–66.

Bosworth, B., Collins, S., and Virmani, A. (2007) Sources of growth in the Indian economy. NBER Working Paper Series, No. 12901. Cambridge, MA: National Bureau of Economic Research.

Chand, S. and Sen, K. (2002) Trade liberalization and productivity growth: evidence from Indian manufacturing. *Review of Development Economics*, 6(1), pp. 120–132.

Chanda, R. (2007) Services, in K. Basu (ed.) *Oxford Companion to Economics in India* (New Delhi: Oxford University Press), pp. 472–479.

De Long, J. B. (2003) India since independence: an analytical growth narrative, in D. Rodrik (ed.) *In Search of Prosperity: Analytical Narratives on Economic Growth* (Princeton, NJ: Princeton University Press).

Farmer, B. H. (ed.) (1977) *Green Revolution? Technology and Change in Rice Growing Areas of Tamil Nadu and Sri Lanka* (London: Macmillan).

Goldberg, P., Khandelwal, A., Pavnik, N., and Topalova, P. (2010) Multi-product and product turnover in the developing world: evidence from India. *Review of Economics and Statistics*, 92(4), pp. 1042–1049.

Haggard, S. (1996) Lessons from successful reformers: Korea and Taiwan. *Economic Reform Today*, 2(1), pp. 15–22.

Harriss-White, B. and Janakarajan, S. (2004) *Rural India Facing the 21st Century: Essays on Long Term Village Change and Recent Development Policy* (London: Anthem Press).

Joshi, P. K., Birthal, Pratap Singh, and Minot, Nicholas (2006) Sources of agricultural growth in India: role of diversification towards high-value crops. International Food Policy Research Institute Markets, Trade and Institutions Division Discussion Paper No. 98.

Kochhar, K., Kumar, U., Rajan, R., Subramanian, A., and Tokatlidis, I. (2006) India's pattern of development: what happened, what follows? *Journal of Monetary Economics*, 53(1), pp. 981–1019.

Kohli, A. (2006) Politics of economic growth in India: 1980–2005. *Economic and Political Weekly*, 61(1), pp. 1251–1259.

Kotwal, A., Ramaswami, B., and Wadhwa, W. (2011) Economic liberalization and Indian economic growth: what's the evidence? *Journal of Economic Literature*, 49(4), pp. 1152–1199.

Krueger, A. (1997) Trade policy and economic development: what have we learned? *American Economic Review*, 87(1), pp. 1–22.

Kundu, A. (2011) Trends and processes of urbanisation in India, IIED and UNFPA Working Paper, New York.

Mazumdar, D. and Sarkar, S. (2012) *Manufacturing Enterprise in Asia: Size Structure and Economic Growth* (Basingstoke: Routledge).

Mookherjee, D. (1995) Introduction, in D. Mookherjee (ed.) *Indian Industry: Policies and Performance* (Oxford: Oxford University Press), pp. 1–43.

Palmer-Jones, R. and Sen, K. (2003) What has luck got to do with it? A regional analysis of poverty and agricultural growth in rural India. *Journal of Development Studies*, 40(1), pp. 1–31.

Panagariya, A. (2008) *India: The Emerging Giant* (New York: Oxford University Press).

Raj, R. and Sen, K. (2012) Did international trade destroy or create jobs in Indian manufacturing? *European Journal of Development Research*, 24(3), pp. 359–381.

Riedel, J. (1988) Economic development in East Asia: doing what comes naturally? in H. Hughes (ed.) *Achieving Industrialisation in East Asia* (Cambridge: Cambridge University Press).

Robertson, Peter E. (2010) Investment led growth in India: fact or mythology? *Economic and Political Weekly*, 45(40), pp. 120–124.

Rodrik, D. and Subramanian, A. (2004) From Hindu growth to productivity surge: the myth of the Indian growth transition, NBER Working Paper No. W10376.

Rogaly, B., Harriss-White, B., and Bose, S. (eds) (1999) *Sonar Bangla: Agricultural Growth and Agrarian Change in West Bengal and Bangladesh* (New Delhi: Sage).

Sen, K. (2007) Why did the elephant start to trot? India's growth acceleration re-examined. *Economic and Political Weekly*, 43, pp. 37–49.

Sen, K. (2008) *Trade Policy, Inequality, and Performance in Indian Manufacturing* (London: Routledge).

Sen, K. (2009) What a long, strange trip it's been: reflections on the causes of India's growth miracle. *Contemporary South Asia*, 17(4), pp. 363–377.

Varshney, A. (1999) Mass politics or elite politics: India's reforms in comparative perspective, in J. D. Sachs, A. Varshney, and N. Bajpai (eds) *India in the Era of Economic Reforms* (Delhi: Oxford University Press).

Virmani, A. (2006) *Propelling India from Socialist Stagnation to Global Power* (Delhi: Academic Foundation).

Walton, M. (2010) Can a social democratic resolution resolve issues of inequality and growth for India? <http://www.michaelwalton.info/wp-content/uploads/2010/11/Social-democracy-and-inequality_Nov2010.pdf> (accessed 20 January 2013).

Wood, A. and Calandrino, M. (2000) When the other giant awakens: trade and human resources in India. *Economic and Political Weekly*, 35(52–53), pp. 4677–4694.

Part II

China, India, and the International Economy

3

The Challenges of China and the International Economy

PETER J. BUCKLEY

ANY ECONOMY'S INTERACTION with the international economy reflects both internal and external changes. It is a fact that, for instance, the difference between savings and investment is identical to the difference between export and imports. So, in examining China and the international economy we need to pay particular attention to the interaction between events in contemporary China and also to changes in the international economy. This is clearly a massive task, and so this chapter concentrates in particular on the role of foreign direct investment (FDI) in linking China to the global economy. FDI involves the control of foreign assets from a particular host country, and in the Chinese case this has two interesting aspects—the important role of inward FDI in modern China and the more recent, but equally fascinating, case of Chinese outward FDI. China has become not only one of the most important host countries for inward FDI but also one of the top five foreign direct investors outside China.

Contemporary China faces a large number of challenges. These include maintaining growth (in particular to maintain (urban) employment), restructuring the domestic economy while moving into higher value activities, competing in the global economy, absorbing and harnessing the IT revolution, innovation, managing the high level of foreign control in the domestic economy while internationalizing Chinese-owned companies, managing societal disparities, institutional reform (particularly of all levels of government), coping with the drastic changes in media relations, environmental challenges, demographic changes, and absorbing the increasing resource costs of growth.

It could be argued that, as all of these issues are interrelated, all of them have an international dimension, and that would be correct. This chapter concentrates in detail on two issues: inward FDI and outward FDI, and the internationalization of Chinese companies. There are particular and direct

Proceedings of the British Academy, **193**, 65–76, © The British Academy 2014

implications for growth and employment, restructuring, global competition, innovation, and resource costs arising out of the effects of both inward and outward FDI.

The first section of this chapter examines inward FDI in China and its relationship with domestic policy. The second part looks at the issues through an examination of outward FDI. A third section looks at underlying trends affecting China's long-run international position, and this is followed by a conclusion.

Inward FDI to China

Micro-economic background

China is undergoing transformation from an export-orientated economy to one based more on domestic consumption. In policy terms, this has amounted to allowing or encouraging wage increases. Minimum wages in many provinces and cities have been rising. The policy intent here is to encourage industries to move west into the interior of China. This is achieved both by raising costs in the coastal provinces, or at least allowing them to rise, while providing incentives to invest in central and western China. This has led to rapid rates of growth in inland Chinese provinces such as Sichuan and Hunan. There has been a massive increase in infrastructural investment to facilitate this development. It is notable, however, that investment still accounts for over 40 per cent of Chinese GDP.

The new role that inward FDI is intended to play is to shift towards serving the Chinese consumer rather than aiming at export-orientated investment. This needs to be managed with care because of the income distribution issue. In fact, household income as a share of GDP has declined from around 55 per cent in the early 1980s to around 34 per cent in early 2011. Reversing this trend involves a massive restructuring effort, which will have profound implications for China in the next decade. It is complicated by the fact that much of consumption is geared towards luxury consumption, and this may exacerbate the already skewed income distribution measured at individual province and regional levels. Reform of the banking sector will increase consumption because the spread of lending and deposit rates gives low returns on savings and constrains household consumption. The central control of interest rates exacerbates this problem, and it is an indication of the interrelated nature of the issues facing China that control of interest rates cannot be relaxed without affecting the foreign exchange markets, which are a major concern for China. An appreciation in the Chinese exchange rate would increase domestic consumption and discourage exports, but again this represents a balancing act, because of the number of Chinese jobs currently connected to the export industries. Reform of the banking sector is also an urgent need, because consumer financing is currently underdeveloped. A further constraining factor on increasing consumption is that many Chinese families maintain a high level of savings because of worries about health care. Reform of the health-care sector and more health-care insurance would have a significant effect on increasing domestic consumption.

Capital market imperfections

In increasing domestic activity, one crucial imperative is to improve the domestic capital market. For our purposes here, it is of considerable interest to note that imperfections in the capital market in China currently have perverse effects. The abundance of capital made available to state-owned enterprises (SOEs) enables them to undertake many investments, including, of course, foreign investments, while the private sector is constrained by lack of access to capital. We should remember here that small and medium enterprises (SMEs) account for fully 80 per cent of the urban labour force. To release China's full potential, these firms need fairer access to capital in order to be able to invest and innovate.

Policy reassertion is a response to complaints of foreign investors

The recent reassessment of strategy towards inward FDI is a response to complaints, arising, among others, from General Electric, Siemens, and BASF (some of the oldest-established foreign investors in China). Policy has begun to respond to the EU Chamber of Commerce in China call to 'remove red tape' and create a 'level playing field'. To some extent this is ironic, in that it is possible to regard past policy as biased in favour of foreign investors in China. This is another of those balancing acts that need to be performed in China—the dynamism of much of the Chinese economy is based on inward FDI, now there is a need to reenergize the domestic sector, but this needs to be done without alienating existing foreign direct investors.

There have been a number of specific complaints made by foreign investors. These include:

1. Not opening up the service sector in accord with World Trade Organization (WTO) agreements: examples include telecoms, travel computer reservation, travel agents, and banking. A particularly egregious example of this is petrol stations, where, in order to operate such a facility, there

is a need to own an oil refinery in order to obtain a wholesale licence. However, oil refineries are 'strategic assets', and it is impossible for foreigners to obtain such a licence.

2. 'Standards'—it is a common complaint among foreign direct investors that restrictions on their activities are brought about by insisting on (possibly 'Chinese') standards. The foreign investment community has requested that the WTO should be notified of such requirements to comply with standards.

3. Legal issues—state secrets and commercial secrets laws are difficult for foreign investors to negotiate, and their impact is not always known in advance.

4. The retrospective introduction of income tax law in December 2009 alarmed many foreign investors.

5. This was compounded by the government's announcement to 'buy Chinese'. The concern was that the promotion of 'indigenous innovation' would mean that only products patented in China would be bought by government agencies. In the face of intense protests, this provision has been considerably watered down.

6. Certification—the EU Chamber of Commerce, backed by a large number of significant foreign direct investors, felt that business licence requirements were 'vague and unprecedentedly broad definitions of public security and critical infrastructure' in the certification of products. This is an example of the Chinese government's obsession with security conflicting with its desire to achieve economic growth, and this links strongly with the desire to achieve long-term restructuring of the Chinese economy without decelerating the rate of growth.

Policy changes in China towards foreign investment

In response to these changes the top decision-makers in China (including the then Premier Wen Jiabao and the then Vice-President Xi Jinping) have moved to reassure foreign investors in China. These statements made it clear that all enterprises registered in China according to Chinese law are Chinese enterprises. Their products are made-in-China products. The equal treatment to foreign-invested enterprises in government procurement would be continued. A key point of national strategy is intellectual property rights protection, which has been previously weak but now is being strengthened, not least because China now has a considerable investment in intellectual property rights of its own. There would be a focus on innovation, upgrading industrial infrastructure, and advances in technology.

Long-term structural shift in the Chinese economy

Underlying many of these issues is the desire of the Chinese government to move the economy from producing labour-intensive products to higher value added activities. This is also expressed in the change of phrase, from 'Made in China' to 'Created in China'. This expresses the need to move from simple production based on cheap labour to design and innovation-intensive products. If such a transformation is to occur, then there is a need to improve the 'soft infrastructure' of China. In particular, this means huge investments in human resources and innovatory capacity. Indeed, this is the intent of the National Medium and Long-Term Talent Development Plan (2010–2020). Around this plan are suggestions that many creative Chinese should be lured back to their homeland to assist in the upgrading of design, production, marketing, financing, and branding of Chinese products. This may have the ring of a protectionist policy to the ears of foreign direct investors in China, but it should be remembered that all threats are also opportunities, creating massive demand in China for automation services, innovation-related activities, and environmental services and products. Consequently, the desire to move to 'Created in China' has secured a large inflow of research and development facilities of foreign firms. It is an interesting issue how far the research and design facilities are solely targeted at the Chinese market and how far these are truly global facilities.

The recent reaction of foreign direct investors suggests that this shift has been communicated to them and that they are responding with alacrity. Companies announcing expansions in China recently include Walmart, Coca-Cola (with a large R&D facility), HSBC, and BMW, all of whom are aiming not for export but to service the Chinese market. It is interesting that global car producers are now focusing on smaller cities and rural demand in China, with products that include new energy vehicles, hybrid electrical vehicles, hydrogen fuel cells, and pure electric cars.

The optimists among Chinese policymakers and observers are already beginning to predict that the next shift in Chinese policy will be towards encouraging smaller Chinese businesses. Such a policy could be carried out in parallel with this major structural shift, but this clearly represents a major undertaking in industrial restructuring.

Implications for foreign-owned companies in China

The current environment for foreign investment in China has therefore undergone a considerable shift in response to the needs of long-term restructuring. This has several implications for foreign companies, both those that are already present in China and those that are considering investing there.

First, as outlined above, there are new opportunities for foreign companies. Second, there is increased pressure to localize, which means that, third, foreign companies are likely to be treated equally and equivalently to Chinese companies if they achieve local identification. Investment in high value added activities, particularly innovation and R&D, is now particularly favoured, and there is immense competition from Chinese cities and provinces to attract it. Local support is even more vital in achieving success in China. Individual governors are incentivized to bring in foreign investors. This means that the choice of location in China is more important than ever. Foreign investors need to consider the choice of city or province as a prime factor in their investment decision.

Does this therefore mean that the era of low wage investment to China is over? This is unlikely to be the case, as labour productivity is likely to grow faster than wages for some time, but the era of privilege for foreign investors in low value added activities is over and opportunities will be restricted to fewer areas, and, of course, these will be in the inland provinces where infrastructure is weaker and associated costs are higher. As mentioned above, this trend will be accelerated by the recent increase in minimum wages, which in some provinces is as much as 30 per cent.

The improvement in intellectual property protection will make China more attractive as a foreign investment destination for activities involving the management of knowledge. The realization that the property rights regime has improved may take some time to impact on inflows and Chinese government policy, and the legal framework will be carefully monitored by potential foreign investors to ensure that there is no backsliding on this issue.

Finally, attracting talent in China has become a key issue. A recent survey shows that college students broadly prefer SOEs to foreign investors. However, several really high-profile foreign investors remain popular. Talented Chinese people now have the opportunity to choose well-paid and rewarding jobs, and the consequence of this is that labour mobility is unprecedentedly high in skilled occupations.

Chinese outward FDI

A major impetus for the growth of Chinese outward FDI arises from the recycling of China's massive export surplus. A high proportion of China's foreign exchange reserves are invested in US Treasury Bonds. China has foreign exchange reserves of approximately US $3.2 trillion. (This is equivalent to excess savings as discussed above.) This is, of course, related to China's undervalued exchange rate against the dollar, which has led to China being vilified as a 'currency manipulator' by the USA, even though the renminbi/yuan has appreciated by more than 20 per cent since July 2005. In terms of the structure of Chinese external trade, it is important to remember that 'processing trade' accounts for more than 50 per cent of China's export revenue. This is largely the result of the activities of foreign-owned firms in China, and because of the narrow profit margins on the supply activities in China, processing activity does not greatly enhance local value added in China.

Outward FDI by Chinese companies is another way of utilizing these reserves. FDI is a means by which Chinese firms can obtain control of the assets they acquire, whereas other forms of investment (foreign portfolio investment) do not entail control. An alternative to FDI is to support Sovereign Wealth Funds to acquire foreign assets. The prime vehicle for this is the China Investment Corporation (CIC), which has assets under management of US $400 billion and has built an extensive portfolio abroad (CIC, 2011). This piece concentrates on outward FDI by Chinese companies.

Outward FDI from China—scale

Chinese FDI is still small in global terms, but is frightening to the rest of the world. The stock of FDI from China was US $298 billion in 2010 (UNCTAD, 2011). However, Chinese FDI has experienced extremely rapid growth since 2003. China's stock of outward FDI has grown from US $4.5 billion in 1990 to US $27.8 billion in 2000 and US $298 billion in 2010 (UNCTAD, 2011).

In fact, even by 2010 China's FDI outflow was still very small in world terms, as it is only 5.1 per cent of the global total. China's FDI stock was only 1.4 per cent of the world total in 2010. However, these figures may significantly underestimate outward investment by Chinese companies, because many of their deals are financed outside China. In addition, we need to add in the outward direct investment that emanates from Hong Kong. Hong Kong's outward stock was US $949 billion in 2010. It is not possible simply to add the outflows or stock from China to that of Hong Kong because some of this FDI is in the form of 'round-tripping', where Chinese firms invest in Hong Kong in order to reinvest in China, usually in a different province. In addition, much of Chinese outward FDI is targeted at tax havens, and has its ultimate destination back in China.

The available figures are therefore fraught with danger for the uninitiated, but on any serious account Chinese FDI is still a relatively small player on the world scene. Moreover, Chinese OFDI and Chinese multinationals are often not in direct competition with Western multinational enterprises (MNEs). The location of Chinese MNEs is often in peripheral regions and countries with little head-to-head competition with Western MNEs. Just this point is made by de Jonquières (2012), who argues that 'Chinese companies necessarily focus heavily on regions where their western competitors are not already entrenched or are, for one reason or another, barred from operation' (p. 4). As he is focusing on extractive firms, he further points out that the 'effect of "Chinese companies'" international expansion is not to "lockup" supplies, but, rather, to augment at the margin those available on world markets' (p. 4). He further notes that most crude oil that Chinese companies extract is swapped or sold on world markets— as little as 10 per cent is shipped back to China.

The threat of China taking over the world is clearly a chimera, at least as far as outward FDI is concerned.

Transformation of SOEs

A high proportion of Chinese outward FDI is that of SOEs. A section above alluded to the bias in the capital market against private companies, and this is manifested in the relative ease by which SOEs can obtain investable funds in order to undertake foreign ventures. This is not a uniform picture, however, in that some private companies are favoured by decision-makers in government and financial institutions, and similarly have access to capital at below equilibrium cost rates. The continued reform of SOEs is likely to include further international investments, and one beneficial result of this is their exposure to competition and international standards.

Need for skilled management

A key requirement for successful internationalization of companies is skilled management. Chinese foreign companies are not well endowed with skilled and internationally experienced managers, nor do foreign managers find it easy to work in Chinese companies, however reputedly internationalized. It is a well-known phenomenon that international companies need to build their top level management in parallel with their internationalization. China is making rapid strides to build a cadre of internationally aware managers by establishing new training programmes, such as setting up Masters degrees in International Business. In parallel with this, Chinese companies that internationalize will need to adapt what is still a fairly insular culture in order to be able to compete globally and to understand foreign consumers and buyers.

The jury is still out on the success or otherwise of Chinese companies that have begun to internationalize. It is to be expected that Chinese companies will make many mistakes as they attempt to internationalize simply because of naivety and a lack of understanding of the various foreign environments to which they are exposed. This not a factor unique to China—every set of companies that internationalizes has to learn by its mistakes. There is a great deal of anecdotal evidence as to the mistakes currently being made by Chinese companies in Africa, and there is consequently the need for more studies where Chinese firms are compared with other multinational enterprises.

One further vital question determining the success of the internationalization of Chinese companies is the degree to which they are able to innovate. This is part of a wider question of how far China can switch from simply making basic products to being a long-run innovator. This question goes to the root of many of the issues around the current organization of Chinese society and polity. There is an argument that innovation is not rewarded in China, and indeed that innovators and entrepreneurs are actively discriminated against and discouraged for political reasons. The obsession of the communist party with the control of information clearly militates against innovatory activity. Control of certain aspects of the Internet, for example, may not be compatible with the freedom of entrepreneurs to adopt new ideas. Lack of innovation will inhibit development, and if not corrected will ultimately stymie the further internationalization of Chinese companies.

Underlying trends affecting China's long-run international position

The need for innovation and creative talent is, therefore, a key problem affecting China's long-run international position. In order to improve its global position, China needs to move from attracting financial capital to attracting human capital. In spite of the encouragement to overseas Chinese to return to China, there is still a net export of highly qualified personnel from China. In order to compete in the long run, China needs to build internationally recognizable brand names. Building brand names is a long-run process which requires continued and sustained investment in product and service quality. It is too early to expect China to have succeeded in this in the short period following its opening up to the world economy, but there are serious concerns about design and quality issues in Chinese production and service activities, so this is a long-run concern.

Demography, of course, is a key long-term issue. The concern about the ageing population that 'China will get old before it gets rich' encompasses a growing anxiety in Chinese society. The 60-plus age group has grown to 167.14 million (12.5 per cent of the population) because of increasing life expectancy and the one-child policy (which is currently under questioning and revision). This provides opportunities for both foreign and domestic companies to invest in health care opportunities, which, apart from first-tier cities, is poor.

A long-run shift from 'hardware' to 'software' requires major changes in the Chinese economy. Investment remains at 45 per cent of GDP, and there are huge infrastructure projects currently being undertaken in high speed railways, airports, education, research and development, public health, energy conservation, environmental protection, and social welfare. This is necessary to move China from an investment-driven economy to a talent-driven one. In parallel with a shift from investment to consumption, this means the rapid growth of services and non-tradable goods in which China has not yet been successful.

Conclusion

'For 18 of the past 20 centuries, China has boasted the biggest economy in the world. Many Chinese see the past 200 years of underdevelopment and colonial occupation as an aberration that must be addressed' (*Financial Times*, 3 Dec. 2002: 17).

Becoming the largest economy in the world now represents a major challenge. China has reached the second position in purchasing parity terms, largely by utilizing standard procedures of production and low value added export-orientated manufacturing, mainly undertaken with the agency of inward FDI. To continue to grow at the historically unprecedented rates that China has achieved in the recent past now requires a radical change in economic structure if China is to avoid the middle income trap. This is against a relatively unpromising labour situation, with increasing militancy and expectations, unemployment among college graduates (6 million each year), and increasing manufacturing costs in coastal regions.

The international position of China is entwined with all these issues as this chapter shows. Inward FDI is likely to continue and possibly to increase somewhat, although its nature will move away from export-orientated manufacturing to more differentiated products and services for the Chinese market. Chinese outward FDI faces a number of challenges, which rely upon the domestic economy becoming more capable of innovation and producing high level human resources. All of the challenges that the domestic Chinese economy faces have international ramifications, and developments in the international economy will codetermine China's future economic path.

References

CIC (China Investment Corporation) (2011) Annual report. <http://www.china-inv.cn/cicen/include/resources/CIC_2011_annualreport_en.pdf> (accessed 5 November 2012).

De Jonquières, G. (2012) What power shift to China? European Centre for International
    Political Economy Policy Briefs, 4/2012. <http://www.ecipe.org/media/publication_
    pdfs/PB201103.pdf> (accessed 5 November 2012).
UNCTAD (United Nations Conference on Trade and Development) (2011) World
    investment report 2011. <http://unctad.org/en/Pages/DIAE/World%20Investment%20
    Report/WIR2011_WebFlyer.aspx> (accessed 5 November 2012).

4

India and the World Economy

VIJAY JOSHI & DEVESH KAPUR

TEN YEARS AFTER achieving independence in 1947, India embarked on an autarkic path of development, with the avowed objective of building its industrial base on the basis of import-substitution and 'self-reliance'.[1] Concurrently, stung by the adverse colonial experience with foreign capital, it also closed itself off from international investment. As things turned out, the second half of the twentieth century coincided with a rapid growth of global trade and investment, and the emergence in East Asia of trade as a growth engine. The consequence was that while India did build a diverse industrial base, by 1990 it had become one of the world's most inward-looking countries, and paid a steep price in foregone investment, technology flows, and economic growth. (Autarkic policies also had other negative consequences; import controls, in particular, encouraged the growth of rent-seeking.) A major goal of India's historic reforms launched in 1991 was to reintegrate India into the global economy and reap the economic benefits of doing so. Since then, India's globalization has proceeded apace. In this chapter, we first examine the evolution and extent of India's global engagement in recent years. We then discuss the impact of India's global engagement on India. Finally, we analyse the effects of India's global engagement on the world.

India's global engagement: evolution and extent

In 1990, India had one of the world's most closed economies. Indeed, on some measures, for example the ratio of exports to gross domestic product (GDP), its economy was more closed in 1990 than it was in 1950. The home market was protected by high tariffs as well as stringent quantitative restrictions on imports. These measures were part of a pervasive and convoluted system of

---

[1] This effort began with the Second Five Year Plan that started in 1956. One of its aims was 'rapid industrialization, with particular emphasis on the development of the basic and heavy industries'.

Proceedings of the British Academy, **193**, 77–92, © The British Academy 2014

controls (the Licence Raj) that accompanied the adoption of a statist model of development. The model was a failure: for 30 years after independence, the growth rate of national income did not budge from a trend of 3.6 per cent a year (the Hindu Rate of Growth), despite a doubling of saving and investment rates. By the second half of the 1970s, it was clear that India's development path had run into the sand. Some tentative and piecemeal deregulatory reforms were then introduced. India was so far inside the efficiency frontier that even these small changes, along with fiscal expansion and foreign borrowing, raised the growth rate to 5.7 per cent a year in the 1980s.[2] The acceleration would have fizzled out in due course, however, because the reforms were very shallow.[3] In the event, it was brought to a halt at the end of the decade by a severe balance of payments crisis. By then, the contrast between East Asian (including Chinese) success and Indian failure had become painfully evident. Moreover, the USSR had collapsed, and with it collapsed the respectability of India's erstwhile strategy. A reform programme, much more radical than anything attempted earlier, was instigated in 1991, aimed at moving the economy decisively away from controls and towards greater market orientation. In the last two decades, India's growth rate has risen to an average of 6.5 per cent a year.[4]

A crucial element of the 1991 reforms was the dismantling of barriers to international trade and foreign investment. Since then, though the pace has varied, the direction of policy has remained unchanged. Over the last two decades, tariffs in the manufacturing sector have been slashed: the average tariff fell from 145 per cent in 1990 to 9 per cent in 2010 (see Table 4.1). As, if not more, important, quantitative import controls on manufactured goods have been almost entirely swept away.[5] Agriculture still remains fairly highly protected, as in most countries. Even so, the average agricultural tariff has come down from 134 per cent in 1990 to 33 per cent in 2010. Restrictions on inward and outward foreign investment have been significantly reduced. The exchange rate used to be fixed; it is now a (heavily) managed float.

These changes have brought about a pronounced increase in the openness of the economy, manifested in a radical change in the structure of the balance

[2] India's decadal average annual percentage growth rates were as follows. 1950s: 3.2; 1960s: 3.9; 1970s: 2.9; 1980s: 5.7; 1990s: 5.7; 2000s: 7.3. It should be noted that the growth rate for the 1990s is dragged down by the sharp slowdown at the start of the decade, which was in turn caused by a crisis that originated in the fiscal profligacy of the 1980s.

[3] In the 1980s, government policy became more business-friendly, but there was little in the way of introducing more competition, domestic or international.

[4] Bhagwati and Desai (1970) is the locus classicus of description and analysis of the 'Licence Raj'. See also Joshi and Little (1994) and Panagariya (2008). The causes and resolution of the 1991 balance of payments crisis are analysed in Joshi and Little (1994, 1996). For a critical examination of India's reforms, see Joshi and Little (1996), Panagariya (2008), and Joshi (2010).

[5] India's trade liberalization since 1991 is examined in Joshi and Little (1996), and Panagariya (2004, 2008).

Table 4.1. India: Structure of Tariffs (unweighted averages, %)

	1990	2006	2010
All Goods	144	16	–
Agriculture	134	43	33.2
Manufacturing	145	14	8.9

Source: World Trade Organization, Trade Policy Review
(India), various years.

of payments (see Table 4.2). Exports of goods and services have tripled as a proportion of GDP from just 7 per cent in 1990 to 22 per cent in 2010 (see Table 4.3). Naturally, imports of goods and services have shown a roughly similar rise. The country has become an attractive destination for foreign investment, so inflows of capital have increased significantly. Capital outflows have also grown, but net capital inflows have been substantially positive. In the present century, except very recently, the overall balance of payments has been in good health, with a modest current account deficit outweighed by a large capital account surplus. As a result, the country has accumulated a sizeable stock of foreign exchange reserves, currently about $300 billion. Aggregate gross external receipts and payments (current and capital combined) have more than tripled as a proportion of GDP from 32 per cent in 1990 to 108 per cent in 2010. India is thus more open than ever before. The rest of this section adds some detail to this broad-brush picture.

On the current account, the most striking feature is the huge surge in invisible exports, particularly exports of information technology (IT) services. India's net IT exports grew from virtually nothing in 1990 to $57

Table 4.2. India: Structure of the Balance of Payments (Current Account)
(% GDP unless otherwise indicated)

	1960	1980	1990	2007	2010	2010 ($ billion)
Current Account	-2.4	-1.6	-3.1	-1.3	-2.6	-44.3
Trade Balance	-3.0	-4.6	-3.0	-7.8	-7.5	-130.5
Exports	3.8	4.9	5.8	14.2	14.5	250.5
Imports	6.8	9.5	8.8	22.0	22.0	380.9
Invisibles Balance	0.6	3.0	-0.1	6.2	5.0	86.2
Software Services	0.0	0	Neg.	3.0	3.3	56.8
Private Remittances	Neg.	1.4	0.7	3.4	3.1	53.4
Other Items	0.6	1.4	-0.8	-0.2	-1.4	-24.0

Source: Reserve Bank of India, *Handbook of Statistics on the Indian Economy 2010/2011.*

Vijay Joshi & Devesh Kapur

Table 4.3. India: Indicators of Openness (% GDP)

	1950	1980	1990	2007	2010
Exports (goods)	6.5	4.9	5.8	14.2	14.5
Exports (services)	1.9	1.3	1.4	7.7	7.6
Exports (goods + services)	8.4	6.2	7.2	21.9	22.1
Imports (goods)	6.5	9.5	8.8	22.0	22.0
Imports (services)	1.3	0.2	1.1	4.5	4.9
Imports (goods + services)	7.8	9.7	9.9	26.5	26.9
Trade (goods + services)	16.2	15.9	17.0	48.4	49.0
Current Account (receipts)	–	–	8.0	26.8	25.9
Current Account (payments)	–	–	11.2	28.3	28.4
Capital Inflow	–	–	7.2	36.9	28.7
Capital Outflow	–	–	5.0	27.7	25.1
Gross Flows (current + capital)	–	–	32.4	119.7	108.1

Sources: Reserve Bank of India, *Annual Report 2008/2009* and Reserve Bank of India, *Handbook of Statistics on the Indian Economy 2010/2011*.

billion (3.3 per cent of GDP) two decades later. Inward remittances from overseas Indians also grew strongly, as will be discussed below. Merchandise exports have advanced along a broad front. However, while the overall export performance is creditable, it is much less spectacular than China's. In 1990, India's share of world exports was 0.5 per cent; in 2010, it had risen, but only to 1.4 per cent. Over the same period, China's share grew from 1.8 per cent to 10.4 per cent (see Table 4.4). Unlike China, India has not conquered the world market for labour-intensive manufactured goods. A stunning example is that of clothing and footwear, in which India's share of world exports grew from 1.4 per cent to 3.2 per cent between 1980 and 2007. In sharp contrast, China's share rose from 1.3 per cent to 37.6 per cent (UN Commodity Trade Database). Another major difference between the export performances of the two countries is that India, unlike China, has not been closely integrated into global manufacturing networks. In other words, India is a successful recipient of cross-border outsourcing in services, but not in manufacturing (Athukorala, 2008).

On the capital account, official aid flows—critical for India's balance of payments in the 1960s—have dwindled in importance, gradually supplanted by flows of foreign direct investment (FDI). Foreign portfolio investment, especially into equities, is also booming (see Table 4.5). Inward FDI was negligible before the 1991 economic reforms because of the autarkic policies of previous governments and their lingering suspicion of multinational

Table 4.4. India, China, Korea: Shares of World Merchandise Exports (%)

	India	China	Korea
1950	2.0	1.3*	0.5*
1980	0.4	0.9	0.9
1990	0.5	1.8	2.0
2000	0.7	3.9	2.7
2007	1.1	8.9	2.7
2010	1.4	10.4	3.1

Source: adapted from International Monetary Fund, International Financial Statistics, various years.
Note: *Chinese and Korean data refer to 1953.

corporations (MNCs). However, after the balance of payments crisis in that year, the Indian government slowly opened up to foreign investment. A Foreign Investment Promotion Board was created to oversee a single-window clearance process for large investments, and the FDI policy regime switched from a positive list to a negative list, thereby expanding the range of industries which could attract foreign money (although the positive list still covered many major industries, and there were often sector-specific caps on the extent of foreign investment in any given enterprise). By the early 2000s, foreign investors under a certain size could invest with minimal government policy barriers (though the transactions costs of investing in greenfield FDI in India still remain high). Inward FDI steadily increased throughout the 1990s, but really took off in the mid-2000s after India partially deregulated its financial sector and started achieving GDP growth rates of 8 per cent a year. (China's FDI flows are much more impressive than India's (see Table 4.6), but it has to be remembered that reform in India began ten years later than in China.) Portfolio equity investments by foreign institutional investors into Indian stock markets were liberalized early on in the reform programme. These inflows have been strong but volatile. Investment in government and corporate bonds has been deregulated very gradually in the last few years.

An interesting development was the growth of outbound FDI from India (Athukorala, 2009). MNCs used to be viewed as the devil's apprentice in Indian intellectual thinking; now there is pride in attracting and nurturing Indian MNCs. As Figure 4.1 shows, in the last ten years, Indian outward FDI has moved more or less in step with inward FDI, albeit at a slightly lower level. In 2010, inward FDI was around $25 billion and outward FDI around $15 billion. In the last few years, large foreign acquisitions by Indian companies have attracted considerable attention. Examples include Tata's acquisition of

Table 4.5. India: Structure of the Balance of Payments (Capital Account) (% GDP unless otherwise indicated)

	1960	1980	1990	2007	2010
Capital Account	2.1	1.0	2.2	9.2	3.3
Loans	1.5	0.8	1.7	3.5	1.6
Ext. Assistance	1.5	0.8	0.8	0.2	0.3
Comm. Borrowing	Neg.	Neg.	0.8	2.0	0.7
Short-term Credit	Neg.	Neg.	1.1	1.4	0.6
FDI (net)	Neg.	Neg.	0.6	1.4	0.4
Inflows	Neg.	Neg.	0.6	3.0	1.4
Outflows	Neg.	Neg.	Neg.	-1.6	- 0.9
Portfolio Investment	Neg.	Neg.	Neg.	2.3	1.8
Other Items	0.6	0.2	-0.1	2.0	-0.5
Memo Items:					
Forex Reserves	1.8	4.0	2.0	24.3	15.8
Forex Reserves ($ billion)	0.6	6.9	5.8	299.1	274.3
Forex Reserves (months)	3.0	5.2	2.5	14.4	9.6
Exchange Rate (Re/$)	4.76	7.9	17.9	40.2	45.7

Source: Reserve Bank of India, *Handbook of Statistics on the Indian Economy 2010/2011*.

Table 4.6. India, China: FDI Inflows and Outflows ($ billion)

	1990	2007	2010
Inflows			
India	0.2	35	25
China	3.5	85	106
Outflows			
India	Neg.	18	15
China	Neg.	25	68

Sources: Reserve Bank of India, *Handbook of Statistics on the Indian Economy 2010/2011* and UNCTAD, *World Investment Report*, various years.

Corus ($12.1 billion) and Jaguar Land Rover ($2.3 billion), Bharti Airtel's acquisition of the African assets of Zain telecom ($10.7 billion), and, more recently, Fortis's expansion in South East Asia, emerging in the process as the largest private tertiary health provider in developing countries. These investments are significant not only because of their large size but also because of the reputational advantages that they give Indian MNCs at home and abroad. As Indian MNCs start to become more visibly active abroad, the ideological justifications for rejecting foreign MNCs' activities and investment in India have become less vociferous (although the political outcry over allowing FDI in retail in 2011 shows that in some sectors political resistance continues to be high).[6]

Despite the liberalization of foreign investment, it is noteworthy that India, like China, has refrained from full-scale capital account liberalization. While direct and portfolio equity inflows were mostly unrestricted, debt inflows, especially of short-term tenure and denominated in foreign currency, were tightly controlled, using multiple instruments—quantitative limits, price-based measures, and administrative measures. The aim has been to avoid the 'original sin' of excessive foreign currency borrowings by domestic entities, particularly the sovereign, as well as to keep a check on excessive dollarization of balance sheets of financial sector intermediaries, particularly banks. As regards capital outflows, restrictions have been lifted only partially, and very gradually. These measures, which have made a major contribution to economic stability, indicate that the Indian version of economic liberalization was not mindlessly wedded to laissez faire.

Another element of India's growing engagement with the world economy, in addition to trade and capital movements, has been international migration. Outward migration from independent India was initially driven by the large demand for unskilled and semi-skilled workers in the United Kingdom, following the end of the Second World War. From the late 1960s onwards, two major streams of migration emerged. The first, to the Middle East, was dominated by unskilled or semi-skilled temporary workers, and nearly four-fifths of these labour flows were to just three Middle Eastern countries (Saudi Arabia, UAE, and Oman). The second stream, comprising skilled professionals, migrated to OECD countries, and especially to the USA. The Indian-born population in the USA grew from around 12,000 in 1960 to 51,000 in 1970. It then climbed to 206,000 in 1980, 450,000 in 1990, 1 million in 2000, and 3.2 million in 2010.

---

[6] In 2011, the central government announced its decision to permit 51 per cent FDI in multibrand retail, and then backtracked in the face of opposition. In September 2012, the central government reintroduced the measure, but with an option for each state to go along with it or not. It remains a politically sensitive issue, given the uncertainties regarding its effects on net labour displacement.

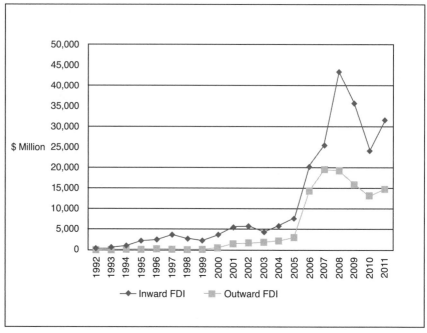

Figure 4.1. India: Inward and Outward FDI
Source: UNCTADSTAT.

India's global engagement: impact on India

The development discourse in post-independent India was dominated by fears of the ruinous effects of foreign exposure, such as deindustrialization, destabilization, and general impoverishment. The opening up of the economy has dispelled these apprehensions: the outcomes of India's globalization have been almost wholly positive. Foreign industry has not destroyed Indian industry, and foreign companies have not devoured Indian companies. Instead, gradual but firm liberalization of trade and foreign investment, along with other reform measures, has led to a sharp increase in the rate of productivity growth (Chand and Sen, 2002; Panagariya, 2004). Entrepreneurial response to the reforms has also been dramatic. India now has world-class companies in many sectors, such as iron and steel, cement, automobiles, pharmaceuticals, and information technology. Indeed, as we saw above, several Indian companies, not content with domestic expansion, have been making large foreign acquisitions.

Opening up did not destabilize the economy. Since 1991, India has not had a major macroeconomic crisis. It escaped the East Asian crisis of 1997 and the global credit crisis of 2008 relatively unscathed. An important reason for this benign outcome is that India rejected full capital account convertibility (even while it was being actively promoted by the IMF and the US Treasury before the East Asian crisis). As discussed earlier, while India's policies towards equity inflows were permissive, those towards debt inflows—particularly of the short-term, unhedged variety, in other words, 'hot money'—were restrictive, thus avoiding the build-up of an unstable debt structure. The capital controls regime also gave the authorities policy space, by enabling them to target the exchange rate at a competitive level and accumulate (sterilized) reserves, without losing control of monetary policy.[7]

While the effects of India's increasing global integration on 'growth with stability' have been demonstrably positive, there is somewhat greater ambiguity about its distributional impact across Indian states, socio-economic groups, and the rural–urban divide. Some studies have claimed that in rural districts whose industries were relatively more exposed to liberalization, poverty reduction was adversely affected, principally because of very limited factor mobility across sectors and states (Topalova, 2007). But this is a strongly disputed matter and other studies do not find such effects (Hasan, Mitra, and Uzal, 2007). Moreover, with time, factor mobility has improved, and the divergence of growth rates across Indian states appears to have been stemmed.

Trade liberalization has clearly not led to general impoverishment, indeed quite the contrary. Even so, it does appear that the response of poverty reduction to increased growth has fallen. Could it be that external liberalization has led to growth that is rapid but not 'inclusive' (despite the theoretical presumption that a move towards freer trade would increase the demand for unskilled labour in a labour-abundant country)? This line of criticism is not persuasive. Inclusivity depends primarily on employment creation and social empowerment, and secondarily on income redistribution. It is indeed true that India's industrialization, unlike that in East Asia, has not been employment-creating for unskilled labour. But the reason for this outcome can be traced to domestic policies. In practice, a host of domestic policy impediments—small-scale industry reservations, rigid labour laws, infrastructure deficiencies, lack of access to credit, weak human capital, and discouragement of FDI in labour-intensive industries—have suppressed the

---

[7] India's capital controls enabled it to combine interest-rate autonomy and exchange rate targeting. This would not have been possible with a fixed or floating exchange rate accompanied by free capital mobility. See Joshi (2003), Joshi and Sanyal (2004), and Joshi (2008), and, for a different perspective, Patnaik and Shah (2011). Of course, as the Indian economy matures, the balance of advantage can be expected to shift towards fuller capital account convertibility. Several gradual moves have been made in that direction and, in consequence, exchange rate management has become more difficult. However, full convertibility is not round the corner, especially with the recent re-emergence of balance of payments weakness.

demand for low-skilled labour (Joshi and Little, 1996; Panagariya, 2008; Joshi, 2010). (In contrast, the demand for skilled labour has risen, and with it the wage premium for skills, which is one reason why income inequality increased over this period.) Income redistribution policies, such as cheap food by way of the public distribution system, and social empowerment policies, such as provision of education and health care, have not worked satisfactorily owing to weak state capacity to deliver public services. India's inclusion deficit has domestic roots, and cannot be blamed on globalization.

A subtle but important outcome of India's increasing global integration is its political impact. India's trade with the USA is set to increase to $100 billion in 2012 (a quadrupling from 2000), and trade with China will probably reach the same level in 2015 (from barely $3 billion in 2000). Naturally, commercial interests now loom much larger in India's bilateral relations with these major powers. Similar considerations have affected the relationship with other trading partners. The emergence of Indian firms as the largest investors in Britain's ailing manufacturing sector cannot but have an effect in shaping the bilateral relationship between the two countries. Both private MNCs and state-owned corporations, particularly in the energy and natural resources sectors, have started investing abroad in a big way in countries ranging from Australia to Indonesia to Bolivia, and, of course, Africa, and these capital flows are opening new avenues in India's bilateral relationships with the countries in question. Unlike China, whose overseas investments are dominated by state-owned enterprises, private firms dominate in the Indian case (with the exception of the oil and gas sector). While the aims of the firms may not be as aligned with national interests as is the case with China, they do appear less threatening to the host countries.

International migration from India has also had multiple economic and political effects.[8] The economic effects of migration work through three mechanisms: financial flows, global networks, and the diaspora's role as reputational intermediaries. The Chinese diaspora has been a critical source of FDI into China. The Indian diaspora's role in this regard has been modest; instead, it has been an important source of financial flows into India in the form of remittances. Remittances emerged as an important component of the country's balance of payments in the mid-1970s, and increased dramatically after the onset of economic liberalization in 1991. They have grown from $2.1 billion (0.7 per cent of GDP) in 1990 to $53 billion (3.1 per cent of GDP) in 2010. These figures reflect both the rise in the stock of Indian citizens residing abroad (especially in North America) and the degree to which their earning power has multiplied. Policy changes over the last two decades, including the devaluation of the rupee, liberalization of gold imports, and rupee

---

[8] This paragraph and the two that follow rely heavily on Kapur (2010).

convertibility for current account transactions, have also made a difference, especially in bringing remittances from the Middle East through official markets rather than underground (*hawala*) channels.

The large remittances into India that have resulted from international migration have also mitigated the effects of external shocks through a range of mechanisms, from increased consumption to provision of social insurance, at both the household and national level. (For instance, remittances enhanced India's ability to withstand sanctions imposed in the aftermath of its nuclear tests.) Remittances have also had significant distributional consequences, affecting income inequalities across states, social groups, and households. In the state of Kerala, remittances account for nearly a quarter of state net domestic product, and appear also to have had considerable effects on policy incentives. (These effects were not always beneficial. Remittances provided an income uplift, which reduced public pressure for desirable policy change.) However, while labour flows from Kerala were dominant in the 1970s and 1980s, by 2010 Uttar Pradesh had emerged as the largest state for low-skilled international labour outflows.

The Indian diaspora has created a web of cross-national networks, thereby facilitating the inflow of tacit information, business ideas, and technologies. It has also facilitated 'home sourcing', as exemplified by the rapid growth of India's diamond cutting and polishing industry on the one hand, and the rapid growth of India's IT sector on the other. The selectivity of recent Indian emigration and the success of migrants abroad have transformed the 'brain drain' into a 'brain bank'. This has resulted in broader spillover effects for India, with diasporic networks acting as reputational intermediaries and as credibility-enhancing mechanisms. The Indian diaspora's success in Silicon Valley has had a considerable cognitive impact on global perceptions of India, particularly as regards India's technology businesses. There is little doubt that, by the 1990s, India's human-capital-rich diaspora, especially in the USA, became an international business asset for the country.

If India's growing integration with the global economy has transformed the country's economy, the success also may have led to an early complacency that has hampered a parallel transformation of domestic institutions to propel the country to the next stage of development. At the time of writing this chapter, we expected the current account deficit in 2012 (around 4 per cent of GDP) to exceed that which led to the balance of payments crisis of 1991, and the fiscal deficit (around 8.5 per cent of GDP) to be nearly as high as just before that crisis. India's rapid growth has exposed the severe resource constraints it faces, be they land, energy, or water. The allocation of these scarce resources through the use of non-market discretionary and opaque government actions has resulted in a severe governance crisis in the country. In the absence of major policy and institutional reforms to address these growing challenges, there is currently a non-negligible risk that India's engagement with the global economy could be derailed.

India's global engagement: impact on the world

India's impact on the world economy has so far been small. If it continues to grow at the present rate, its global presence will become much more significant. Indeed, it is likely to emerge as the world's third-largest economy by around 2030.[9] While India's overall consumption and production levels are still at levels that are too low to shape world prices, in certain areas such as oil (where it is a major importer) or cotton and sugar (where it is a major exporter), its impact is already being felt. Moreover, the more India integrates with the global economy, the more its emerging demographic bulge will impact on global labour markets. And if trends such as 'frugal engineering' — the development of low-cost innovative processes and products, such as cheap cars and cheap generic pharmaceuticals—continue to deepen in India, they could disturb the existing market strategies of other countries and major international companies. Of course, these outcomes are by no means certain. India has significant assets but also major liabilities. If, however, India's advance continues, it would raise the question: What kind of power will India want to be? Will it seek to uphold the international order established by the Western powers, and especially the USA, in the aftermath of the Second World War? Or will it seek to change this order, and, if so, in which ways? The predicament that India will face is that, as a major global economic power, the world will expect India to shoulder the burden of providing global public goods, such as climate change mitigation, even while it will continue to be a relatively poor country (in terms of per capita income), with major internal challenges.

A major change that is already occurring is India's transformation from foreign aid recipient (indeed the largest aid recipient, in absolute terms, in the second half of the twentieth century) to foreign aid donor (Kapur, 2012). A key inflexion point in Indian foreign aid was the decision in 2003 to repay its bilateral debt to all but four countries, not to accept tied aid in the future, and accept bilateral aid from only five countries and the EU. With India becoming a lower middle-income country, it is also poised to graduate from International Development Association (IDA) soft loans, which are one of the

---

[9] This would be so at both market and purchasing power parity (PPP) exchange rates. Currently, India has the world's fourth highest national income at PPP exchange rates and the tenth highest at market exchange rates. See Maddison (2007) and Wilson and Purushothaman (2003). Needless to say, in 2030, India's per capita income will be well below that of advanced countries.

cornerstones of the global multilateral aid system. India's activity as aid donor is acquiring quantitative weight. Between 2003 and 2010, India provided $5.1 billion in lines of credit, of which $3.3 billion went to Africa, $1.8 billion to South Asia, and $131 million to Caribbean countries. In May 2011, India announced $5 billion of low-interest loans over the next three years for Africa and an additional $1 billion to pay for education, railways, and peacekeeping, a massive increase from the $25 million that India provided as aid to Africa a year ago. While one part of this aid package is tied aid, linked to export subsidies for Indian goods, another part has focused on technical cooperation, for example in setting up broadband networks. India also provided $2.1 billion to its South Asian neighbours in grants and loans, and $346 million to other developing countries. In addition, it has emerged as a significant contributor to multilateral assistance, through financial contributions to the UN system and multilateral organizations. It remains to be seen whether India will strive to marshal its limited foreign aid resources through bilateral channels and those small multilateral institutions where it has a leadership role, or operate through large global institutions where its voice is relatively limited.

On international trade policy, India's changing stance is reflected in increasing willingness to commit to binding international commitments. Although it was seen in some quarters as a spoiler in the Doha Round, other major powers have been at least as responsible. With global trade talks at an impasse, India has become surprisingly (at least by its own past record) aggressive in pursuing bilateral and regional trade agreements, reversing its earlier stance: that committing to long-term trade agreements would constrain domestic policy choices. Table 4.7 shows the marked rise in India's trade agreements in the last decade. Before 2000, India had signed just one inconsequential agreement (with the Maldives); another three were negotiated from 2000 to 2005; no fewer than 16 followed in the next five years. At the end of 2011, India was negotiating another seven agreements (including, significantly, one with the EU). While most of these are Free Trade Agreements, some are Preferential Trade Agreements, and a few are Comprehensive Economic Partnership Agreements (which include services as well as trade).

Table 4.7. India's Trade Agreements

Before 1990	1
1990–99	0
2000–05	3
2006–11	16
Under Negotiation	7

Source: Government of India, Ministry of Commerce, Annual Reports.

At the macro level, India's impact on the world has to be seen in the context of China's simultaneous rise. There will be not one but two emerging giants in the world economy, with India the smaller of the two. China and India will provide rapidly growing markets for advanced as well as developing countries. Indeed, they are already acting as global engines of growth. Even so, the effects of their rise on the rest of the world are likely to be complex: some favourable, others unfavourable. Three types of effect can usefully be distinguished: on global stability, on overall living standards, and on the distribution of income in other countries.

The effects on global stability will depend, inter alia, on exchange rate policy in China and India. In the last decade, China's policy raised hackles. An influential account runs as follows. China followed an export-led growth strategy on the back of an undervalued exchange rate and, in consequence, ran large current account surpluses and accumulated a mountain of foreign exchange reserves. This, in turn, led to excessive 'global imbalances' that played an important part in causing the global credit crisis. Of course, this statement is simplistic and controversial, but it does indicate how an emerging giant could damage the international balance of payments adjustment. India's policies have so far not been open to such strictures. Its growth strategy has been much more balanced between domestic and foreign markets than China's. Its moderate current account deficits, offset by capital inflows, have been a stabilizing force in the global economy, albeit in a modest way. The point to note is that in future years India's exchange rate policy will matter to the rest of the world. Any scheme for global exchange rate and monetary coordination will have to involve India because it will be a 'systemically important' country.

The long-run effect of the rise of China and India on overall living standards in various countries could turn out to be substantial, but is hard to predict. This effect will operate principally through the terms of trade, which could move favourably or unfavourably. For example, China's and India's voracious appetite for commodities promises to raise world commodity prices. This would be good for commodity producers, for example in Africa and the Middle East, but bad for commodity importers. China's and India's success in producing goods and services cheaply will make consumers in many countries better off. By the same token, countries which compete with China and India in third-country markets may be adversely affected owing to a worsening of their terms of trade. The distribution of income within countries will also be influenced by the integration of China and India into the world economy, and the consequent 'doubling of the world's labour force'. The eventual impact is likely to be favourable. But in the short run, unskilled wages in the West could be adversely affected. Equally important, as skills in China and India improve, there will also be downward pressure on skilled wages in electronically offshoreable jobs in Western countries.

No serious discussion of the impact of China and India can exclude consideration of the climate change issue. Though the responsibility for putting the accumulated stock of carbon in the atmosphere rests mainly with the advanced countries, China and India will be increasingly important in future carbon emissions production. While it is right that all countries should make efforts to counter global warming, it is also fair and reasonable that the associated financial burden should be borne by the advanced countries for a couple of decades (Joshi, 2009; Joshi and Patel, 2009; Kapur, Khosla, and Mehta, 2009). Since this is a deeply contested matter, reaching an international agreement will be far from easy.

It seems likely that on all the major global economic issues, such as exchange rates, trade, and climate change, global action will have to involve the participation of China and India. The optimistic vision for the future is of a world in which the great powers, old and new, cooperate to supply global public goods. The pessimistic vision is one of disharmony and conflict between the major powers, similar to that which has accompanied some power transitions in the past. For good or ill, China and India will matter in the twenty-first century for each other and for the world.

References

Athukorala, P. (2008) Export performance in the reform era: has India regained the lost ground? ASARC Working Paper No. 2008/03, Australian National University.

Athukorala, P. (2009) Outward direct investment from India. *Asian Development Review*, 26(2), pp. 125–153.

Bhagwati, J. and Desai, P. (1970) *India: Planning for Industrialization* (Oxford: Oxford University Press).

Chand, C. and Sen, K. (2002) Trade liberalization and productivity growth. *Review of Development Economics*, 6(1), pp. 120–132.

Hasan, R., Mitra, D., and Uzal, B. (2007) Trade liberalization, labour market institutions, and poverty reduction: evidence from Indian states. *India Policy Forum*, 3, pp. 71–110.

Joshi, V. (2003) India and the impossible trinity. *World Economy*, 26(4), pp. 555–583.

Joshi, V. (2008) Convertibility now? No, thanks, in R. Kumar (ed.) *India and the Global Economy* (New Delhi: Academic Foundation), pp. 285–304.

Joshi, V. (2009) How to share the burden of combating climate change. Vox. <http://www.voxeu.org/> (accessed 5 August 2013).

Joshi, V. (2010) Economic resurgence, lopsided reform and jobless growth, in A. Heath and R. Jeffery (eds) *Diversity and Change in Modern India: Economic, Social and Political Approaches* (Oxford: The British Academy and Oxford University Press), pp. 73–106.

Joshi, V. and Little, I. M. D. (1994) *India—Macroeconomics and Political Economy 1964–1991* (Washington, DC and New Delhi: World Bank and Oxford University Press).

Joshi, V. and Little, I. M. D. (1996) *India's Economic Reforms, 1991–2001* (Oxford and New Delhi: Oxford University Press).

Joshi, V. and Patel, U. (2009) India and climate change mitigation, in D. Helm and C. Hepburn (eds) *The Economics and Politics of Climate Change* (Oxford: Oxford University Press), pp. 167–196.

Joshi, V. and Sanyal, S. (2004) Foreign inflows and macroeconomic policy in India. *India Policy Forum*, 1, pp. 135–187.

Kapur, D. (2010) *Diaspora, Development, and Democracy: The Domestic Impact of International Migration from India* (Princeton, NJ: Princeton University Press).

Kapur, D. (2012) Graduation day at Bretton Woods. *Business Standard*, 12 March. <http://www.business-standard.com/article/opinion/devesh-kapur-graduation-day-at-bretton-woods-112031200077_1.html> (accessed 5 August 2013).

Kapur, D., Khosla, R., and Mehta, P. (2009) Climate change: India's options. *Economic and Political Weekly*, 64(31), pp. 34–42.

Maddison, A. (2007) *The Contours of the World Economy 1–2030 AD: Essays in Macroeconomic History* (Oxford: Oxford University Press).

Panagariya, A. (2004) India's trade reform. *India Policy Forum*, 1, pp. 1–57.

Panagariya, A. (2008) *India: The Emerging Giant* (New York: Oxford University Press).

Shah, A. and Patnaik, I. (2011) India's financial globalization. Working Paper No. 79, National Institute of Public Finance and Policy, New Delhi.

Topalova, P. (2007) Trade liberalization, poverty and inequality: evidence from Indian districts, in A. Harrison (ed.) *Globalization and Poverty* (Chicago: University of Chicago Press), pp. 291–336.

UN Commodity Trade Database. <http://comtrade.un.org/> (accessed 5 August 2013).

Wilson, D. and Purushothaman, R. (2003) Dreaming with the BRICS: the path to 2050. Global Economics Paper No. 99, Goldman Sachs.

Part III

Changing Demographic Profiles

5

The Social Consequences of Demographic Change in China

DELIA DAVIN

CHINA, LIKE INDIA, has experienced rapid demographic change in recent decades. Combined with the dramatic economic growth which started with the introduction of market-orientated economic reforms from the late 1970s, demographic change has had enormous and still ongoing impacts on Chinese society, marriage, family relations, and family building. This chapter starts by offering a general overview of the major forms of this demographic change: rising life expectancy and lowered fertility, the distorted child sex ratio, and migration and urbanization. It moves on to a discussion of some of the actual and potential consequences of these changes, focusing on marriage, the shortage of brides, and marriage finance; marriage migration; the implications of lowered fertility for women; and population ageing and its challenge to the intergenerational contract. Labour migration is given less attention than it would otherwise deserve because it is discussed elsewhere in this volume.

Forms of demographic change

Rising life expectancy and fertility decline

Mortality decline and increased life expectancy began in China in the 1950s as a result of greater food security, peace, and the introduction of grass-roots level medical services focused on the fight against infectious disease. Progress was fastest in the early years. Life expectancy, which was about 35 years in 1949, rose to 47 in 1956, and 65.1 in 1978 on the eve of the economic reforms. The one terrible reverse in this progress was the result of famine from 1959 to 1961, when life expectancy fell for three consecutive years, reaching its nadir in 1960 at 25.6. It had resumed its upward progress by 1962, when it stood at

Proceedings of the British Academy, **193**, 95–114, © The British Academy 2014

53 (Banister, 1987: 352).[1] Life expectancy continued to rise under the economic reforms, though more slowly, and had reached 73.8 by 2005 (Banister, 2009: 18). The Chinese record in the reform decades compares well with that of the USSR and various Eastern European countries, where catastrophic rises in mortality followed the move to market economies (Chen, Wittgenstein, and McKeon, 1996). Nonetheless, the rising inequalities in income distribution and access to health care which have characterized the reform decades may have slowed mortality decline (Zhao and Fei, 2007: 3). There are large regional and rural/urban variations in life expectancy. At the census of 2000, it was over 76 in Beijing and 78 in Shanghai. By contrast, eight of China's 31 provincial-level administrations still had life expectancies of less than 70. All eight were border provinces or particularly poor provinces, or both; Tibet, at 64.4, was the lowest (NBS, 2010: 100).

Fertility remained high through the 1950s and 1960s. Total fertility rate (TFR) was above 5.3 except in 1959–61, the years affected by the famine. It underwent an extraordinarily rapid decline in the 1970s from 5.8 at the start of the decade to 2.24 by 1980 (adjusted figures from Banister, 1987). This has continued. Official estimates drawn from unadjusted census and survey results gave TFRs of 1.2 and 1.4 at the end of the 1990s, but official adjustments raised this to between 1.8 and 1.9. Independent scholarly reconstructions produced rates of between 1.5 and 1.7 children per woman (Scharping, 2007). All estimates agree that fertility is now well below replacement level.[2]

Fertility decline in China as elsewhere was part of demographic transition from a society with high death rates and high birth rates to one in which both were low. As in other countries, the fall in death rates came first, and included striking falls in infant mortality, providing the reassurance to parents that it was not necessary to have large numbers of children to ensure that some survived to adulthood. China's fertility decline has also been associated with the spread of education and the rise in the aspirations of ordinary people for their children, high rates of female participation in education and the workforce, urbanization, the development of a consumer society, and efforts by the state to bring about a rapid fall in the birth rate.

The distinctive feature of China's fertility decline is that it has been accompanied by a sustained campaign on the part of the state to reduce family size. This began in the 1950s and continued into the twenty-first century with

---

[1] Banister's figures are computer reconstructions which adjust for factors such as under-registration of deaths. They produce lower expectancy of life than the official Chinese figures from which they are derived.

[2] The introduction of the one-child family policy with its attendant fines for second or higher parity births, visited both on the parents and on local officials in whose areas too many 'out-of-plan' children are born, has given large numbers of people an interest in concealing births to avoid fines. As a result, quality of statistics is believed to have deteriorated, and there is room for much debate about them.

only short periods of relaxation at the time of the Great Leap Forward (1958–62) and the first years of the Cultural Revolution (1966–69) (Scharping, 2003; Greenhalgh and Winkler, 2005; White, 2006). The family planning information campaigns of the 1950s were followed by stronger exhortations in the 1960s. From the early 1970s, a two-child family model was widely advocated, and 1980 saw the beginning of the one-child family policy backed up by a range of incentives and penalties. Ironically, this policy was introduced when fertility had already fallen to an all-time low. It was justified, however, with reference to the extreme youth of the Chinese population at that time, which, it was claimed, would function as a demographic time bomb unless fertility could be reduced.

The one-child policy was not universally observed. In the first decade of the policy, around half of all births were first births, rising to around 70 per cent by the turn of the century. Of the remainder, the great majority were second children. Third and higher parity births dropped from over 50 per cent of all births in 1975 to around 20 per cent by 1990, and only 5 per cent by 1997 (White, 2006: 74). Some second births and even a few third parity ones are permitted births or births 'within the plan'. The one-child regulations have never been uniform. They are stricter in the urban areas than in the rural ones and they vary by province. The exemptions allowed, as well as the severity of the sanctions and the strictness of implementation, have all varied from one province to another and from one period to another since 1980 (Scharping, 2003). The most important change, introduced in 1988 after some experimentation and considerable debate, was to allow rural couples whose first child was female to have a second child after a gap of four years (Davin, 1990).

The precise contribution of the one-child campaign to fertility decline is disputed. Clearly some decline was to be expected; the factors that brought about fertility decline elsewhere in the world (including India) were also present in China. However, the severity of state policies and the power of the state to enforce them probably contributed to the exceptional speed and extent of fertility decline in China. Whatever its causation, it is calculated to have averted 300 million births since the 1970s (Zhao and Fei, 2007: 5). Yet a UN population projection of 2004 indicated that China's total population would not start to decline until 2030, at which point it will have reached 1.45 billion (Zhao and Fei, 2007: 5). The Sixth National Census of 2010 found a population total of 1.39 billion (NBS, 2012: 10).

Child and infant sex ratios

The child sex ratio, which was near normal from the 1950s to the 1970s at around 106 boys to 100 girls, became increasingly distorted from the 1980s.[3]

---

[3] Unlike their colleagues working on India, demographers of China follow international practice by expressing the sex ratio in terms of numbers of boys per 100 girls.

It was 107.1 in 1982, 110.2 in 1990, and 120.2 in 2000 (Cai and Lavely, 2003 and 2007; Das Gupta, 2005).[4] The 2010 census reported a sex ratio at birth of 117.96 (NBS, 2012: 265).

The ratio is thought to have been high in the past in China especially in times of war and shortage (Lee and Wang, 1999; Hudson and Boer, 2004). In a society where girls were married out, parents were determined to have sons. In hard times, infant survival, and thus the child sex balance, was affected by preferential treatment of boys and the neglect and abandonment, or even infanticide, of girls. In the Maoist period, improving food availability and high fertility produced a more even child sex ratio. However, since the 1980s, in the context of greatly reduced fertility and average families of around two children, raised sex ratios have become an ever more serious problem. Parents do not mind having a daughter, but remain determined to have at least one son. Under the one-child policy, if the first child is a girl, they may, especially if they are rural, get permission to have a second child after a gap of four years or may resolve to go ahead without permission and risk a fine. In either case, they will try to ensure that the second child is a boy. This is reflected in the sex ratio, which is not far from normal for first parity births but becomes progressively elevated with birth parity, particularly if the first child has been a girl (Zeng et al., 1993; Scharping, 2003; Das Gupta, 2006; Attané, 2013).

There is debate both about what underlies the distorted child sex ratio in China and whether the figures are accurate. It is known that both parents and local officials who wish to escape sanctions for 'out of plan' births may conceal female births. However, it is generally agreed that concealment, and excess female infant and child mortality, explains only part of the distortion, and that sex-selective abortion has become an increasingly important mechanism, as is true elsewhere in Asia. Sex determination of the foetus is illegal for other than medical reasons (Population and Birth Planning Law, 2001), but as medical services have been extensively privatized and scanning machines are widely available, the prohibition is unenforceable.

The phenomenon of missing girls in China is often blamed on the one-child family policy. There is considerable evidence that, given the choice, Chinese families would choose to have a mix of sons or daughters, but that when parents are allowed only one child a son is still seen as a necessity. This, indeed, is the reason that, since 1988, the rural population has been allowed a second child if the first is a girl (Davin, 1990). However, the attribution of the phenomenon of the missing girls in China solely to the one-child family policy seems perverse when other Asian countries have developed the same

---

[4] I follow Cai and Lavely (2007) by using the child sex ratio based on census returns for children aged one to four (whenever available), in the belief that these figures are likely to be less affected by the desire to conceal births than infant sex ratios derived from birth registrations.

problem in the same period (Croll, 2000; Jeffery, Chapter 6, this volume). A better explanation would seem to be that in societies with a strong son preference, where fertility falls steeply for whatever reason, parents having only one, two, or at most three children will be determined to have at least one boy. The development and spread of ultra-sound techniques in the last decades of the twentieth century made this possible to achieve with sex-selective abortion. The problem is particularly severe in China, where extraordinarily low fertility is the result not only of parental decisions but also of strong and effective state intervention.

Migration and urbanization

Large-scale migration and urbanization have contributed greatly to the transformation of Chinese society since the 1980s. Rural urban migration was effectively proscribed in Maoist China. As a result, a huge labour surplus developed in the countryside, and the considerable rural/urban inequalities could not be mitigated by peasants seeking more income in the towns. As restrictions eased, a labour market developed, and the burgeoning economy created a huge demand for labour. Peasants responded by moving into the urban areas (Davin, 1999; Solinger, 1999; Fan, 2008; Solinger, Chapter 7, this volume).

Migrants temporarily resident in urban areas numbered around 30 million at the time of the 1990 census, and perhaps there were around 140 million by the early twenty-first century (Liang, 2007). The findings of the 2010 census imply a total of over 226 million (NBS, 2012: 460–462). At first, this migration was largely circular. More recently, although the status of migrants in the urban areas remains poor, they lack entitlements, and are generally required to pay for time-limited urban resident permits, more and more of them are succeeding in settling in the urban areas. They thus contribute to the growth of the urban population.

The census of 2010 found that 49.7 per cent of the population lived in the urban areas, up by nearly 13.5 per cent since the census of 2000 (NBS, 2011). The pace of urbanization is difficult to calculate with certainty, as the definitions of what is urban and the regulations for enumerating rural migrants have changed from one census to another, but it is clearly extraordinarily rapid. The growth in the urban population owes nothing to fertility, which is well below replacement level in the urban areas. The redesignation of industrializing rural areas as urban areas certainly contributes something, but the main cause of growth is migration.

Social consequences of demographic change

Falling death rates and birth rates, changes in the child sex ratio, migration, and urbanization have together brought about enormous changes in many areas of Chinese life. The age structure of the population and the dependency ratio already reflect China's demographic transition. As Figure 5.1 shows, working age adults predominate in the population. The elderly are still a small percentage of the total, but will grow rapidly in future given the large size of the middle-aged cohorts. The small size of the cohorts under 20 years old already reflects the fall in fertility that China has experienced. Males outnumber females in all but the oldest age groups. This difference is striking in the youngest age groups.

Average household size in the census of 2010 was 3.10 persons, down from 3.44 in 2000 and 3.96 in 1990 (NBS, 1993, 2003, 2012: 3). The decline no doubt reflects lowered fertility and the fact that three-generational families are less common. This is partly due to urbanization, but even in the rural areas young couples are increasingly less inclined to live with their ageing parents (Yan, 2003). Migration also separates older people from their adult children. Returning migrants, bringing back urban ideas about how life should be lived, are gradually changing rural life.

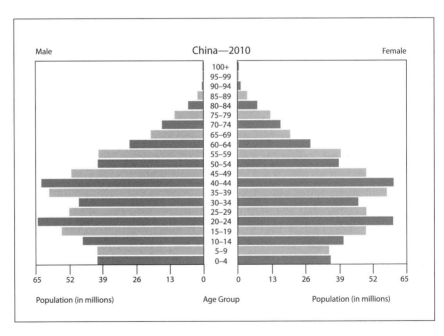

Figure 5.1. Estimate of Population of China by Age and Sex, Mid-2010
Source: US Census Bureau, International Data Base <http://www.census.gov/population/ international/ data/idb/region.php>.

Children, the vast majority of whom are singletons or have only one sibling, perhaps benefit from their rarity value. Care, attention, and economic resources are lavished on them. Parents invest heavily in them and are desperate for them to achieve educationally, get good jobs, and marry well. The shortage of young women is making it harder for men to marry and is changing the nature of the marriage market. For the moment, a young and increasingly well-educated workforce may bring a demographic dividend (Wang and Mason, 2007). However, in the longer term, China faces the challenge of an ageing population at a time when attitudes to the intergenerational contract may be changing (Banister, 2009). The following discussion focuses on five aspects of the social impact of demographic change: the competitive society; the bride shortage and the marriage market; marriage migration and its gendered impacts; the impact of lowered fertility on women; and the intergenerational contract in the context of an ageing society.

The demographic dividend and the competitive society

The 2010 census revealed that over 70 per cent of the Chinese population were in the 15–59 age group, up by 3.3 per cent over the 2000 census (NBS, 2012: 265-266). The advantageous age structure is also reflected in China's population dependency ratio (the ratio of those under 15 or over 65 to the working population), which the World Bank put at 37.8 in 2011 (World Bank, 2012) compared with India at 54.3, the UK at 52, the USA at 50, and many African countries at over 80 or even 90. China's low ratio offers its economy the demographic dividend, the temporary window of opportunity (discussed by Riskin and Jeffery in Chapters 1 and 6 respectively) that occurs in the course of demographic transition, when the majority of the population is of working age, can be productive, and pays taxes. The problem for China, as Riskin shows in Chapter 1, is that to realize the dividend fully, large numbers of new jobs must be generated every year that the working-age population increases. From the point of view of the individual, the large size of the working-age population means fierce competition in the labour market. In an age where labour has been commoditized, and the old social contract—whereby the authoritarian socialist state guaranteed the urban population certain entitlements—has been swept away, the competitive society creates real difficulties and anxieties (Lee, 2007).

Increasing income inequality has created a tier of people in China who live very well. The market economy, mobility, improved communications, and the media have together created awareness of their prosperous lifestyle and of the consumer goods available to those who can afford them. Chinese people have become ambitious to live better themselves and to see their children do so. This is reflected in the willingness of ordinary people to migrate for better-paid jobs, however hard and disagreeable, to accept long-term family separations, to leave the land if there are superior opportunities elsewhere, and to spend very considerable sums of money on education for children.

Yet secure employment is at a premium. Many of the workers laid off as state industry closed were never able to work again or found only casual work, and the huge migrant labour force is highly casualized (Lee, 2007; Bramall, 2009: 426–430). It is difficult for workers to fight for better conditions as there are so many who are waiting to step into their shoes. There is no longer a shortage of high school or even college graduates. Contemporary China is dominated by fierce competition for jobs, as everyone rural or urban tries to retain or improve their own place on the occupational ladder and to ensure that their children have one that is as good or better. At all levels, people deploy what social capital they have—qualifications, experience, family connections, and the influence of friends—as they struggle for their place.

Sex ratios and marriage markets

In China as elsewhere in Asia, marriage is regarded as essential for men and women. Historically, Chinese marriage rates were high. In the nineteenth century, 98–99 per cent of Chinese women had married by the age of 30, compared with only 75–85 per cent in Europe (Maynes and Waltner, 2001: 11–21). Men's marriage rates were lower, because son preference created a deficit of marriageable women (Lee and Wang, 1999). It was the poorest or those with severe disabilities who failed to marry. They were referred to as bare branches—*guanggun* 光棍—a derogatory term for a bachelor that also means a failure or idler (Hudson and den Boer, 2004).

Traditionally, marriages were arranged by families, often with the help of a broker. The government and the Communist Party have long campaigned against arranged marriage, and the practice has also come under pressure from social and economic change. It would now be unusual for a bride and groom to marry as strangers, although in the rural areas marriages are often still arranged, albeit in consultation and with approval from the young couple. In the urban areas, young people may find their own partners, but most would want family approval. Many also ask friends or family for introductions or use lonely hearts advertisements. By whatever means partners are found, the process of selection includes the conscious use of criteria which include economic factors as well as personality and physical attraction.

The contemporary marriage market is already highly competitive for men, and will become more so as the cohorts in which the sex imbalance is greater reach marriageable age. The shortage of women of marriageable age makes marriage an additional way for women to seek upward mobility. There is ongoing inflation in the expectations of brides and their families, who look for men with prospects whether based on wealth, education, jobs, or access to resources.

The reform decades saw inflation in brideprice (Siu, 1993; Bossen, 2002; Murphy, 2002; Yan, 2003). Although Chinese brides traditionally bring a dowry, this is normally worth less than the brideprice paid by the boy's family. Most of the brideprice and dowry now goes towards setting the young couple up with the increasingly expensive household goods that are now seen as necessary. In the cities, where the details of marriage finance are not always arranged by families, there may be no reference to brideprice or dowry, but young men who cannot provide a home properly equipped for a modern life will find it difficult to marry. Education also plays an important part in the marriage market. The general expectation is that women will marry men a little older and perhaps somewhat more educated than themselves.

Table 5.1, using data from the censuses of 1990 and 2000, shows that the vast majority of the Chinese population marry, but men are more likely to be unmarried at the age of 40 than women. The minimum legal age for marriage is 20 for women and 22 for men, but most marry a few years later. The minority of men who were married in the 20–24 age group tended to be the least educated. A majority of less-educated women in this age bracket were married, whereas a majority of better-educated women remained unmarried. However, by the age of 25–29, the majority of both men and women were married. For men, education was a clear predictor of the ability to marry. Almost all of the most educated men were married by their late 30s, whereas very significant proportions of the least educated remain unmarried. Each added level of education tended to make bachelordom less likely. The least-educated men were clearly finding it more difficult to marry by the time of the 2000 census. For women, poor education was not a significant impediment to marriage. Very few women remained single into their 30s. Interestingly, a slightly higher proportion of the best-educated women did so. We do not know whether this was because education and economic independence made remaining single a viable personal choice, or because by the time these women were ready to marry, single men of suitable levels of education were in short supply. The male figures reflect the market power conferred by education. As the shortage of women becomes more serious, more poor uneducated men will have to remain single.

There is also a spatial aspect to the marriage market. Patrilocal marriage has always been the norm in China, and in the rural areas women did not often marry men within their own villages. On the other hand, they did not normally marry at a distance of more than a few hours' walk or bicycle ride away. A woman's visits to her natal home were restricted by custom, which varied greatly by locality, but she could and did make them. In some regions, indeed,

Delia Davin

Table 5.1. China: Percentage of Population Never Married, by Educational Level and Sex for Selected Age Groups: Censuses of 1990 and 2000

Males

Age	15–19	20–24	25–29	30–34	35–39
Education	(1990) 2000	(1990) 2000	(1990) 2000	(1990) 2000	(1990) 2000
Illiterate or semi-literate	(95.1) 97.0	(66.6) 71.9	(40.1) 45.0	(26.0) 35.7	(21.8) 33.7
Primary	(97.6) 98.8	(60.8) 70.2	(21.6) 26.1	(10.8) 11.6	(6.7) 9.2
Junior middle	(98.4) 99.8	(57.1) 74.5	(13.3) 19.9	(4.8) 5.2	(2.7) 2.7
Senior middle	(99.6) 100	(76.0) 86.8	(14.0) 29.3	(3.5) 6.43	(1.9) 2.0
Vocational school	(99.8) 100	(84.5) 89.0	(22.7) 32.0	(2.6) 5.9	(0.57) 1.4
College	(100) 100	(94.6) 95.6	(35.8) 38.2	(5.5) 6.5	(0.96) 1.5
All levels	(98.2) 99.7	(62.5) 78.6	(16.7) 24.6	(7.2) 7.45	(5.7) 4.1

Females

Age	15–19	20–24	25–29	30–34	35–39
Education	(1990) 2000	(1990) 2000	(1990) 2000	(1990) 2000	(1990) 2000
Illiterate or semi-literate	(87.3) 88.1	(24.6) 28.0	(2.4) 5.7	(0.5) 2.0	(0.28) 1.2
Primary	(93.8) 95.8	(35.0) 38.1	(2.5) 4.2	(0.2) 0.64	(0.9) 0.24
Junior middle	(97.3) 99.0	(42.2) 54.7	(4.2) 8.0	(0.6) 1.2	(0.5) 0.39
Senior middle	(99.4) 99.9	(66.0) 72.2	(6.8) 14.7	(1.3) 2.8	(0.8) 0.8
Vocational school	(99.7) 99.9	(74.5) 76.7	(13.3) 15.1	(3.0) 2.6	(0.25) 0.09
College	(100.0) 100	(88.7) 87.4	(22.0) 27.3	(7.2) 4.0	(2.9) 1.5
All levels	(95.2) 98.8	(41.4) 57.5	(4.3) 8.7	(0.6) 1.3	(0.34) 0.5

Source: Calculations from the censuses of 1990 and 2000 made by the author.

women spent a considerable amount of time at their natal home, at least until the birth of their first child (Judd, 1994). The maintenance of such contact eases the transition a bride must make in becoming a member of a new family.

Lavely (1991) showed that in the 'spatial economy' of marriage, men from the poorest, least desirable villages, where incomes were low and agricultural work hard, found it difficult to attract brides. Women would not want to go there, nor would their families want to send them. It was much easier for men in rich fertile villages to find wives. Not only could they could attract women from poorer areas, but they could also retain women from the immediately surrounding villages, who were happy to stay in their own area upon marriage. It was the poorest men who tended to remain single, and there were more single men in the poorest villages, for there were no communities from which they could import brides.

Marriage migration and its gendered impacts

In post-reform China, mobility has made the enlargement of marriage markets possible, and marriage migration over considerable distances has become commonplace (Tan Lin and Gilmartin, 2001; Davin, 2008; Fan, 2008). A significant minority of women now traverse much greater distances, crossing provincial or even regional boundaries to join their husbands. Working through marriage-brokers or through female relatives who have already married into far-off places, brides or their families can seek a good economic match not just by moving a few miles but to destinations sometimes hundreds of miles away. For some, the market is now national, or even occasionally involves crossing frontiers (Tran, 2001; Lu, 2008; Lu and Yang, 2008).

The census of 2000 recorded 1.30 million female marriage migrants among a total of 6.52 million female migrants who had moved since 1995 (NBS, 2003: 1818–1824). The 1 per cent sample census of 2005 found 64.57 million women had moved within their province in the previous five years, of whom 10.8 million had moved for marriage. Of the 31.67 million female migrants who had taken up residence in another province, 2.28 million had moved because of marriage (NBS, 2007: 720–726). The census of 2010 found that 12 per cent, over 10.4 million of the 124 million women living outside the areas in which they were registered, had migrated for marriage.

Migrant brides have enormous adjustments to make. In addition to their new roles as wives and mothers, they have to learn new languages or dialects, new ways of life and customs, new jobs, and different ways of cooking. All this must be accomplished and new relations established with husbands and in-laws without the support of their own families or, in many cases, any person whom they knew in their former lives. The ethnographic evidence on the outcomes of marriage migration for women indicate that they vary enormously. Huang's study of two villages on the North China Plain (Huang, 2007) reported that migrant wives did well, although their husbands were from the next poorest group in their communities apart from the bachelors. Better-educated and more forceful than local women in villages that had been poor before the new cashmere-processing industry was introduced, the migrant brides were well thought of for their hard work. They integrated successfully, especially if they had a son, and they created comparatively balanced conjugal relationships.

By contrast, Tan and Short (2004), looking at women from the poorest provinces of China who had married into a prosperous county-level city in Jiangsu province, found that these women felt inferior—yet they rarely expressed regret. Living better than they would have in their natal villages, they worked hard at being accepted, and tried to bring in relatives to expand their networks and reduce their isolation. They had planned for themselves and seemed to have a sense of agency. The migrant wives in Han and Eades's (1995) study, on the other hand, had come from poor parts of south-west China, often conveyed by brokers, into what had long been one of the wealthiest and most sophisticated regions in China. They also felt despised, but lacked confidence and suffered the difficulties of not knowing how to do the local agricultural work, speak the local dialect, or cook the local dishes.

In China's poorest regions, marriage migration has dire implications for the ability of men to find wives. In the past, every village had some unmarried men, although poorer ones had more. Huang observed that in order of numerical importance in northern villages, the causes of men's failure to marry were: poverty, disability and mental illness, bad class status, and 'missing the age for marriage'. The worsening sex ratios in China, together with increased marriage mobility, imply that the distribution of unmarried men will become increasingly concentrated. Poor or otherwise disadvantaged men in the wealthier, better-developed areas of China can import brides from the poorest areas of China, while poor counties and provinces are net exporters of brides to the richer areas, especially in the coastal provinces (Davin, 1999, 2008). The working of the marriage market will thus produce a tendency for large numbers of lifetime bachelors to be concentrated in the poorest areas of the country where adult sex ratios will become increasingly skewed.

The spatial aspect of the market will be further complicated by the fact that the child sex ratio is far from uniform nationally. According to one county-level study (Cai and Lavely, 2007), about 10 per cent of the Chinese population live in counties with a normal child sex ratio. Of the remaining 90 per cent, 40 per cent live in counties with a seriously imbalanced ratio of 120 or more boys to girls. Approximately 5 per cent are in counties where the ratio is over 150. Clearly such ratios will complicate the effects of the marriage squeeze, creating areas where a high proportion of men have no chance of finding a local bride, and perhaps triggering an outflow of men from areas where they have no hope of finding a wife.

Bachelors lack status in Chinese rural society. They are looked down on and not seen as proper adult men (Huang, 2007: 72–75). Without children, they have no-one to carry on their family line or care for them in old age. More immediately, they have no-one to help them care for their own parents in old age. Usually impoverished to start with, these men will stay poor, for they have no-one to help them on the land or in household industries, and no-one to cultivate their plot if they seek temporary work as migrants. It is a matter of concern that demography will condemn so many Chinese men to this fate in future.

Implications of fertility decline for women

Lowered fertility and the shortage of women have specific consequences for women. Women have suffered in particular ways from the state-sponsored family planning campaign. When the one child they were allowed to bear was a girl, they frequently carried the blame for what was regarded as the family's misfortune and might be beaten, ill-treated, or abandoned. In the struggle between the state and the family to control women's fertility, women themselves may lack agency (Davin, 1987). Some come under family pressure to conceive a second or higher parity child without the necessary official permission. Then, if the pregnancy is discovered, they may be coerced into an abortion. More positively, most women now have their child or children in their early or mid-20s and finish childbearing early. They are far less likely to die in childbirth than earlier generations or to suffer ill-health from repeated and over-close pregnancies.

Mean age at first marriage increased almost continuously in the second half of the twentieth century in China, owing in part to socio-economic development and in part to the state campaign for later marriage. The minimum age for marriage, set at 18 for women and 20 for men in the marriage law of 1950, was raised to 20 and 22 respectively in 1980. From the 1970s, the family planning campaign set marriage age targets, often reinforced by sanctions, of 23 for women and 25 for men (or in some areas even higher), which were intended to postpone first births. Delayed marriage played an important part in the fertility decline of the 1970s. Ironically, with the disappearance of these targets, the 1980 law produced a slight fall in average age at marriage. However, in general the trend has been a slow rise. For women it was just over 20 years in 1970, 21.8 in 1991, 23.6 in 2000 (Zhang and Gu, 2007). In 2005, it was 23.49 (NBS, 2007: 421).

We do not yet know whether the marriage squeeze will bring about more significant falls in the age at marriage for women in future. This may occur as men search to secure a bride early. On the other hand, women and their parents may seek to maximize girls' education to improve their chances in both the labour and the marriage markets. Young women and their families also sometimes wish to delay marriages so that the women can enjoy a period of independence or bring their wages to home to their natal families before acquiring the responsibilities of married women.

Trafficking

The shortage of marriageable women is often blamed in the press for the flourishing state of prostitution in contemporary China. Media and scholarly reports alike have also attributed the increasing problem of abductions and trafficking of women on the demand for wives (Zhao, 2003; *The Guardian*, 2012). Both suppositions are plausible, although these are difficult subjects on which to obtain reliable information. Much of the visible growth of prostitution over the past three decades has been of establishments catering for upmarket business trade rather than poor bachelors (Zheng, 2009a, 2009b). The Ministry of Security recognizes the problem of trafficking, and indeed ran a National Plan of Action on Combating Trafficking in Women and Children from 2008 to 2012 (HumanTrafficking.org, 2011). Many traffickers were arrested and punished, but it seems unlikely that it will be possible to eliminate the practice in the near future.

Women's paid employment

In Maoist China, it was the accepted norm that women should work outside the home on the land in rural areas, and in waged employment in urban areas. This generally remains the case since the economic reforms and in the era of lower fertility. Indeed, it is often reported that agriculture is becoming ever more feminized as men participate in labour migration or in the non-farm economy locally. Women's workforce participation is extraordinarily high by international standards, at 90 per cent between the ages of 20 and 45, but falls sharply after that, as women leave the workforce earlier than men (Stockman, Bonney, and Sheng, 1995). Jobs for women increased in many sectors in the 1990s, although there was a minor decline in the employment of young women, some of whom apparently stayed at home to look after young children (Parish and Busse, 2000).

Low fertility reduces the years that women commit to childcare but intensifies concerns about child welfare. Parents are understandably anxious about the health, care, and education of the one or two children they are permitted to have. Although kindergarten provision for the over three-year-olds remains common in urban areas, the crèches provided for under threes in the urban areas in the Maoist era have almost disappeared. Very young children are cared for at home, but not necessarily by the mother. Better-off families often employ a nanny, usually a rural migrant. Often another family member helps out. The care that grandmothers are expected to give and women's lower retirement ages bring about a precipitate decline in employment of women in their 40s and early 50s (NBS, 2007: 228–257). Even increased geographical mobility does not necessarily interfere with this practice. Young couples who have moved great distances away from their parents may send babies to live with the grandparents for months or even years at a time. Alternatively, the grandparents may come to stay until the child is old enough for kindergarten.

Population ageing and the intergenerational contract

In China, it is expected that when the elderly are no longer able to work and be self-sufficient, their sons and their sons' wives will take care of them. In the traditional ideal, old people share a household with one of their sons and the others contribute to their upkeep either in cash or in kind. Even in the 1980s, when the one-child policy was first mooted, people began to worry about how the singleton generation would manage to look after two sets of parents and even grandparents from both sides. It is now clear that the considerable increase in life expectancy combined with fertility reduction will produce accelerated population ageing in years to come.

The 2010 census found that 13.3 per cent of China's population was over 60, almost 3 per cent more than in 2000 (NBS, 2012: 266–267). By 2050, this is projected to reach 50 per cent. Clearly, such demographic change will necessitate policy adjustments. China's leadership has so far resisted calls to drop the one-child policy formally, but national and local relaxations have, in effect, made it a one- or two-child policy. In the past, if both parents were themselves only children they could usually get a permit to have a second child. In 2013, it was announced that this concession was to be extended to couples in which only one was an only child. Thirty years on from the introduction of the policy this will in fact include the majority of young parents.

The suggestion that China should raise the retirement age, generally set at the low level of 60 for men and 50–55 for women has so far been resisted (Song, 2010), but may well be accepted at a later date. Social welfare is far from complete. Most of the urban employed pay into social insurance schemes, but few migrant workers are covered and the majority of the rural population is unprotected. The urban elderly often have pensions, and are entitled to various forms of income support and health cover. If they need help from their children, the children are likely to be in a position to offer something, although well-off pensioners may still offer support to their adult children. The rural elderly, by contrast, make up a high proportion of the poor. Most spent their working lives as low earners on the land. In recent decades, they have also often been carers for their grandchildren, whose parents have migrated elsewhere in search of higher earnings. Social welfare reforms to relieve rural poverty are much discussed, but the problems remain immense. It would certainly be feasible for China to redirect some of its ample household, societal, and private sector savings towards funding future retirements (Banister, 2009).

There is as yet little research to show how the long years of separation between grandparents, parents, and grandchildren will affect family relations. The level of migrant remittances sent to the villages seems to indicate an impressive degree of family solidarity, yet some ethnographic studies indicate that younger rural people may be grudging in the support they give their parents. As early as the 1980s, it was noticeable that in peasant houses the room occupied by the young couple was often well equipped with a colour TV and brightly coloured silk bedding. The older couple would have a black and white set and shabby quilts. In the north-eastern village studied by Yan (2003), half the elderly couples in the village lived on their own. Those who shared with married sons tended to be relegated to rooms which were dark and unheated—the least pleasant in the compound. He attributed this treatment to the individualization of Chinese society and the growing strength of the conjugal bond, which directs men's primary loyalty to their wives rather than to their parents. What Yan calls the 'crisis of filial piety' has been noted in various studies (Zhang, 2004).

Changes in the way the elderly are supported are recorded in other sources. In some villages, there is an apparent increase in the support that women are able to give their elderly parents, contrary to the tradition by which women cared for their parents-in-law and left the care of their own parents to their brothers (Judd, 1994). Huang (2007) found that siblings took turns to send food to elderly parents who did not move in with their children. Parents who did live with their children might be rotated from one child to another as a way of sharing the burden. In other cases, elderly couples were split up, with one brother's household taking in the mother while the other took the father.

As we know little about the variations in how the elderly were actually cared for in the past, it is hard to know which of these practices are really innovations. Much of the discourse concerning the treatment of the elderly in China in the past is based on the normative ideals of respect, obedience, care, and support. It is possible that few of the rural elderly received all this once they became too old and weak to contribute much to the household.

At present, with the over 60s numbering only just over 13 per cent and the over 80 population still very small (see Figure 5.1), the elderly do not pose a huge problem in China. However, the picture will be quite different in 30 years' time. Not only will the over 60s be more numerous, there will be many who survive to extreme old age. It seems probable that in China, as elsewhere in the world, the real difficulties will come not with the care of reasonably fit family members in their 60s and 70s but with those in their 80s and 90s, who are likely to be less able and less capable of making any contribution to the household. In the past, such survivors have been the exception and the intergenerational contract—or the filial piety of the Chinese—has hardly been tested by the difficulties of dealing with them. This is another of the social challenges that lies ahead.

Acknowledgements

Delia Davin would like to thank Barbara Harriss-White and Patricia Uberoi for their close reading and useful comments on her chapter, and all the kind and competent staff of the National Health Service who kept her functioning throughout the project.

References

Attané, I. (2013). *The Demographic Masculinization of China. Hoping for a Son.* Dordrecht: Springer.

Banister, Judith (1987) *China's Changing Population* (Stanford, CA: Stanford University Press).

Banister, Judith (2009) Health, mortality and longevity in China today. Paper presented at the XXVI IUSSP International Population Conference, Marrakech, Morocco, September. <http://iussp2009.princeton.edu/papers/90481> (accessed 21 July 2013).

Bossen, Laurel (2002) *Chinese Women and Rural Development: Sixty Years of Change in Lu Village, Yunnan* (Lanham, MD: Rowman & Littlefield).

Bramall, Chris (2009) *Chinese Economic Development* (London: Routledge).

Cai, Yong and Lavely, W. (2003) China's missing girls: numerical estimates and effects on population growth. *The China Review*, 3(2), pp. 1–17.

Cai, Yong and Lavely, W. (2007) Child sex ratios and their regional variation, in Zhongwei Zhao and Fei Guo (eds) *Transition and Challenge: China's Population at the Beginning of the 21st Century* (Oxford: Oxford University Press), pp. 1–17.

Chen, Lincoln C., Wittgenstein, F., and McKeon, E. (1996) The upsurge of mortality in Russia: causes and policy implications. *Population and Development Review*, 22(3), September, pp. 517–530.

Croll, Elisabeth (2000) *Endangered Daughters: Discrimination and Development in Asia* (New York: Routledge).

Das Gupta, Monica (2005) Explaining Asia's 'missing women': a new look at the data. *Population and Development Review*, 31(3), pp. 529–535.

Das Gupta, Monica (2006) Cultural versus biological factors in explaining Asia's missing women: response to Oster. *Population and Development Review*, 32(2), pp. 328–332.

Davin, D. (1987) Gender and population in the People's Republic of China, in Haleh Afshar (ed.) *Women, State and Ideology: Studies from Africa and Asia* (London: Macmillan), pp. 111–129.

Davin, D. (1990) Never mind if it's a girl, you can have another try: the modification of the one-child family policy and its implications for gender relations in rural areas, in

J. Delman, C. Ostergaard, and F. Christiansen (eds) *Remaking Rural China: Problems of Rural Development and Institutions at the Start of the 1990s* (Aarhus: Aarhus University Press), pp. 81–91.

Davin, D. (1999) *Internal Migration in Contemporary China* (Basingstoke: Macmillan).

Davin, D. (2008) Marriage migration in China: the enlargement of marriage markets in the era of market reforms, in Rajni Palriwala and Patricia Uberoi (eds) *Marriage, Migration and Gender* (New Delhi: Sage Publications), pp. 63–77.

Fan, Cindy (2008) *China on the Move: Migration, the State and the Household* (London: Routledge).

Greenhalgh, Susan and Winkler, Edwin (2005) *Governing China's Population: From Leninist to Neoliberal Biopolitics* (Stanford, CA: Stanford University Press).

Guardian, The (2012) Thousands of Chinese trafficking victims rescued by police: police freed more than 24,000 abducted women and children across the country as nearly 3,200 gangs were broken up: report from the Ministry of Public Security, 11 March <http://www.guardian.co.uk/world/2012/mar/11/chinese-trafficking-victims-rescued> (accessed 5 November 2012).

Han, Min and Eades, J. S. (1995) Brides, bachelors and brokers: the marriage market in rural Anhui in an era of economic reform. *Modern Asian Studies*, 29(4), pp. 841–869.

Huang, Xiyi (2007) *Power, Entitlement and Social Practice: Resource Distribution in North China Villages* (Hong Kong: Chinese University Press).

Hudson, Valerie and den Boer, Andrea (2004) *Bare Branches: Security Implication of Asia's Surplus Male Population* (Cambridge, MA: MIT Press).

HumanTrafficking.org (2011) <http://www.humantrafficking.org/countries/china/> (accessed 5 November 2012).

Judd, E. (1994) *Gender and Power in Rural North China* (Stanford, CA: Stanford University Press).

Lavely, W. (1991) Marriage and mobility under rural collectivisation, in R. S. Watson and P. Ebrey (eds) *Marriage and Inequality in Chinese Society* (Berkeley: University of California Press), pp. 286–312.

Lee, J. and Wang, F. (1999) *One Quarter of Humanity: Malthusian Mythology and Chinese Reality 1000–2000* (Cambridge, MA: Harvard University Press).

Lee, Kwan Ching (2007) *Against the Law: Labor Protest in China's Rustbelt and Sunbelt* (Berkeley: University of California Press).

Liang, Zai (2007) Internal migration: policy changes, recent trends, and new challenges, in Zhongwei Zhao and Fei Guo (eds) *Transition and Challenge: China's Population at the Beginning of the 21st Century* (Oxford: Oxford University Press), pp. 197–215.

Lu, Melody Chia-Wen (2008) Gender, marriage and migration, contemporary marriages between mainland China and Taiwan. PhD thesis, Leiden University.

Lu, Melody Chia-Wen and Yang, Wen-shan (eds) (2008) *Asian Cross-Border Marriage Migration: Demographic Patterns and Social Issues* (The Hague: IIAS Publications Series).

Maynes, M. J. and Waltner, A. B. (2001) Women's life-cycle transitions in world-historical perspective: comparing marriage in China and Europe. *Journal of Women's History*, 12(4), pp. 11–21.

Murphy, Rachel (2002) *How Migrant Labor is Changing China* (Cambridge: Cambridge University Press).

NBS (National Bureau of Statistics) formerly SSB (State Statistical Bureau) (1993). *Tabulation of the 1990 Population Census of the People's Republic of China (Zhongguo 1990 nian renkou pucha ziliao)* (Beijing: China Statistics Press).

NBS (National Bureau of Statistics) (2003) *Tabulation of the 2000 Population Census of the People's Republic of China* (*Zhongguo 2000 nian renkou pucha ziliao*) (Beijing: China Statistics Press).

NBS (National Bureau of Statistics) (2007) *Materials from the 2005 One Per Cent Sampling Census of the People's Republic of China* (*2005 nian quanguo 1% renkou chouyang pucha cailiao*) (Beijing: China Statistics Press).

NBS (National Bureau of Statistics) (2010) *China Statistical Yearbook* (*Zhongguo tongji nianjian 2010*) (Beijing: China Statistics Press).

NBS (National Bureau of Statistics) (2011) Communiqué of the NBS of the PRC on the major figures of the 2010 National Census, 24 and 28.4.2011, nos 1 and 2. <http://www.stats.gov.cn/english/newsandcomingevents/t20110428_402722244.htm> (accessed 17 July 2012).

NBS (National Bureau of Statistics) (2012) *Tabulation of the 2010 Population Census of the People's Republic of China* (*Zhongguo 2010 nian renkou pucha ziliao*) (Beijing: China Statistics Press).

Parish, William L. and Busse, Sarah (2000) Gender and work, in Wenfang Tang and William L. Parish (eds), *Chinese Urban Life under Reform: The Changing Social Contract* (Cambridge: Cambridge University Press).

Population and birth planning law (2001) (Translated in) *Population and Development Review* 28(3), pp. 579–585.

Scharping, Thomas (2003) *Birth Control in China 1949–2000* (London: Routledge Curzon).

Scharping, Thomas (2007) The politics of numbers: fertility statistics in recent decades, in Zhongwei Zhao and Fei Guo (eds) *Transition and Challenge: China's Population at the Beginning of the 21st Century* (Oxford: Oxford University Press), pp. 34–53.

Siu, Helen F. (1993) Reconstituting dowry and brideprice in south China, in Deborah Davis and S. Harrell (eds) *Chinese Families in the Post-Mao Era* (Berkeley: University of California Press), pp. 165–188.

Solinger, Dorothy (1999) *Contesting Citizenship in Urban China: Peasant Migrants, the State and the Logic of the Market* (Berkeley: University of California Press).

Song, Wei (2010) China won't postpone retirement age: official. *China Daily*, 16 September. <http://www.chinadaily.com.cn/china/2010-09/16/content_11312771.htm> (accessed 5 November 2012).

Stockman, Norman, Bonney, Norman, and Sheng, Xuewen (1995) *Women's Work in East and West: The Dual Burden of Employment and Family Life* (London: UCL Press).

Tan, Lin and Gilmartin, C. K. (2001) Fleeing poverty: rural women, expanding marriage markets and strategies for social mobility in contemporary China, in Esther Nganling Chow (ed.) *Transforming Gender and Development in East Asia* (New York: Routledge), pp. 203–216.

Tan, Lin and Short, Susan E. (2004) Living as double outsiders: migrant women's experiences of marriage in a county-level city, in Arianne M. Gaetano and Tamara Jacka (eds) *On the Move: Women in Rural to Urban Migration in Contemporary China* (New York: Columbia University Press), pp. 151–174.

Tran, Dinh Lam (2001) China's booming trade in Vietnamese brides. *Asia Times*, 12 September. <http://atimes.com/se-asia/CI12Ae02.html> (accessed 21 July 2013).

Wang, Feng and Mason, Andrew (2007) Population aging: challenges, opportunities and institutions, in Zhongwei Zhao and Fei Guo (eds) *Transition and Challenge: China's Population at the Beginning of the 21st Century* (Oxford: Oxford University Press), pp. 177–196.

White, Tyrene (2006) *China's Longest Campaign: Birth Planning in the People's Republic, 1949–2005* (Ithaca, NY: Cornell University Press).

World Bank (2012). Dependency ratios. <http://search.worldbank.org/data?qterm=Depen dency%20ratio&language=EN> (accessed 21 July 2013).

Yan, Yunxiang (2003) *Private Life under Socialism: Love, Intimacy and Family Change in a Chinese Village, 1949–1999* (Stanford, CA: Stanford University Press).

Zeng Yi, Tu Ping, Gu Baochang, Xu Yi, Li Bohua, and Li Yongping, 'Causes and implications of the recent increase in the reported sex ratio at birth in China' *Population and Development Review* 19 (2), June 1989, pp. 283–302.

Zhang, Guangyu and Gu, Baochang (2007) Recent changes in marriage patterns, in Zhongwei Zhao and Fei Guo (eds) *Transition and Challenge: China's Population at the Beginning of the 21st Century* (Oxford: Oxford University Press), pp. 124–139.

Zhang, Hong (2004) 'Living alone' and the rural elderly: strategy and agency in post-Mao rural China, in Charlotte Ikels (ed.) *Filial Piety: Practice and Discourse in Contemporary East Asia* (Stanford, CA: Stanford University Press), pp. 63–87.

Zhao, Gracie Ming (2003) Trafficking of women for marriage in China: policy and practice. *Criminology and Criminal Justice*, 3(1), pp. 83–102.

Zhao, Zhongwei and Fei, Guo (eds) (2007) *Transition and Challenge: China's Population at the Beginning of the 21st Century* (Oxford: Oxford University Press).

Zheng, Tiantian (2009a) *Red Lights: The Lives of Sex Workers in Postsocialist China* (Minneapolis: University of Minnesota Press).

Zheng, Tiantian (2009b) *Ethnographies of Prostitution in Contemporary China: Gender Relations, HIV/AIDS, and Nationalism* (New York: Palgrave Macmillan).

6

The Social Consequences of
Demographic Change in India

PATRICIA JEFFERY

SINCE THE MID-1960s, India's population dynamics have been characterized by several notable shifts that will have social implications for decades to come. This chapter sketches some of the central parameters of a complex demographic picture—in particular: marked interregional differences in the timing and extent of fertility decline (earlier and deeper in much of the south, later and still ongoing in the large northern states); complex intraregional variations associated with rural–urban residence, economic position, caste, and religious community; and striking regional contrasts in 'daughter aversion' (most extreme in parts of north-west India, though with pockets in the south and evidence of spread to new regions). The main body of the chapter addresses the likely impact of these demographic processes through the following themes: the demographic dividend, the marriage squeeze, the implications of fertility decline for women, population ageing, and the intergenerational contract.

Declining mortality, declining fertility

After independence, death rates began declining, largely owing to greater access to preventive and curative medical care, reductions in childhood diseases, and greater food security (Dyson, 2010). Subsequently, fertility rates also began declining, owing initially to the rising age of marriage for women, later because of increased use of 'modern' contraception (Visaria, 2004a).

India's fertility transition is, however, marked by persistent regional differences (Guilmoto and Rajan, 2001; Dyson, 2004; Visaria, 2004a). Since 1951, fertility decline has gradually spread from coastal areas (especially in the south and south-east) to most of India, arriving most recently in the Gangetic plain (Guilmoto and Rajan, 2001). Parts of southern India already have below-replacement fertility, while continuing population growth in the north is largely attributable to the lag in fertility decline. Visaria (2004a), however, predicts a gradual regional convergence as preferred family size approaches two children and unmet need for contraception declines everywhere. Nevertheless, regional contrasts in fertility decline will mark the population age and sex profiles for some decades, with young populations and slower population ageing in the north, but more rapid population ageing in the south.

Intraregional differences in fertility decline are also striking. Census and survey data do not always permit firm conclusions on the relationship between fertility and economic position, but, broadly speaking, fertility is lowest among the wealthiest urban dwellers and highest among poor villagers, especially in the northern states. Generally, fertility remains higher among Scheduled Castes and Tribes (SCs and STs) and Muslims (Jeffery and Jeffery, 1997; Dharmalingam and Morgan, 2004; Jeffery and Jeffery, 2006; Jeffery, Jeffrey, and Jeffrey, 2008), although these profiles are heavily marked by regional differences.

Explanations for fertility decline are diverse. Most accounts prefer to see it as an outcome of people's responses to the consequences of mortality decline (Visaria, 2004a; Bhattacharya, 2006), rather than India's family programme, whose major demographic impact has been providing contraception to couples who wish to limit their fertility. Increased certainties about child survival may generate fears about the costs of childrearing and encourage parents to adopt contraception swiftly after having their desired number of children (Basu, 1999). Additionally, rising aspirations—for fewer, 'better-quality' (for example, more educated) children, for more consumer goods—raise childrearing costs (Basu, 1999, 2002). Caldwell (2005: 736), for instance, considers that 'the pressure to have fewer children results principally not from forward-looking educated parents but from forward-looking investing parents'.

Another approach, following Dyson and Moore (1983), focuses on regional differences in fertility decline in relation to kinship organization and women's autonomy, with northern areas characterized by patrilocal marriage and women's low bargaining power in their marital homes (Krishnan, 2001), and low levels of women's autonomy and formal education that hamper women's capacity to make decisions about fertility (e.g., Drèze and Murthi, 2001; Drèze and Sen, 2002). Yet, if regional differences in gender politics and kinship may give some handle on *regional* differences in fertility decline, there is little firm evidence that *intraregional* differences, such as those between Hindus and Muslims, reflect consistent differences in women's autonomy (Jejeebhoy and Sathar, 2001; Morgan et al., 2002). Indeed, defining 'autonomy' is as complex as evaluating what its relationship might be to education and fertility decision-making (Jeffery and Basu, 1996; Visaria, 2004a). Moreover, educated women initially predominated in fertility decline figures, but about 65 per cent of fertility decline by 1990 was among illiterate women, attributed to rising aspirations (Bhat, 2002) or a diffusion effect within households and local communities (McNay, Arokiasamy, and Cassen, 2003). Furthermore, fertility decline seems not to necessitate improvements in women's autonomy or educational status, and is often more readily understood in relation to rising aspirations and wider economic changes (Basu, 2002; Bhattacharya, 2006). Perhaps, though, people's motives and the available means to limit fertility are extremely varied and there is no single grand narrative, whether one resting on women's autonomy or on social and economic parameters (Basu, 1999).

Additionally, India's fertility decline has been sex-biased. This is an important downside of 'prosperity optimism' (Agnihotri, 2000: ch. 8), which again suggests that fertility decline does not necessarily *require* improvements in women's autonomy. The sex bias in fertility decline has been spatially non-random (Guilmoto and Attané, 2007): India's increasingly masculine child sex ratios (CSRs) are most striking in what Oldenburg (1992) notably termed the 'Bermuda triangle for girls', parts of north and north-west India that have historically had masculine CSRs (Visaria, 2004b; Arokiasamy, 2007), with gradual spatial diffusion to contiguous areas as couples aim both to limit their fertility and affect the sex balance of their children (Guilmoto and Attané, 2007; Guilmoto, 2008). Parts of south India not previously noted for masculine CSRs now also have increasingly masculine CSRs, however (Basu, 1999; Agnihotri, 2001).

Until the 1980s, masculine CSRs were basically explicable in terms of the differential care of girls and boys. In the northern states, female disadvantage still sets in very soon after the neonatal period (Arokiasamy and Gautam, 2008). From the mid-1980s, new technologies to determine foetal sex in utero became widely available and affordable, and sex-selective abortions now account for some of the increasingly masculine CSRs (Patel, 2007)— a phenomenon that raises uncomfortable questions about women's agency (Bhattacharya, 2006).[1] Reliable information about the incidence and social distribution of sex-selective abortions is scarce, however (see Guilmoto, 2009). Some argue that sex-selective abortion is replacing differential care (e.g., Goodkind, 1996). Others consider that girls face 'double jeopardy' from neglect compounded by sex-selective abortion (Sudha and Rajan, 2003) and that sex-selective abortion can coexist with the continuation of discrimination against those girls who are born (Agnihotri, 2003). Das Gupta and Bhat (1997) consider that discrimination against girls increases when fertility declines

---

[1] Indian demographers generally present sex ratio statistics in terms of females per 1,000 males. A normal sex ratio at birth (SRB) would be 930–960 (or 104–107 males per 100 females).

faster than the desired number of sons, and they predicted that sex-selective abortions would play an increasing role in determining the CSR, while Bhat and Zavier (2003) consider that the 'son preference' effect can more effectively be put into practice because of available technology. It seems that educated, wealthy urban residents are more likely than poorer rural residents to practise sex-selective abortions, but that they do not discriminate against girls they allow to be born; by contrast, excess female child mortality is more marked for children of poorer and uneducated mothers (Agnihotri, 2003; Arokiasamy, 2007). It also appears that the economically advantaged pioneer sex-selective abortions. The practice gradually seeps down the class hierarchy within localities (Guilmoto and Attané, 2007; Guilmoto, 2008). while the spread of masculine CSRs to new areas begins in urban centres and gradually spreads to rural areas (Agnihotri, 2003). Sex ratios at birth are most masculine for Sikhs and Jains, followed by Hindus (Bhat and Zavier, 2007; Guilmoto, 2008). Masculine CSRs among SCs are intensifying, narrowing the gap between them and the general population (Bhat and Zavier, 2003; Siddhanta, Agnihotri, and Nandy, 2009). Broadly, Muslims match the overarching regional patterns, yet within regions Muslims have less masculine CSRs than their neighbours (Guilmoto, 2008): Muslims express lower son preferences, rarely practise sex-selective abortion (Bhat and Zavier, 2003, 2007), and their children (including girls) have a mortality advantage that cannot readily be explained by wealth and education differentials (unlike among caste Hindus and SCs) (Bhalotra, Valente, and van Soest, 2010).

Son preferences and 'daughter aversion' are often explained by reference to parental fears about having to provide daughters with dowries—the jewellery, household goods, cash, and so on provided by the bride's parents and wider kin network that go to the bride's husband's home.[2] Dowry has a long history, especially in northern India, a region with longstanding masculine sex ratios. More recently, writers and activists have addressed dowry: its escalation, dowry demands, the harassment and even murder of young married women whose dowries are deemed insufficient, and its recent spread to areas where it was rare previously (or only an urban elite phenomenon), such as parts of the south.[3]

Further, in most of India marriage is patrilocal, that is, the bride moves to her husband's home) (e.g., see Banerjee and Jain, 2001; Agrawal and Unisa,

[2] Some items are given before the wedding (e.g., at engagement ceremonies), and gifts continue to go from the bride's family to her in-laws on various occasions throughout her life. The dowry is not straightforwardly the bride's personal property: some items are designated for specific individuals in her husband's family, and her ability to control even household items is not necessarily complete: Sharma (1984) and Srinivas (1984).

[3] Basu (2005) and Bradley, Tomalin, and Subramaniam (2009) contain useful collections of papers addressing these issues.

2007), and outlays made by the groom's parents—such as providing a residence for their son and daughter-in-law—remain within the groom's family. Marriage migration also occurs in less prestigious marriages involving brideprice or bride purchase. Typically, the groom's family reaps long-term advantages: the daughter-in-law's labour, her childbearing and childrearing capacity, and care in old age (see below). Daughters, then, benefit their in-laws rather than their parents (e.g., see Sudha and Rajan, 2003) and women's marriage migration provides a strong disincentive to rearing daughters *even when there is no dowry system* (Das Gupta et al., 2003).

Social consequences of India's demographic transition

Fertility will probably continue to decline in India, with a gradual convergence between the different regions, but predictions about the gender bias in this process are contested. Some demographers predict that India's sex ratios will continue to become more masculine (Das Gupta and Bhat, 1997; Mayer, 1999) and that son preferences will continue to be manifest for some decades, especially if the social and economic root causes are not removed (Guilmoto and Attané, 2007). Others predict that son preferences will decline (Visaria, 2004a), and there are indications that the sex ratio at birth has begun to plateau (Bhat and Zavier, 2003). Regional differences will probably persist, with the north-west having masculine CSRs for some years before they begin to plateau (Das Gupta, Chung, and Li, 2009) and regions where fertility decline is coming later (much of the rest of north India) showing a worsening of CSRs, at least for a time (Guilmoto, 2009).

Perhaps the one safe prediction is that fertility decline, population ageing, and masculine CSRs will leave their stamp on social and economic life, but their impact will operate at different paces in different regions and for different social groups, and India's demographic profile will be marked by regional, class, and other diversities well into the twenty-first century. With this in mind, I now explore some implications for family life and household processes. Obtaining employment, marrying, and having children are major aspects of people's transitions to adulthood in India. Many people in much of India will find it difficult to achieve these transitions successfully, however, because of how demographic processes intersect with other social and economic phenomena. I organize the discussion first around how the demographic dividend and the marriage squeeze affect people's ability to achieve these transitions. I then consider how these issues and fertility decline impact on women, before turning to population ageing and the intergenerational contract.

Demographic dividend

The demographic dividend (or bonus) refers to a short-term window of opportunity that may arise when fertility declines. The child dependency ratio falls because there are proportionally more people in the working age groups (usually 15–59 or to 64) to provide for smaller proportions of dependent children. This may generate savings at both national and household level that can be devoted to social and economic investment, for instance in education and health care. Gradually, though, with increasing longevity and as people of working age exit from economic activity, the old-age dependency ratio rises (see below), and this window of opportunity closes.

It is very unlikely, however, that the demographic dividend will materialize for India as a whole (Acharya, Cassen, and McNay, 2004: 204–205). Put simply, being of 'working age' is not the same as being 'economically active' (Basu, 2011). The agricultural sector has not absorbed all the new potential workers, over 90 per cent of workers are in the informal sector, employment is increasingly casualized (with particularly high levels of youth unemployment, including among educated young people), and income inequalities are widening (McNay, Unni, and Cassen, 2004). Yet the working-age population will increase by 1.5 times between 2001 and 2026 (McNay, Unni, and Cassen, 2004: 170), probably not all of whom will obtain secure or well-paid employment (Acharya, Cassen, and McNay, 2004: 206 ff.). Indeed, India's apparently spectacular economic performance in recent years has been characterized as 'jobless growth', with jobs in IT and its spin-offs recruiting only small numbers of highly trained people (for example, Joshi 2010). And, crucially, women of 'working age' continue to have relatively low rates of economic activity, especially in the north (Desai, 2010; Basu, 2011) (see below). The *demographic* dividend, then, will not necessarily generate an *economic* and *social* one.

There will, however, be considerable interregional contrasts, and very different employment prospects and trajectories for people in different class positions within regions. Some demographic dividend may be experienced in parts of the south with relatively long histories of fertility decline and considerable job creation in industrial and other economic enterprises. Some of the large northern states, by contrast, are characterized by late and slow fertility decline and a record of sluggish job creation (Acharya, Cassen, and McNay, 2004: 217; Dyson, 2010: 40–41): increasingly fragmented landholdings become less viable and reduce job opportunities for the landless/ land-poor, and the bulk of the potentially employed experience 'informal' employment, often poorly paid and insecure, and/or extended periods of under- and unemployment. Education provides no guaranteed route into secure employment (Jeffrey, Jeffery, and Jeffery, 2008), and young men may wait for years to achieve economic independence (Jeffrey, 2010). Such employment difficulties have significant implications for young men's ability to marry and create families (to which I now turn), and the intergenerational contract (see below).

Marriage squeeze

The 'marriage squeeze' refers to imbalances in the numbers of men and women in the potential marriage pool. In India, men usually marry women a few years younger, and assessments of the marriage squeeze thus necessitate comparing the relevant age cohorts. In post-independence India, reductions in child mortality before fertility declined meant that younger cohorts were larger (although the potential 'surplus' of females was somewhat reduced by excess female child mortality). Moreover, improvements in adult women's survival reduced levels of widowerhood, and thus the proportions of men seeking second marriages (Bhat and Halli, 1999). Gradually, 'shortages' of potential bridegrooms developed. With fertility decline, especially when this is rapid, however, the number of younger cohorts begins to be smaller than older ones, creating 'shortages' of potential brides that are further exacerbated, in some regions, by sex-selective abortion and excess female child mortality.

A commonsense understanding has developed positing that dowry escalation is linked to 'surpluses' of females and increasing competition for bridegrooms. Some commentators have also suggested that the increasing 'shortages' of brides could result in the tapering off of dowry (e.g., Bhat and Halli, 1999; Das Gupta and Li, 1999; Das Gupta et al., 2003). The relationship between numerical 'surpluses' and 'shortages' of brides and marriage payments (such as dowry and its escalation) is much more complex than this approach suggests, however. As Sudha and Rajan comment, shortages of marriageable women will not enhance their value on the marriage market: the 'marriage squeeze' has been associated with an increase and spread in dowry to regions and social groups where it had not been common, and 'shortfalls in the "supply" of women will lead to their being subject to greater restrictions, control and violence' (Sudha and Rajan, 2003: 4368).[4]

It is far from straightforward to predict what will happen to marriage practices—people's ability to marry, economic exchanges, and so on—because so many crucial considerations are not factored into demographic statistics. Large-scale studies usually enable disaggregation between rural and urban

---

[4] For a more extensive critique of the 'marriage squeeze' in relation to marriage payments, especially dowry, see Jeffery (forthcoming).

residents down to the district level, and SCs and STs are routinely detailed separately, but other castes tend to be enumerated in combined lists, people's religious community membership is not always registered, and estimating people's economic position is fraught with complexity. Yet these and other criteria (such as appearance and education) channel people's decisions when selecting marriage partners.

Most marriages in India are negotiated by parents and family elders, for whom a demographic 'shortage' of females may not map onto a *perceived* shortage of females in the relevant marriage pool. Indeed, throughout my own research in rural western Uttar Pradesh since the early 1980s, villagers have insisted that there is a shortage of (suitable) grooms. Aziz (1983: 604) attributed the element of compulsion in dowry to a shift from the 'normal eligible bachelor to a "fancy" product' (with English education, formal sector job, etc.). Educated and employed young men receive more offers of marriage than uneducated unemployed young men—and they can hold out for a substantial dowry, too. Grooms' parents often regard the dowry as recompense for the expenses of educating sons and getting them into employment (bribes, the costs of establishing a business), and particular occupations and castes may have specified rate charts (Banerjee and Jain, 2001). More generally, men are increasingly unwilling to marry without a cash incentive because of the growing uncertainties about men's livelihood prospects, while some men aim to fulfil their desire for consumer goods by way of their wife's dowry (Banerjee and Jain, 2001: 106–108).[5] Additionally, concerns over girls' 'security' pressurize girls' parents to settle them quickly in good marriages, even if that curtails their education (Banerjee and Jain, 2001; cf. Aziz, 1983: 604, who describes girls as 'perishable commodities'). Providing a generous dowry also enhances their social standing, and may protect brides from harassment by in-laws who wished for larger dowries.[6] All told, the families of well-placed grooms tend to have the upper hand in marriage negotiations. Given the employment prospects outlined in the previous section, this is likely to be even more common in the decades to come. In other words, the relative sizes of age cohorts of males and females *alone* can give little insight into how marriages come about (Billig, 1991).[7]

Das Gupta and Li (1999) comment that poor people are particularly badly hit by marriage squeezes: when men are in surplus, poor men find it hard

[5] Indeed, Das Gupta and Li (1999) note that dowry can attain a normative status—which would perhaps negate the tapering off in dowry inflation that they predict. See also Das Gupta et al. (2003).
[6] There is evidence that young men implicated in dowry murders can make second marriages relatively easily—which suggests that women are quite easily replaceable rather than being in short supply, at least in the upper economic reaches.
[7] To the best of my knowledge, there are no reliable national or even regional data on marriage payments, including whether dowry payments are increasing in real terms and the social and economic profiles of people making particular types and sizes of payments. See AIDWA (2003) for an account of people's *perceptions* of how dowry has altered in character in recent decades.

to marry, and when women are in surplus, poor women cannot compete for the few marriageable men. I would put it somewhat differently. It is more productive to visualize a sliding scale of multiple marriage squeezes within caste and religious communities operating at different levels of the class hierarchy simultaneously, favouring 'suitable boys' at the top, who are sought out as grooms, and compromising the marriage chances of men without resources or employment prospects. Virtually all young women can marry, but they tend to be siphoned up the system, dowry continues to be a sine qua non for marriage higher up the class hierarchy, and poor men experience shortages of women (Billig, 1991). The available data are not always sufficiently detailed and disaggregated to allow for an analysis incorporating economic and social diversities as well as demographic data. Yet it is vital to think in terms of diverse and fragmented marriage markets (not one marriage market), because that is how marriage negotiations play out on the ground.

Interregional differences in the timing and extent of fertility decline (and other demographic parameters) are echoed in longstanding regional differences in marriage practices and employment generation. The 'crisis of masculinity' (Chowdhry, 2005) and wide class differences in men's ability to marry at a conventionally appropriate age, and the economic exchanges associated with marriage are likely to be most acute in the populous states of north and north-west India, where employment opportunities are particularly limited. In the south, fertility declined sooner and with less sex bias than in the north, and there are generally more employment opportunities. Further, urban India may look rather different from the rural areas: for instance, urban middle-class consumption ambitions put greater pressure on brides' families to provide generous dowries much earlier than in the rural areas. Yet, even in villages, dowries now include new consumer goods and large sums of cash. In addition, marriages continue to be mainly arranged by family elders, and this will probably remain the norm for many years to come. Although 'love marriages' are widely regarded as dishonourable, they do occur, probably more commonly in urban areas, and they rarely entail dowry or brideprice payments. To the extent that such marriages become more common, we might expect to see a shift in marriage practices.

Overall, however, recent data suggest that economic inequality has increased during the period of economic liberalization, so we should not expect the homogenization of marriage markets in the near future (Sarkar and Mehta, 2010). Educated and securely employed men will probably continue to command large dowries when they marry. And increasing numbers of poor men will probably have to wait many years to marry or will simply fail to marry at all, which Guilmoto (2010) predicts will undermine the patriarchal system from which son preferences derive—although he also predicts more forced marriage, trafficking of women, and rape. One does not need to agree with all the predictions of Hudson and den Boer (2004) that the growing numbers of unmarried young men in India (and Asia more generally) pose a threat to national and international security through rising levels of criminality and violence (in general, as well as against women). But this does not mean that we should ignore the crisis of masculinity faced by young men who cannot achieve the respectable adult roles of husband and breadwinner.

Implications of fertility decline for women

In the middle of the twenty-first century, most young women will still marry, since parents will probably continue to arrange most marriages and few women will be able to opt out of marriage. Typically, rural and uneducated women in the north marry at younger ages than urban women, those who complete secondary and tertiary education, and women in the south. Overall, however, women's age of marriage has increased in recent decades, but only to the late teens or early 20s, partly because girls' education is now an important counter in marriage negotiations. This is unlikely to increase greatly in the foreseeable future, since girls' parents are juggling girls' education (which might delay marriage) against family honour (which pushes towards earlier marriage).

Well-educated young men in secure employment will probably have little difficulty in attracting brides with a dowry, and they may continue to marry in their 20s. Young men who lack sufficient economic security to attract offers of marriage face a very different situation. Where there are several brothers, one may be married relatively young, in order to meet the household's needs for women's labour, with the remaining brothers delaying their marriage until their 30s or later (or possibly sharing their brother's wife in de facto fraternal polyandry: Jeffery and Jeffery, 1997: 229ff.) In addition, local shortages of brides can be shortcircuited by importing brides from other regions, with payments being made by the groom and his kin rather than dowry coming from the bride's family. Long-distance brides generally come from the northern hills, the eastern Gangetic plain, north-east India, Bangladesh, and, more recently, Kerala. Such a class-differentiated scenario has a long history in north-west India. Nevertheless, long-distance brides have been attracting increasing attention in recent years (Jeffery, Jeffery, and Lyon, 1989: 39–40; Jeffery and Jeffery, 1996: 231–244; Das Gupta and Li, 1999; Kaur, 2004, 2008; Blanchet, 2005; Jeffery, forthcoming). In such instances, age gaps between spouses would probably widen and hamper the development of more companionate marriage; this is likely to be particularly conspicuous in the north and north-west, where age gaps between spouses have generally been smaller than in the south.

Nevertheless, some demographic changes may have positive implications for women. Rising age of first pregnancy and low fertility reduce the incidence of maternal mortality as well as maternal depletion owing to pregnancy, childbirth, and lactation. Increasingly, young women are having their children in quick succession shortly after marriage and then being sterilized. Nowadays, young women in India have often completed their childbearing before their mid-20s (Visaria, 2004a: 60ff.; Dyson, 2010: 36, 43). The *social* impact of lowered fertility and early completion of childbearing is hard to predict, however.

Paid employment for women

Some authors predict women's greater involvement in the labour force, with the potential to enhance their position within their husbands' families (McNay, Unni, and Cassen, 2004: 171; Visaria, 2004a: 73). But it is not inevitable that the time seemingly liberated by women's abridged fertility will be devoted to paid employment, not least because job creation is not keeping pace with the increasing numbers of young *men* seeking employment. Despite class differences and locally specific employment opportunities, most young women will be unlikely to obtain suitable occupations (Desai, 2010). Poor women have long been compelled to perform dirty, ill-paid, insecure, and undesirable paid work; low fertility may make it easier to combine such employment with domestic and childrearing duties. In general, however, paid employment for married women is still considered rather undesirable, and women are commonly withdrawn from paid employment outside the home if the household's economic position improves. For highly educated women, completing childbearing quickly may enable them to enter the labour force on favourable terms. But most women will probably continue to be largely based in their homes.

These presumptions mesh with parental perceptions that girls' education is important primarily because it enhances marriageability (not employability). In contemporary India, potential grooms and their parents seek educated brides who possess refined housewifery skills and (especially) have 'better-quality' childrearing capacity: overseeing children's homework and reducing outlays on tuitions, and investing huge effort in their children's progress in the extremely competitive educational market (Donner, 2008).

Women's marriage migration

Women's marriage migration to their in-laws' homes will almost certainly continue to be the norm, especially in the rural areas but also in many urban settings. To the extent that patrilocal residence persists, the buttresses and rationales for daughter aversion and son preferences will remain, given the need for care in old age (in addition to the costs of rearing and providing dowries for daughters). Indeed, as Guilmoto (2009) argues, fertility decline does not reduce the need for a son, rather it increases the risk of being sonless. In a low-fertility regime, then, masculine CSRs are probably not a thing of the past, for the premium on ensuring that a small family has at least one son impacts on whether female infants are born or will survive childhood.

Furthermore, marriage migration has implications for girls who survive to become married women themselves. Especially in the south and also often among Muslims in the north, marriage distances are lower than for most women in the north, where large marriage distances, poor transport and communication facilities, and normative restrictions on who can visit women in their in-laws' homes all hamper ready contact with outmarried daughters. Young married women's disempowerment by virtue of their dislocation from their supportive childhood networks and the emotional upheaval that marriage brings is further heightened by controls over their mobility.[8]

But how will patterns of marriage migration fare in the wake of other social and economic changes? Das Gupta (2009) argues that the rationale for son preferences is 'unravelling', because expectations that brides will migrate to their in-laws' home are being undermined, particularly by urbanization (which detaches people from the land) and by the state's supplanting of the political importance of patrilineal clans. These processes, however, are likely to be uneven and very slow in much of India. Parts of south India are already significantly more urbanized than much of the north, and marriage patterns there generally do not entail as much separation of a married woman from her natal kin. In the large northern states, however, over 70 per cent of the population lives in rural areas.[9] For landowners, women's marriage migration has a strong economic rationale: sons remain in their natal village to farm, while their inmigrant wives bear sons to continue the patriline and perform other household services. The land-poor and landless have fewer economic reasons for continuing to marry their daughters out. Yet, while parents acknowledge the grief of separation from their married daughters, hegemonic taken-for-granted ideas about giving a daughter in marriage and receiving nothing in return serve to perpetuate women's marriage migration.

In other words, especially in India's north and north-west, women's marriage migration is likely to be quite resilient, thus continuing young married women's subordination and vulnerability to dowry demands, and violence and harassment in their marital homes. And, in a low-fertility regime, women will need to bear at least one son. Women are sometimes

---

[8] See for instance, Dyson and Moore (1983), Jeffery, Jeffery, and Lyon (1989), Palriwala and Uberoi (2005). Palriwala (1999) notes the importance of visiting the natal home to work there and also to receive gifts for the in-laws.

[9] Definitional problems, however, mean that many 'rural' areas deserve reclassification as urban. See Dyson (2010) and Dyson and Visaria (2004).

coerced into sex-selective abortions—but they also have a significant stake in bearing sons to support them in old age. Without major improvements in women's access to education, employment, property rights, and health care, 'daughter aversion' will probably persist. As Harriss-White (1999) argues, fertility decline coupled with increasing needs for old age support—a form of 'demographic "structural adjustment" without precedent' (pp. 148–149)—pull in the opposite direction from the Indian government's piecemeal (and ineffective) efforts to eradicate dowry and sex-selective abortion. The changes set in motion by fertility decline, then, are not unambiguously beneficial to women.

Population ageing and the 'intergenerational contract'

Much of India is unlikely to experience the breathing space of a demographic dividend. Declining fertility and increasing longevity will inexorably result in increasing proportions of elderly people outside the normal working ages, many of them infirm, although some will undoubtedly need to be economically active, or would wish to be. And the problems that men of working age face in obtaining employment and family building are likely to persist. There will, then, be considerable challenges in meeting the day-to-day subsistence needs of those who can no longer earn and in providing health care for the elderly infirm. Crucially, there is little prospect of comprehensive provision of adequate state or occupational pensions, or of affordable good-quality health care or residential care for the infirm or destitute.

Few employed men are in occupations that provide pensions or health insurance, or indeed the surplus income that would enable substantial savings. Additionally, as cohorts age, poor unmarried men will be more prominent among the elderly, disproportionately men unable to marry because of their poor employment prospects. More strikingly, though, adult women's life expectancies are now higher than men's (partly owing to reductions in female mortality in the reproductive ages because of declining fertility) (Das Gupta and Bhat, 1997). This 'feminization' of old age raises several issues connected with women's positions in the labour market and family systems. Disproportionately, women are *not* economically self-sufficient, and they are less likely than men to be in paid employment or to possess assets (land, shelter, savings, etc.) in their own right (Visaria, 2004b: 54). As is already the case, widows will probably be in the most difficult situations (Chen, 2000). Existing widows' state pensions are inadequate to enable widows to subsist alone (and corruption in low level officialdom means that widows often cannot access all or even any of the state pension to which they are entitled). This means that most elderly people in India cannot be economically independent.

With increasing proportions of the elderly, this situation will worsen through the next few decades at least.

This takes us to the 'intergenerational contract' (or bargain), in which people in the working 'generation' transfer resources both to the young and to the elderly. In India, without significant social provision from either the state or the market, the intergenerational contract basically operates *within the family* (Collard, 2000). This is a long-term 'contract', as individuals move through the generations, sometimes providing for others, sometimes being provided for. Potentially, people in different generations have conflicting interests, so the robustness of the contract — the extent to which those who fail to fulfil their side of the bargain can be sanctioned — is crucial (Collard, 2000). Croll (2006) notes the widespread fear in Asia generally that 'modernization' will increase individualism. Young couples may be caught between wishing to invest heavily in their own children and their obligation to repay their debt to their parents. She argues, however, that people are reinterpreting and renegotiating the intergenerational contract, which becomes increasingly based on the benefits that accrue to all the parties. Parental investments in children may be *intensified* (which increases the sense of obligation), *protracted* to include helping adult children (childcare for grandchildren, domestic work), and *spread* (to include daughters). And parents may delay the transfer of resources (land, house, etc.) to retain a hold over their adult children. For Kabeer (2000), though, the intergenerational contract is risky, even when parents have some hold over their children, whether it be economic or emotional.

Somewhere between 80 and 90 per cent of India's elderly live with adult children or other relatives, even in the urban areas (Croll, 2006), but predicting how long the intergenerational contract will continue to operate like this is complex. With young women these days increasingly completing their childbearing by their mid-20s, most people are grandparents by their late 40s (several years earlier would be typical in rural north India). While the grandchildren are small, the grandparents may still be economically active and/or able to provide childcare. For a while, the intergenerational contract may function to everyone's benefit, although it cannot be guaranteed to operate straightforwardly to the benefit of the elderly. Sons might fail to support their ageing parents, and declining fertility only reduces parental options about sources of care. From the other side, low fertility and rising longevity both increase and protract the financial burden on each adult son of caring for elderly parents. With the burden of carework — of children as well as the elderly — falling predominantly on inmarried women, increasingly concentrated care responsibilities will present an additional obstacle to women's labour force participation. Moreover, by the time the grandchildren's education becomes most costly and they need to be settled in marriage, the grandparents will have become increasingly reliant on their adult children for subsistence and meeting their health-care needs. To the extent that marriage ages rise, especially for men, this pincer effect is likely to be even more apparent. All these considerations could exacerbate the potential for conflicts, and might compromise the care that the elderly receive.

Of course, there will probably be multiple intergenerational contracts in India. Given regional differences in the timing and extent of fertility decline, population ageing also has regional dimensions, with ageing occurring most rapidly in states where fertility has been lowest for longest: Tamilnadu and Kerala, for instance, will be experiencing a decline in people aged 15–49 by 2026 (Dyson, 2004: 99ff.). In the north, by contrast, population ageing is proceeding more slowly, and for some decades to come most elderly people will continue to have several sons on whom they might rely.

Further, people's capacity to provide for their elderly family members relates closely to their economic position (Collard, 2000; Kabeer, 2000). Poor people may be faced with particularly painful dilemmas — whether to provide for their children or care for their parents. While the wealthy might employ domestic servants and nursing staff to look after their elderly kin, men at the other end of the economic scale would struggle to spare the necessary resources even to feed their parents. Indeed, they may even have remained unmarried and thus have no wife to perform carework for their own parents, as well as having no children to care for them in their own old age. The working conditions and low incomes of the poor also mean that their health status is liable to be compromised at much younger ages than among the more wealthy (despite the rise in 'diseases of affluence'). Yet the latter and their adult children will be least well placed to weather their need for health care or their inability to be economically active. In rural areas, people with land may try to retain a hold over their sons by deferring the transfer to ownership. The landless and land-poor, however, can exert little leverage over their sons, who may be employed locally but refuse to contribute to their parents' upkeep, or may migrate in search of work and fail to send remittances. On the other hand, to the extent that people are increasingly detached from the land, we might also expect some shift in expectations that parents should rely on sons rather than daughters — although this seems to be a limited and mainly urban phenomenon so far.

Concluding comments

Regional differences have been historically important in India's demographic transition, although they may narrow in the decades to come. But intraregional differences, of economic position, caste, religious community, and so on show no sign of waning. Thus, declining fertility and population ageing, in both of which gendered processes are central, will play out in very different ways.

Predicting how social processes will operate over time is always a risky affair. That said, India as a whole is unlikely to benefit from the demographic dividend (although parts of the south may do so), because of the intractable problems of job creation that have dogged India's economy for decades, and because women's paid employment is so low. Enduring employment difficulties are also likely to be reflected in the continuing differentiation of marriage markets, with well-placed young men able to command high dowries when they marry, while poor young men finding it increasingly hard to marry. Although women may experience health benefits from low fertility, the *social* impact of low fertility is more ambiguous. Enhanced labour force participation by women is not guaranteed, but greater investment in 'quality' childrearing and increased responsibilities for care of the elderly are likely. If women's marriage migration continues, the considerations that contribute to 'daughter aversion' will persist, with various adverse effects for gender politics. The gender and class implications of population ageing also suggest that 'intergenerational contracts' will be both diverse and characterized by tension and renegotiation.

There are, of course, numerous other issues on which there can be even less certainty: for instance, how India's national and regional economies will intersect with global events in coming decades, or how social movements such as women's activist groups might impinge on the various gender issues that have been alluded to above. And India does not readily lend itself to grand narratives: its diversity renders it all the more important not to simplify what is bound to be a complex and heterogeneous future.

Acknowledgements

This chapter was made possible by a British Academy/Leverhulme Trust Senior Research Fellowship and a Leverhulme Trust Research Fellowship (2009–10). I am grateful for the support of these institutions. They do not, of course, bear any responsibility for what I have written here. Thanks are also due to colleagues who have provided helpful comments on earlier drafts, in particular Delia Davin, Tim Dyson, Barbara Harriss-White, Patricia Uberoi, and an anonymous reviewer.

References

Acharya, Shankar, Cassen, Robert, and McNay, Kirsty (2004) The economy—past and future, in T. Dyson, R. Cassen, and L. Visaria (eds) *Twenty-First Century India: Population, Economy, Human Development, and the Environment* (New Delhi: Oxford University Press), pp. 202–227.

Agnihotri, Satish Balram (2000) *Sex Ratio Patterns in the Indian Population: A Fresh Exploration* (New Delhi: Sage).

Agnihotri, Satish Balram (2001) Unpacking the juvenile sex ratio in India, in V. Mazumdar and N. Krishnaji (eds) *Enduring Conundrum: India's Sex Ratio (Essays in Honour of Asok Mitra)* (Delhi: Rainbow Publishers, for Centre for Women's Development Studies), pp. 36–72.

Agnihotri, Satish Balram (2003) Survival of the girl child: tunnelling out of the Chakra-vyuha. *Economic and Political Weekly* 38(41), pp. 4351–4360.

Agrawal, Sutapa and Unisa, Sayeed (2007) Discrimination from conception to childhood: a study of girl children in rural Haryana, India, in I. Attané and C. Z. Guilmoto (eds) *Watering the Neighbour's Garden: The Growing Demographic Female Deficit in Asia* (Paris: Committee for International Cooperation in National Research in Demography (CICRED)), pp. 247–266.

AIDWA (All India Democratic Women's Association) (ed.) (2003) *Expanding Dimensions of Dowry* (New Delhi: All India Democratic Women's Association).

Arokiasamy, Perianayagam (2007) Sex ratio at birth and excess female child mortality in India: trends, differentials and regional patterns, in I. Attané and C. Z. Guilmoto (eds) *Watering the Neighbour's Garden: The Growing Demographic Female Deficit in Asia* (Paris: Committee for International Cooperation in National Research in Demography (CICRED)), pp. 49–72.

Arokiasamy, Perianayagam and Gautam, Abhishek (2008) Neonatal mortality in the Empowered Action Group states of India: trends and determinants. *Journal of Biosocial Science*, 40, pp. 183–201.

Aziz, Abdul (1983) (No title). *Economic and Political Weekly*, 18(15), pp. 603–604.

Banerjee, Nirmala and Jain, Devaki (2001) Indian sex ratios through time and space: development from women's perspective, in V. Mazumdar and N. Krishnaji (eds) *Enduring Conundrum: India's Sex Ratio (Essays in Honour of Asok Mitra)* (Delhi: Rainbow Publishers, for the Centre for Women's Development Studies), pp. 73–119.

Basu, Alaka Malwade (1999) Fertility decline and increasing gender imbalance in India, including a possible south Indian turnaround. *Development and Change*, 30(2), pp. 237–263.

Basu, Alaka Malwade (2002) Why does education lead to lower fertility? A critical review of some of the possibilities. *World Development*, 30(10), pp. 1779–1790.

Basu, Alaka Malwade (2011) Demographic dividend revisited: the mismatch between age and economic activity-based dependency ratios. *Economic and Political Weekly*, 46(39), pp. 53–58.

Basu, Srimati (ed.) (2005) *Dowry and Inheritance* (New Delhi: Women Unlimited).

Bhalotra, Sonia, Valente, Christine, and van Soest, Arthur (2010) The puzzle of Muslim advantage in child survival in India. *Journal of Health Economics*, 29, pp. 191–204.

Bhat, P. N. Mari (2002) Returning a favor: reciprocity between female education and fertility in India. *World Development*, 30(10), pp. 1791–1803.

Bhat, P. N. Mari and Halli, Shiva S. (1999) Demography of brideprice and dowry: causes and consequences of the Indian marriage squeeze. *Population Studies*, 53(2), pp. 129–148.

Bhat, P. N. Mari and Zavier, A. J. Francis (2003) Fertility decline and gender bias in northern India. *Demography*, 40(4), pp. 637–657.

Bhat, P. N. Mari and Zavier, A. J. Francis (2007) Factors influencing the use of prenatal diagnostic techniques and sex ratio at birth in India, in I. Attané and C. Z. Guilmoto (eds) *Watering the Neighbour's Garden: The Growing Demographic Female Deficit in Asia* (Paris: Committee for International Cooperation in National Research in Demography (CICRED)), pp. 131–160.

Bhattacharya, Prabir C. (2006) Economic development, gender inequality, and demographic outcomes: evidence from India. *Population and Development Review*, 32(2), pp. 263–291.

Billig, Michael S. (1991) The marriage squeeze on high-caste Rajasthani women. *Journal of Asian Studies*, 50(2), pp. 341–360.

Blanchet, Thérèse (2005) Bangladeshi girls sold as wives in north India. *Indian Journal of Gender Studies*, 12(2/3), pp. 305–334.

Bradley, Tamsin, Tomalin, Emma, and Subramaniam, Mangala (eds) (2009) *Dowry: Bridging the Gap between Theory and Practice* (New Delhi: Women Unlimited).

Caldwell, John C. (2005) On net intergenerational wealth flows: an update. *Population and Development Review*, 31(4), pp. 721–740.

Chen, Martha Alter (2000) *Perpetual Mourning: Widowhood in Rural India* (New Delhi: Oxford University Press).

Chowdhry, Prem (1997) Enforcing cultural codes—gender and violence in northern India. *Economic and Political Weekly*, 32(19), pp. 1019–1028.

Collard, David (2000) Generational transfers and the generational bargain. *Journal of International Development*, 12, pp. 342–351.

Croll, Elisabeth J. (2006) The intergenerational contract in the changing Asian family. *Oxford Development Studies*, 34(4), pp. 473–491.

Das Gupta, Monica (2009) Family systems, political systems, and Asia's 'missing girls': the construction of son preference and its unraveling, Policy Research Working Paper No. 5148, World Bank, Washington.

Das Gupta, Monica and Bhat, P. N. Mari (1997) Fertility decline and increased manifestation of sex bias in India. *Population Studies*, 51(3), pp. 307–315.

Das Gupta, Monica and Li, Shuzhuo (1999) Gender bias in China, South Korea and India 1920–1990: effects of war, famine and fertility decline. *Development and Change*, 30(3), pp. 619–652.

Das Gupta, Monica, Chung, Woojin, and Li, Shuzhuo (2009) Evidence for an incipient decline in numbers of missing girls in China and India. *Population and Development Review*, 35(2), pp. 401–416.

Das Gupta, Monica, Jiang, Zhenghua, Li, Bohua, Xie, Zhenming, Chung, Woojin, and Bae, Hwa-Ok (2003) Why is son preference so persistent in East and South Asia? A crosscountry study of China, India and the Republic of Korea. *Journal of Development Studies*, 40(2), pp. 153–187.

Desai, Sonalde (2010) The other half of the demographic dividend. *Economic and Political Weekly*, 45(40), pp. 12–14.

Dharmalingam, A. and Morgan, S. Philip (2004) Pervasive Muslim–Hindu fertility differences in India. *Demography*, 41(3), pp. 529–545.

Drèze, Jean and Murthi, Mamta (2001) Fertility, education, and development: evidence from India. *Population and Development Review*, 27(1) pp. 33–63.

Drèze, Jean and Sen, Amartya (2002) *India: Development and Participation* (New Delhi: Oxford University Press).

Dyson, Tim (2004) India's population—the future, in T. Dyson, R. Cassen, and L. Visaria (eds) *Twenty-First Century India: Population, Economy, Human Development and the Environment* (New Delhi: Oxford University Press), pp. 74–107.

Dyson, Tim (2010) Growing regional variation: demographic change and its implications, in A. Heath and R. Jeffery (eds) *Change and Diversity: Economics, Politics and Society in Contemporary India (Proceedings of the British Academy 159)* (Oxford: Oxford University Press), pp. 19–46.

Dyson, Tim and Moore, Mick (1983) On kinship structure, female autonomy and demographic behavior in India. *Population and Development Review*, 9(1), pp. 35–60.

Goodkind, Daniel (1996) On substituting sex preference strategies in East Asia: does prenatal sex selection reduce postnatal discrimination? *Population and Development Review*, 22(1), pp. 111–125.

Guilmoto, Christophe Z. (2008) Economic, social and spatial dimensions of India's excess child masculinity. *Population-E (English)*, 63(1), pp. 91–118.

Guilmoto, Christophe Z. (2009) The sex ratio transition in Asia. *Population and Development Review*, 35(3), pp. 519–549.

Guilmoto, Christophe Z. (2010) Longer-term disruptions to demographic structures in China and India resulting from skewed sex ratios at birth. *Asian Population Studies*, 6(1), pp. 3–24.

Guilmoto, Christophe Z. and Attané, Isabelle (2007) The geography of deteriorating child sex ratio in China and India, in I. Attané and C. Z. Guilmoto (eds) *Watering the Neighbour's Garden: The Growing Demographic Female Deficit in Asia* (Paris: Committee for International Cooperation in National Research in Demography (CICRED)), pp. 109–129.

Guilmoto, Christophe Z. and Rajan, S. Irudaya (2001) Spatial patterns of fertility transition in Indian districts. *Population and Development Review*, 27 (4), pp. 713–738.

Harriss-White, Barbara (1999) Gender-cleansing: the paradox of development and deteriorating female life chances in Tamil Nadu, in R. Sunder Rajan (ed.) *Signposts: Gender Issues in Post-Independence India* (New Delhi: Kali for Women), pp. 125–154.

Hudson, Valerie M. and den Boer, Andrea M. (2004) *Bare Branches: The Security Implications of Asia's Surplus Male Population* (Cambridge, MA: MIT Press).

Jeffery, Patricia (forthcoming 2014) Supply-and-demand demographics: Dowry, daughter aversion and marriage markets in contemporary north India, *Contemporary South Asia*.

Jeffery, Patricia and Jeffery, Roger (1996) *Don't Marry me to a Plowman! Women's Everyday Lives in Rural North India* (Boulder and New Delhi: Westview Press and Vistaar).

Jeffery, Patricia and Jeffery, Roger (2006) *Confronting Saffron Demography: Religion, Fertility and Women's Status in India* (New Delhi: Three Essays Collective).

Jeffery, Patricia, Jeffery, Roger, and Jeffrey, Craig (2008) Disputing contraception: Muslim reform, secular change and fertility. *Modern Asian Studies*, 42(2/3), pp. 519–548.

Jeffery, Patricia, Jeffery, Roger, and Lyon, Andrew (1989) *Labour Pains and Labour Power: Women and Childbearing in India* (London: Zed Books).

Jeffery, Roger and Basu, Alaka (eds) (1996) *Girls' Schooling, Women's Autonomy and Fertility Change in South Asia* (New Delhi: Sage).

Jeffery, Roger and Jeffery, Patricia (1997) *Population, Gender and Politics: Demographic Change in Rural North India* (Cambridge: Cambridge University Press).

Jeffrey, Craig (2010) *Timepass: Youth, Class, and the Politics of Waiting in India* (Stanford, CA: Stanford University Press).

Jeffrey, Craig, Jeffery, Patricia, and Jeffery, Roger (2008) *Degrees without Freedom? Education, Masculinities and Unemployment in North India* (Stanford, CA: Stanford University Press).

Jejeebhoy, Shireen J. and Sathar, Zeba A. (2001) Women's autonomy in India and Pakistan: the influence of religion and region. *Population and Development Review*, 27(4), pp. 687–712.

Joshi, Vijay (2010) Economic resurgence, lopsided reform and jobless growth, in A. Heath and R. Jeffery (eds) *Diversity and Change in Modern India: Economic, Social and Political Approaches* (Oxford: Oxford University Press), pp. 73–106.

Kabeer, Naila (2000) Inter-generational contracts, demographic transitions and the 'quantity–quality' tradeoff: parents, children and investing in the future. *Journal of International Development*, 12, pp. 463–482.

Kaur, Ravinder (2004) Across-region marriages: poverty, female migration and the sex ratio. *Economic and Political Weekly*, 39(25), pp. 2595–2603.

Kaur, Ravinder (2008) Dispensable daughters and bachelor sons: sex discrimination in north India. *Economic and Political Weekly*, 43(30), pp. 109–114.

Krishnan, Pramila (2001) *Culture and the Fertility Transition in India* (United Nations University, World Institute for Development Economics Research (WIDER)).

McNay, Kirsty, Arokiasamy, Perianayagam, and Cassen, Robert (2003) Why are uneducated women in India using contraception? A multilevel analysis. *Population Studies*, 57(1), pp. 21–40.

McNay, Kirsty, Unni, Jeemol, and Cassen, Robert (2004) Employment, in T. Dyson, R. Cassen, and L. Visaria (eds) *Twenty-First Century India: Population, Economy, Human Development and the Environment* (New Delhi: Oxford University Press), pp. 158–177.

Mayer, Peter (1999) India's falling sex ratios. *Population and Development Review*, 25(2), pp. 323–343.

Morgan, S. Philip, Stash, Sharon, Smith, Herbert L., and Mason, Karen Oppenheim (2002) Muslim and non-Muslim differences in female autonomy and fertility: evidence from four Asian countries. *Population and Development Review*, 18(1), pp. 33–60.

Oldenburg, Philip (1992) Sex ratio, son preference and violence in India: a research note. *Economic and Political Weekly*, 27(49/50), pp. 2657–2662.

Palriwala, Rajni (1999) Transitory residents, invisible workers: rethinking locality and incorporation in a Rajasthan village, in K. Sangari and U. Chakravarti (eds) *From Myth to Markets: Essays on Gender* (New Delhi: Manohar, for Indian Institute of Advanced Study, Shimla), pp. 237–273.

Palriwala, Rajni and Uberoi, Patricia (2005) Marriage and migration in Asia: gender issues (introduction to special issue on marriage and migration in Asia). *Indian Journal of Gender Studies*, 12(2/3), pp. v–xxix.

Patel, Tulsi (ed.) (2007) *Sex-Selective Abortion in India: Gender, Society and New Reproductive Technologies* (New Delhi: Sage Publications).

Sarkar, Sandip and Mehta, Balwant Singh (2010) Income inequality in India: pre- and post-reform periods. *Economic and Political Weekly*, 45(37), pp. 45–55.

Sharma, Ursula (1984) Dowry in north India: its consequences for women, in R. Hirschon (ed.) *Women and Property, Women as Property* (London and Canberra: Croom Helm), pp. 62–74.

Siddhanta, Suddhasil, Agnihotri, Satish Balram, and Nandy, Debasish (2009) Sex ratio patterns among the Scheduled Castes in India 1981–2001. Paper presented at IUSSP World Congress, Marrakech.

Srinivas, M. N. (1984) *Some Reflections on Dowry* (New Delhi: Oxford University Press, for Centre for Women's Development Studies).

Sudha, S. and Rajan, S. Irudaya (2003) Persistent daughter disadvantage: what do estimated sex ratios at birth and sex ratios of child mortality risk reveal? *Economic and Political Weekly*, 38(41), pp. 4361–4369.

Visaria, Leela (2004a) The continuing fertility transition, in T. Dyson, R. Cassen, and

L. Visaria (eds) *Twenty-First Century India: Population, Economy, Human Development, and the Environment* (New Delhi: Oxford University Press), pp. 57–73.

Visaria, Leela (2004b) Mortality trends and the health transition, in T. Dyson, R. Cassen, and L. Visaria (eds) *Twenty-First Century India: Population, Economy, Human Development, and the Environment* (New Delhi: Oxford University Press), pp. 32–56.

Part IV

Migration and the Regimes of Labour

7

The Modalities of Geographical Mobility in China and their Impacts, 1980–2010

DOROTHY J. SOLINGER

GEOGRAPHICAL MOBILITY in China—the critical component of which is rural–urban movement—and the weighty problem of inclusion for the migrants into the ranks of city citizens have always been, at base, primarily matters of the expenditure and transfer of state resources. A secondary but related dimension has been about the institutionalized discrimination (Feagin and Feagin, 1993: 15; Chan, 1996: 145–147) that incomers from the countryside have faced in the metropolises, the result of a set of state-devised barriers (and the attendant attitudes among municipal officials and dwellers that have grown up around and bolstered these barriers). These blockages, and the biases and behaviours that have developed over some 50 years in conjunction with the blocks, in short, have been grounded in the command of material resources and in struggles over their disposition.

Victimization and exploitation of peasants moving into municipalities have been the very visible byproducts of these people's efforts to leave home in search of a higher wage and a better life. Consequently, issues of the human rights of newcomers into the towns and cities and the way these rights are trampled on cannot be ignored. But more central to the dynamics of the drama of China's internal migration have been the disposal of and conflicts over material interests. Unless the fundamental clashes of financial interests that drive the bigotry, biases, and injustices are resolved institutionally, charges of poor treatment and calls for redress and equity are unlikely to be effective.

In the discussion that follows, I first lay out what migration has been about in China, where there are a set of decidedly unique understandings of what a cityward 'migrant' is, and what s/he experiences and might hope or not be able to hope to become. This will entail explaining the official framework in which geographical mobility takes place. I then spell out the causes behind the remarkable exodus of farmers from the rural areas that has refashioned

Proceedings of the British Academy, **193**, 139–156, © The British Academy 2014

the shape of Chinese society over the past 30 years. I go on to offer official statistics on the ever-growing numbers of these people, along with data on the nature of their regional flows, and provide demographic information on their ages, educational background, marital status, and so forth. I then describe the lives of migrants in the urban areas, discussing the kinds of jobs they hold, their living and working conditions, and their wages; and the treatment meted out to transients once in the cities. Next, under the heading of the consequences of their transfer, I touch on their remittances home, and also on responses to the discriminatory practices under which they live and labour—from social critics and from the migrants themselves. Finally, I list some recent reforms, and explain why, in the past decade or so, these have been announced to deal with ills in the system. I end by noting recent developments that portend a possible alteration of the overall situation.

Chinese migrants and migration: definitions

Because of the now 60-year-old household registration system (*huji zhidu*, popularly known as the *hukou* system) in China, unlike elsewhere in the world, people who relocate to urban areas comprise two distinct categories: first, there are people who are formally recognized by the state to have migrated (*qianyi*), who have their *hukou* officially switched from rural to urban. After 1960 and before 1980, only those who changed their place of residence with the permission (indeed, usually at the instigation of) the government fell under this classification. And then there is the far more prevalent, and for this chapter relevant, body of those who move without having had the blessing or validation of the authorities; what is often labelled the 'floating population'. The census of 2000 recognized as 'migrants' those who had lived for more than six months under a particular 'street' or neighbourhood authority (*jiedaohui*) other than the one in which s/he was registered (Chan, 2012). But up until 1990 (when the census allowed that the term be given to those who had remained in a county *(xian)*, a much larger unit, for a year or longer), persons outside their homes were simply seen as transients.

Transients who are considered as 'floating', and whose registration has not been authoritatively altered, are defined on three criteria: they have crossed over some territorial boundary; they have not been able to alter their permanent registration (their *hukou*); and, at least in theory, they 'flow in and out' (Wu, 1990: 53–55, 27). Given the restrictions, a switch from rural to urban registration can by no means be made just by moving one's place of habitation; only an official decision based on very limiting regulations can effect this shift, an event that happens only rarely (Potter and Potter, 1990:

307–310; Cohen, 1993; 159).[1] By the end of the twentieth century, both researchers and the Chinese government were directing their attention to a specific subgroup among the 'floating population', the members of the group known as 'rural migrant labour', or *nongmingong*, and gathering statistics just on them. The term 'rural migrant labour' is used to designate those still possessing a rural *hukou* who have transferred to cities and towns to work, whether for long periods, permanently, seasonally, or in a circulating fashion (Watson, 2009: 88, 90).[2]

This registration system was initially devised in the interest of shoring up capital-intensive, heavy industrialization, which was targeted to occur only in the cities, and of conserving key resources and food grain to sustain urban labour. To meet these objectives, it was considered critical to prevent an unplanned increase in the numbers of persons permanently resident in urban areas (Li and Hu, 1991: 30). As a result, the share of the urban population was held constant at about a fifth of the total population for at least 20 years (Fan and Mukherjee, 2005: 7). This arrangement found its justification in the planned economy; as one scholar noted in 1990, 'At all levels and in all localities, administrative management agencies plan their work and projects in accord with the size of the registered permanent population within their respective jurisdictions' (Wu, 1990: 43). Therefore, during the period of the planned economy, urban bureaucrats were vitally concerned with the numbers of people present in and impacting upon what they conceived as their resource systems (Ostrom, 1990: 29–33). As Chan and Zhang (1999: 821) explained, the *hukou* is 'a mechanism to block the free flow of resources (including labour) between ... the cities and countryside'.

In the pre-1992 period, when the urban economy was still largely state-planned, owned, and administered, and when rationing still dictated the supply of many critical commodities in urban areas, city bureaucrats closely guarded the goods for which they were responsible—whether grain, water, heating and cooking oil, transport vehicles, housing, or natural gas—and begrudged any diminution of their supply that might attend the entry into their jurisdictions of 'outsiders', those not locally registered (Solinger, 1999: Chapter 4, this volume; Chan and Wang, 2008: 28). Clearly, this was a case of peasant migrants being seen and treated as if they were second-class or even non-citizens in their own countries.

---

[1] Official changes from rural to urban *hukou* historically occurred when a person was officially recruited for an urban work assignment; peasants generally could become urbanites through serving in the army, rising within the party organization, or making great scholastic achievements. Also, peasants whose land was requisitioned for the use of urban work units were compensated with urban status (often on a one-status-change-per-family basis).

[2] Watson (2009: 90) notes that 20 per cent may be settling permanently in urban places, 60 per cent are mobile, often switching jobs and locations, and 20 per cent tend to be seasonal.

Thus, at that time, keeping peasants out or minimizing their presence was engineered chiefly in order to hoard resources for urban development and the 'proper' (or de jure) populace of the cities. The obvious superiority that the richer provision of public goods lent the cities fostered an arrogance and disdain among urbanites for people they, along with their administrators, perceived to be interlopers. This perspective lay at the core of the discrimination against and exclusivist policies aimed at peasants in towns that continue to obtain to the present. The mistreatment of rural people in urban workplaces was (and is) a function of their lower-status registration, their lack of belonging to the city, and their consequent vulnerability (Solinger, 1999; Chan, 2009: 207).

By the twenty-first century, however, it has become normal for rural people to live in urban areas. As the state plan atrophied and some dimensions of the national economy opened further and further to market forces in the latter half of the 1990s, the contention over migration and migrants became structured less in the old *horizontal* way of rivalry between rural areas and cities (or between one set of provinces and their cities against others) over resources that were allocated by plan (Solinger, 1999: ch. 3);[3] instead, the axis of antagonism and strain became more a *vertical* one.

That is, once the central government delegated to local governments the financial responsibilities for welfare and urban management that it had previously shouldered itself, but without, at the same time, disbursing to the localities the funds to pay for these services, cities became jealous of their resources for a new reason (Wong, 1991, 2009). Given ongoing duties to educate and keep healthy and housed their official residents, they have often refused to nurture people from the outside, whom they perceived as trespassers who would strain their budgets. The stress that today prevents municipalities from absorbing migrants on a permanent basis has less to do with city officials rejecting people from rural areas and poorer provinces in order to make do with a planned allotment of public goods; instead it has to do with inadequate budgets on which cities have to manage services and benefits, once the central government ceased subsidizing these activities.

Indeed, Chan and Wang have found that what might be termed *horizontal*, or interprovincial (or rural versus urban), issues became less salient causes for migration by the late 1990s, when migration itself worked to reduce inequalities among regions. Additionally, after 1995, the gap in living standards diminished, if only painfully slowly, after the central government began offering additional investment funding and some of the wherewithal for welfare services to the countryside (Chan and Wang, 2008: 39–44). Through

---

[3] Solinger (1999: ch 3) details the interprovincial battles of the 1990s over incoming and outgoing migrants, with the poorer areas keen to export surplus labour and the wealthier provinces and cities anxious to prevent the inflow.

the 1990s, there was also an increasing convergence in wages for low-skilled migrant labour across regions (Chan, 2001: 139–142; Park, Cai, and Du, 2008: 15). So in the past 15 years or so, the tensions that make cities oppose long-term settlement by outsiders and disappoint incoming peasants' hopes for more hospitable treatment has had to do mainly with the burdens placed on urban budgets, rather than fighting off encroachments by residents of other regions on a planned supply of material goods.

Thus, whether because of the strictures of the plan or as a result of the incursion of market rationality among urban administrators, people not formally a part of their assigned population have always appeared to these governors, at least in part, as unwelcome invaders. The bottom line is that China's migrants of the past 30 years began as captives of the state plan, with its allocations by region and unit, and end as hostages of the changed financial relations between central and local levels that came with market reforms.

Causes behind geographical movement

The initial impetus for the sudden breakdown of the pre-1980 blockade against farmers' exit from the country was the Chinese leadership's decision in 1979 to dissolve the two-decade-old commune system. That system had forbidden farmers to leave their rural community (unless as part of a working team whose temporary jobs were contracted between the commune and an urban factory), and, given the ubiquity of rationing all the necessities of life and the limited resources in the cities, had kept them locked into place.

Once the communes disappeared, and each farm household was assigned a plot of land to cultivate on its own, it was soon apparent that the rural areas contained many more labourers than there was work or land to occupy. Around the same time, restrictions on marketing were eased, and by the mid-1980s the beginnings of a development craze arrived, with a demand for cheap and eager low-skilled workers to fill newly available construction, service, and manufacturing jobs. As top politicians observed the economic payoffs of this shift, they steadily liberalized the rules around urban markets (Solinger, 1985). Together, these forces drove ever more farmers into the urban areas. Meanwhile, it quickly became evident to the millions of now relatively idle peasants that there were opportunities in the cities to enhance their incomes on an unimaginable scale. As the state implemented preferential policies after 1980 to attract foreign investment along the south-east coast, funds increasingly poured into the provinces there. The multitudinous posts created in light industrial processing and manufacturing firms by such investment offered yet one more incentive to migrants.

The extent of migration: numbers and regional flows

Numbers

Before the market reforms of the late 1970s onwards took effect, a mere 0.6 per cent of the total population lived in a place that was not their site of official residence (Chan, 2009: 202).[4] Moreover, in the 1980s and 1990s, the annual volume of people moving officially (what has been termed *hukou* migrants) was kept constant, at between 16 and 20 million people, through the use of a quota system (Chan, 2001: 130). But in the realm of unofficial movement, according to the state's reckoning, by 1982, 30 million farmers had become migrant workers, a number that shot up, almost steadily, to around 70 million by 1988, and to over 100 million at the beginning of 2001 (Chan, 2001: 130; *China Daily*, 2003).[5]

The average annual flow volume had reached close to 70 million by the late 1990s, producing an annual mobility rate (the percentage of the population that changed its usual residence in a given year) of 6 per cent, up from only 2 to 3 per cent 20 years earlier. Kam Wing Chan has calculated that 40 per cent of the rural labour force left its home township at least once (many later returned home to their villages) over the decades 1980–2000 (Chan, 2001: 132, 133). A national population survey conducted in 2005 found that about 11.3 per cent of China's entire population was 'floating', of whom 86.7 million had registered their presence in cities with the police (Li and Li, 2010: 189; Chan, 2012). By mid-2007, a government survey of nearly 3,000 villages found that in 74 per cent of the villages examined there were no fit workers left to go out to work in distant cities (Bradsher, 2007).

While China's Agricultural Census of 2006 showed a total of 132 million 'rural migrant labourers' (Chan, 2009: 207), if people working in enterprises in the countryside near their own homes were to be counted, that number would have been as high as 225 million by 2008 (Chan, 2010: 362). At the end of August 2010, the National Bureau of Statistics (NBS) released a comprehensive report on rural migrant labour, giving year-end figures for 2009. Its investigation revealed that the total was 148.89 million. Among these, whole families accounted for 29.66 million people, while 84.45 million had left their homes but remained within the same township (NBS, 2010).[6]

As for the direction of the flow, since its beginnings in the 1980s it has primarily been towards the south-east coast, in response to the foreign

---

[4] Chan (2001) offers this figure for the early 1980s.

[5] An illustration of the complexities of interpreting the data is that the official newspaper *China Daily*, on 23 January 2003, noted that 94 million migrated in 2002, a number that was up by 4.7 million over 2001, according to the Ministry of Agriculture (*China Daily*, 2003). Chan suggested (pers. comm.) that data from surveys are defined differently from those derived in other ways.

[6] My thanks to Kam Wing Chan for bringing this to my attention.

investment that poured in there (Wang, 2005: 110; Chan, 2010: 359).[7] According to an NBS study, in 2009, 62.5 per cent of the migrants could be found in the 11 provinces and centrally governed municipalities of east China, 17 per cent were in central China's eight provinces, and the remaining 20 per cent were in the 12 western provinces (Chan, 2001: 140).[8] An interesting finding was that, of those leaving home, 8.9 per cent fewer entered the east than in the previous year; while those whose destination was in the central and western regions rose by 3.8 and 4.8 per cent respectively. This is of interest because central China is considerably less well off than the east, and the west is even poorer. These are the regions from which most migrants come. That more migrants are finding work in these regions represents a major shift.

A related trend was the growing numbers who were migrating but staying within their own province by the year 2009. These represented 48.8 per cent of the national total of migrants in 2009, a rise of 8.2 per cent but a considerable fall from 16 years earlier, when as many as 71 per cent stayed in their own provinces (Chan, 2001: 139). The report also indicated that 9 per cent were working in the centrally governed municipalities (Beijing, Shanghai, Tianjin, or Chongqing); 20 per cent in provincial capitals; 34 per cent in prefecture-level cities (generally, those with populations between half a million and one million); 18.5 per cent in county-level cities; and 18 per cent in smaller cities and 'other places' (NBS, 2009).

Demography of the migrants

The 2009 NSB survey found that 41.6 per cent were in the age group 16–25, with those aged 26–30 accounting for 20 per cent, those aged 31–40 amounting to another 22 per cent, and those aged 40 and over representing 16 per cent. Married people were 56 per cent of the total. Earlier surveys showed a similarly youthful age structure. As of early 1995, according to a national survey of leavers drawn from a rural population of 35,000, 76 per cent were under the age of 35 (Zhang, Zhao, and Chen, 1995: 27).

The 2009 NSB survey found that men accounted for 65 per cent of migrants, while earlier estimates portrayed migrants as overwhelmingly male. Findings vary, but it is clear that sex compositions differed between migration streams. In the export zones of the south-east coast and in the Pearl

[7] As of 1998, 88 per cent of foreign direct investment was located in eastern, coastal China, pulling peasants from the interior into the positions it created. Chan reported that 70 to 80 per cent of the labour force in two major cities of the Pearl River Delta, Shenzhen and Dongguan, was composed of migrant labour.

[8] According to Chan, the east was the destination for 83 per cent of migrants in 1998; this has clearly changed in recent years.

River Delta, females always predominated (Li and Hu, 1991: 13). Young, impoverished peasant women are hired in droves to turn out toys, electronics products, and textiles in foreign-invested firms. A study carried out under the auspices of the Ministry of Agriculture in 1995 reported an increase in the percentage of women migrants nationwide, from 30 per cent in 1987 up to 40 per cent just eight years later (Bajia, 1995).

Migrants tend to be drawn from the better-educated farmers. According to the 2009 NSB survey, the illiterate were only 1 per cent, those with just a primary education accounted for 10.6 per cent, 65 per cent had junior high schooling, and 23.5 per cent education of senior high or above. It would seem that the educational levels of the migrants (like those of the whole rural population) had risen over time. An early 1995 survey found that 3.8 per cent were illiterate or semiliterate, and that 31.6 per cent had only primary school education (Zhang, Zhao, and Chen, 1995: 27). A Ministry of Agriculture study found in early 1994 that just 45.4 per cent had been to junior high and 10.3 per cent senior high (Nongyebu, 1995: 45).

By the end of the first decade of the twenty-first century, a new breed of migrant workers had emerged. The offspring of the original migrants, they were younger, better educated, raised with a higher standard of living than the previous generation, and often born in the cities. These workers have been found to be far more aware of their rights, and so more assertive than were their parents (CLB, 2010b; Yin, 2010).

Migrants' living and working conditions in cities

Like migrants anywhere, those in China tend to be relegated to the dangerous, dirty, and debilitating lines of work. And, as has been the case for nearly 30 years now, their conditions of daily life can be characterized as 'wage exploitation, inadequate food and housing and unsafe working conditions' (Adams, 2009; CLW, 2010).[9] The 2009 NBS report reported that 39 per cent were in manufacturing; 7.3 per cent in construction work; 12 per cent were service workers; 8 per cent were involved in the hotel, catering, and wholesale and retail trades; and 6 per cent were in transport, communications, packaging, and storing. Of the total, 93.5 per cent were employed and a mere 6.5 per cent self-employed. Put differently (and perhaps calculated somewhat differently), migrants accounted for 90 per cent of construction labour in the country and 80 per cent of mining, 60 per cent of all textile workers, and 50 per cent of

---

[9] China Labor Watch reported that the workers continue to suffer from 'low pay, long hours, and no job security', with 11-hour days and six-day weeks common (CLW, 2012). The NBS report for 2009, however, states that the average work week comprised just 58.4 hours.

those in the urban service trades (Watson, 2009: 90). The NBS study showed that 60 per cent work without a contract (Kuhn, 2004: 32).[10]

As for their pay, an average wage of about 470 yuan per month was the estimate of the NBS in 1997, but the average net income per person per month amounted to just 300 yuan around that time, remarkably modest but still three to four times the average rural income (Wang, 2005: 145). In 2006, despite improvements, interviews with 2,500 migrant workers revealed that the average monthly income—of 1,077 yuan per month—amounted to just 62 per cent of the average for an urban worker (Guan, 2008: 151–152). But according to Watson, more than half of all migrants earned under 800 yuan per month, with a third of them getting between 200 and 600 yuan per month in that same year (Watson, 2009: 93). Du Runsheng, a central government official in the agricultural sector, is quoted as having said that for the two decades following 1980 there had been 'hardly any increase in the wages of migrant workers in the coastal areas' (Chan, 2009: 208). And in 2009, two researchers report, average income dropped to as low as 765 yuan per month (down from 850 the year before), after the global financial crisis hit in late 2008 (Orlik and Rozelle, 2009: 21).

The 2009 NBS study did indicate some improvement: it claimed the average monthly income was as high as 1,417, while those receiving under 600 yuan per month represented only 2 per cent of the total. Those getting 800 to 1,200 per month accounted for 32 per cent, while those whose income was 1,200 to 1,600 were another third. Those with incomes between 1,600 and 2,400 yuan per month constituted 20 per cent of the total.

However, an even more important issue than wage levels has been the ongoing problem of wage arrears. A survey announced by the official Xinhua News Agency in 2003 admitted that three-quarters of migrants were having trouble collecting their pay (Pan, 2003); by the end of that year, an official campaign initiated by the then premier, Wen Jiabao demanded that employers pay some 100 billion yuan in back pay owed to migrant workers (Fu, 2004). By January 2004, official sources claimed that about 44 per cent of wages overdue the previous year had been paid, amounting to the astonishing sum of 5.7 billion yuan (*China Daily*, 2004). However, there are regular reports that unpaid wages remain a problem. As of early 2009, migrant surveys indicated that 20 per cent of workers continued not to be fully compensated for their labour each year (Wang, 2009). Oddly, however, the 2009 NBS report alleges that among migrants hired to work, those owed wages represented just 1.8 per cent of the total, having fallen by 2.3 percentage points from the year before.

---

[10] If so, this appears to be a big improvement, since 2004 NBS figures showed up to 80 per cent of migrants were working without contracts (Wang, 2008).

Again relying on the NBS survey of 2009, a third of the migrant workers were living in dormitories supplied by their employer or work unit, while another 18 per cent were residing on their worksite, with half of the total getting free housing and another 7.4 per cent drawing a housing subsidy. Over a third were renting, spending 245 yuan per month on average for this. About 10 per cent were returning home each day, and only a tiny 0.8 per cent had bought their own housing.

The two most serious difficulties faced by migrants in cities are the high cost—or even the impossibility—of arranging standard education for their children, and their low level of access to social security. Urban governments are stingy with these benefits, hoping to conserve their resources for the locally registered, as always, and experiencing this as an issue of strain on their own finances since the economic reforms began. A report by the NGO Human Rights in China, released in May 2002, revealed that at least 1.8 million migrant children were not receiving any education at all, though the group assumed that the number was likely to be much higher. In Beijing's Fengtai district alone, in the autumn of 2001, 50 private schools that migrants had set up themselves were closed by local authorities; Shanghai shut down at least 70 such schools over the three years from 1999 to 2002. Meanwhile, special annual fees that these students were charged were they to attend public schools could range as high as $1,250 at that time (Fackler, 2002; Human Rights in China, 2002). Not surprisingly, an autumn 2006 survey in five major cities found that just 14 per cent of migrant workers had children in schools in the city where they were then working (Guan, 2008: 153).

In early 2008, the *Christian Science Monitor* reported that, with the assistance of private charitable groups, as many as 500,000 children were attending special migrant schools in Beijing. But these were schools of uneven quality, mostly unsanctioned by the state, and yet were the only educational option for the majority of migrant children unless they were to return to their rural homes (Donohue, 2008). As recently as February 2010, plans were afoot to demolish about 20 'unauthorised' private migrant schools serving some 6,000 students in Beijing's Chaoyang district, with local officials there advising parents to send their children back to their hometowns (CLB, 2010). The ulterior motive was to use the space these buildings occupied for economic development (Jacobs, 2010: A11).[11]

Even where cities have been willing to allow migrants to participate in social security programmes—and local experiments with this have appeared in the past decade—high fees, lengthy residence requirements, and lack of portability discourage the transients, most of whom are young and in decent

---

[11] This article also states that about 250,000 children born in Beijing to migrant parents in recent years have no legal right to a public education.

health, from joining (Davies and Ramia, 2008; Saich, 2008: 89; Watson, 2009; Chan, 2012). Official statistics in the NBS 2009 study admit that the percentages who partake of the benefits constitute only a negligible proportion of all migrants: only 7.6 per cent, 21.8 per cent, 12.2 per cent, 3.9 per cent, and 2.3 per cent contribute to pension, work injury, medical, unemployment, and maternity insurance respectively. Even these low figures could well represent only nominal 'participation', and do not by any means indicate that the actual numbers are as high as they appear.[12]

Another conspicuous form of mistreatment includes onerous and ubiquitous fees assessed by local officials, who—despite the central government's repeated orders against this practice—have been unable to resist the opportunities for graft that the presence of powerless peasants in their jurisdictions offers (Yang, 2003).[13] And besides this fleecing, urban authorities, also against both local regulations and orders from higher levels, have persisted in arresting, detaining, and chasing from their municipalities transients found to be without their necessary papers and permits, and also at times of national celebrations and major events. Demolishing their dwellings is one more typical form of harassment (Eckholm, 1999: 1, 4; Cambreleng, 2002; Liu, 2002; Bequelin, 2003; Ransom, 2008).[14] In sum, as Kam Wing Chan has written, 'Because of policy discrimination, most cannot settle in permanently in the urban destination place and have to engage in seasonal migration or eventually return to their home villages' (Chan, 2001: 145).

Consequences of migration

Aside from the obvious, indispensable role migrants have played in building the skyscrapers and roads that mark modern Chinese metropolises, in staffing their hotels and restaurants, and in fuelling the country's export machine, migrants have helped out the countryside as well. Though the movement does suck the young and better-educated rural-born from the agricultural sector, at the same time it cuts down population pressure on the land (Chan, 2001: 146). Although one survey in the year 2000 found that 68 per cent of the 1,000 workers questioned disclosed that after meeting their own expenses they had little money left to send home (CLB, 2000), the *China Daily* claimed two years later that 327.4 billion yuan had been remitted (*China Daily*, 2003).

[12] Pers. comm. from Kam Wing Chan.

[13] One example is a ruling from the Ministry of Finance and the State Development Planning Commission of October 2001, cited in Chen (2003).

[14] Bequelin (2003) notes more than 3 million cases of detention and repatriation per year as of early 2003.

The 370 billion yuan sent back in 2003 was said to contribute a full 40 per cent of rural income, based on interviews with over 20,000 rural households conducted by the Ministry of Agriculture (Kuhn, 2004: 32; Kynge, 2004).[15] A different account, however, notes that the percentage might have been as low as 8.5 to 13 per cent (Watson, 2009: 93).

Given the enormous contribution that migrants have made to China's economic growth and achievements over the past three decades, it is not surprising that voices have been raised in criticism of the limitations and harshness imposed on them by the *huji*, or household registration, system. The censure dates back to at least the late 1980s (Liu, 1990: 34–35). In early 2008, an internet petition urged the National People's Congress to cancel the restrictions associated with the residence permit, and a rights lawyer associated with the letter disappeared soon after (Buckley, 2008). An editorial printed simultaneously in 11 newspapers in March 2010 requested that reform of the system be hastened (Chan, 2010; Ng, 2010: 4),[16] but internet versions were rapidly removed and the editors of several of the papers were chastised. Ignoring the danger, two months later a group of lawyers and scholars posted a letter to the State Council decrying the tight bond between the *huji* system on the one hand, and public services and welfare rights on the other. The letter pointed to three major cities that had set up regulations amounting to new barriers against migrants, thereby contravening orders of the premier and the State Council.[17]

Protests from the victims of the system, though increasing over time, date back decades (Solinger, 1999: 284–285),[18] and do appear to have had some effect (Chang, 2009; Lee, 2009). Probably, however, neither these nor the objections of intellectuals have been the most influential factors in producing official promises and efforts to ameliorate the situation for the 'outsiders' in the past decade or so. Materially based concerns have probably been more potent. One of these was the labour shortages that began in 2004 in the Pearl River Delta and led to revisions of rules in individual localities. As wages, the prices of agricultural products, and job opportunities in the inland countryside all improved around that time, and as word spread of the poor treatment and low wages accorded transient labour in the Delta, fewer migrants chose to relocate to the south-eastern coast in that period (Harney, 2004; Johnson, 2004; Bradsher, 2010).[19] Accordingly, welfare enhancements and higher

---

[15] Kuhn states that the wages make up 40 per cent of total income for *some rural* areas (italics added).

[16] A translation of the editorial appeared in *Population and Development Review*, 36(2) (2010).

[17] The letter, dated 26 May 2010, is in the author's possession, thanks to Kam Wing Chan.

[18] The conclusion to this book contains information on organized agitation among migrants going back to the mid-1980s.

[19] The 2008–09 governmental economic stimulus packages funnelled huge sums into infrastructural projects in the interior, which also worked to keep more manual labour at home.

wages were soon granted to the workers in that area (Cai, 2007; Watson, 2009: 92; *The Economist*, 2010).[20]

The panoply of reforms promulgated by the central government since the late 1990s began with a 1997 State Council policy permitting pilot towns to extend their *hukou*, and one allowing family members (especially children) to acquire the *hukou* if one of their members already possessed it, in 1998 (Chan and Zhang, 1999; Chinese Reform Paper, 2000; Kwan, 2003; Yang, 2003; Tao, 2010; Zuo, 2010). After the new millennium began, reforms intensified. Measures such as the elimination in 2001 of the quota system for registration in small cities and towns, stepped up efforts to terminate detentions for being caught without identification papers, and a crusade to end delays in paying wages and to force the payment of existing arrears, culminated at the national level in 2006 with a comprehensive document that included the bestowal of educational and welfare rights on the migrants and their families, and a plan to substitute residence permits (*juzhuzheng*) for the old *hukou* as a way of keeping track of migrants (and other citizens) that would be less detrimental to their status, and give them access to basic welfare services (although at a steep and likely prohibitive price) (Wang, 2005: 93–97; Watson, 2009: 105–106; Chan, 2012).

Despite the central government's frequent rulings and good intentions, and even in spite of announced revisions of their own practices, for the most part localities have failed to observe and enforce the changes, perceiving the new programmes as contrary to their own financial interests (CLB, 2008; Davies and Ramai, 2008: 141; Saich, 2008: 89; Watson, 2009: 104–105; Pilling, 2010; Tao, 2010; Chan, 2012). As Professor Wang Daben, a population expert from East China Normal University explained, 'Cities could not afford to grant the urban *hukou* to all migrant workers because of the huge cost of extending social welfare, including education, housing, and medical services' (Tam, 2010). An additional disincentive since the mid-1990s has been a desire on the part of cities to reserve any job openings they might have for laid-off local residents (Solinger, 2004).

The history of repeated noncompliance at the grass roots suggests that it is more than a lack of will or an absence of a concern for human rights and justice that has prevented cities from accepting and underwriting the residence of farmers within their fold. It will be only when cities find a reason that links proffering the normal privileges and rights of local citizenship to rural outsiders with their own self-interest that there can be any hope for fundamental change in the attitudes and practices of municipal officials.

---

[20] According to Kynge (2001), an earlier version of this same plan had already been announced for smaller cities and towns in October 2001.

It may be that a programme pioneered in the major inland metropolis of Chongqing in August 2010 could become a model. That city, then equipped with the financial wherewithal to support an enlarged population, mounted an intriguing initiative. This was a drive to entice into its borders a mass of rural people, who would be permanently present to perform the service work essential for sustaining the burgeoning industrial powerhouse that the place was becoming (Zhang and Zhang, 2010). That Chongqing's leaders were also contending to see the city become the 'Hong Kong of the interior' and to have its development zone ranked third nationwide only added to the impetus. It is just such a joining of the vital interests of urban governors with those of the migrants that might be the key to inspiring some confidence in a different future for China's still transient labour.

Acknowledgements

I extend much gratitude to Kam Wing Chan for supplying some references, sharing his own work, giving a very careful reading, and for extending generous advice.

References

Adams, B. (2009) Economic crisis increases risks for migrant workers. Human Rights Watch, 23 January. <http://www.hrw.org/news/2009/01/23/china-economic-crisis-increases-risks-migrant-workers> (accessed 10 December 2012).

Bajia (1995) 'nongxun laodongli liudong yanjiu' keti weituo nongyebu nongcun jingji yanjiu zhongxin ketizu bianji (Eight 'Rural Labor Force Mobility Research' Tasks, Commissioned by the Ministry of Agriculture Rural Economic Research Center Task Groups (ed.), (1995) *Nongcun laodongli jingji yanjiu tongxun* (*Bulletin of Rural Labor Mobility Studies*) (n.p.), pp. A-02, A-07.

Bequelin, Nicholas (2003) Migrant workers: without residency rights, millions wait in limbo. *South China Morning Post*, 27 February, p. 15. Reproduced (with Bequelin misspelt Becquelin) at <http://www.accessmylibrary.com/coms2/summary_0286-22558204_ ITM> (accessed 3 August 2013).

Bradsher, K. (2007) Wages up in China as young workers grow scarce. *New York Times*, 29 August. <http://www.nytimes.com/2007/08/29/business/worldbusiness/29labor. html? pagewanted=print&_r=0> (accessed 10 December 2012).

Bradsher, K. (2010) Defying global slump, China has labor shortage. *New York Times*, 26 February. <http://www.nytimes.com/2010/02/27/business/global/27yuan.html>.

Buckley, C. (2008) Chinese rights lawyer disappears, feared detained. Reuters, 7 March. <http://www.theusdaily.com/articles/viewarticle.jsp?id=326407> (accessed 10 December 2012).

Cai, F. (2007) The formation and evolution of China's migrant policy, in Xiaobo Zhang, Shenggen Fan, and Arjan de Haan (eds) *Narratives of Chinese Economic Reforms: How Does China Cross the River?* (New Jersey: World Scientific Publishing Co. Pte Ltd), pp. 71–90.

Cambreleng, B. (2002) Migrants bear the brunt of police wrath at China's 16th party congress. AFP, 12 November. <http://www.sino.uni-heidelberg.de/archive/documents/humanrights/cambreleng021118.txt> (accessed 18 November 2002).

Chan, K. W. (1996) Post-Mao China: a two-class urban society in the making. *International Journal of Urban and Regional Research*, 20(1), pp. 134–150.

Chan, K. W. (2001) Recent migration in China: patterns, trends, and policies. *Asian Perspectives*, 25 (4), pp. 127–155.

Chan, K. W. (2009) The Chinese *hukou* system at 50. *Eurasian Geography and Economics*, 50(2), pp. 21–56.

Chan, K. W. (2010) The household registration system and migrant labor in China: notes on a debate. *Population and Development Review*, 36(2), pp. 405–407.

Chan, K. W. (2012) Internal migration in China: trends, geography and policies, in United Nations, *Population Distribution, Urbanization, Internal Migration and Development: An International Perspective* (New York: United Nations), pp. 81–102.

Chan, K. W. and Wang, M. (2008) Remapping China's regional inequalities, 1990–2006: a new assessment of *de facto* and *de jure* population data. *Eurasian Geography and Economics*, 49(1), pp. 21–56.

Chan, K. W. and Zhang, L. (1999) The *hukou* system and rural–urban migration in China: processes and changes. *The China Quarterly*, 160, pp. 818–855.

Chang, A. (2009) China: up to 26 million rural migrants now jobless, Associated Press, 2 February. <http://www.utsandiego.com/news/2009/feb/02/china-stability-020209/> (accessed 10 December 2012).

Chen, Yang (2003) Shenzhen government disregards migrant workers' rights, China Labor Watch, 2 May. <http://www.chinalaborwatch.org/en/web/article.php?article_id=50038> (accessed 10 December 2012).

China Daily (2003) Rural-to-town labour force on the rise. *China Daily*, 23 January. <http://app1.chinadaily.com.cn/chinagate/opinion/rural_development/opinion/20030123ggef.htm> (accessed 10 December 2012).

China Daily (2004) China's construction payment in arrears accumulates to 336.6 bln yuan, 14 January. <http://english.peopledaily.com.cn/200401/14/eng20040114_132568.shtml> (accessed 10 December 2012).

CLB (China Labour Bulletin) (2010a) China's 'good news' for workers cannot hide harsh reality. China Labour Bulletin, 3 February. <http://www.clb.org.hk/en/content/chinas-good-news-workers-cannot-hide-harsh-reality> (accessed 20 August 2010).

CLB (China Labour Bulletin) (2010b) China's 'labour famine': hype and reality. China Labour Bulletin, 5 March. <http://www.clb.org.hk/en/content/chinas-labour-famine-hype-and-reality> (accessed 30 August 2010).

CLW (China Labor Watch) (2012) An investigation of eight Samsung factories in China: is Samsung infringing upon Apple's patent to bully workers? 4 September. <http://www.chinalaborwatch.org/pro/proshow-177.html> (accessed 10 December 2012).

Chinese Reform Paper (*Zhongguo gaigebao*) (2000), 1 August, in Summary of World Broadcasts, FE/4014, 4 December, p. G/5.

Cohen, M. L. (1993) Cultural and political inventions in modern China: the case of the Chinese 'peasant'. *Daedalus*, 122(2), pp. 151–170.

Davies, G. and Ramia, G. (2008) Governance reform towards 'serving migrant workers': a case study of the local implementation of central government regulations. *The China Quarterly*, 193, pp. 140–149.

Donohue, A. (2008) Unofficial schools aim to boost prospects of China's migrant children.

Christian Science Monitor, 11 July. <http://www.csmonitor.com/World/Asia-Pacific/2008/0711/p05s01-woap.html> (accessed 10 August 2013).

Eckholm, E. (1999) A glitch as China sets its 50th birthday party. *New York Times*, 3 September, pp. 1, 4.

Economist, The (2010) China's labour market: the next China, *The Economist*. 1 August. <http://www.economist.com/node/16693397> (accessed 10 December 2012).

Fackler, M. (2002) China cracks down on migrant schools. Associated Press, 7 May. <http://www.apnewsarchive.com/2002/China-Cracks-Down-on-Migrant-Schools/id-592a3bea3416bf0d19927af3bf366395> (accessed 10 December 2012).

Feagin, J. R. and Feagin, C. B. (1993) *Racial and Ethnic Relations*, 4th edn (Englewood Cliffs, NJ: Prentice Hall).

Fu, J. (2004) (Vice Premier) Zeng: pay all owed wages to migrant workers, *China Daily*, 24 August. <http://www.chinadaily.com.cn/english/doc/2004-08/24/content_368132.htm> (accessed 10 December 2012).

Guan, X. P. (2008) Equal rights and social inclusion: actions for improving welfare access for rural migrant workers in Chinese cities. *China Journal of Social Work*, 1(2), pp. 149–159.

Harney, A. (2004) China's economic growth shrinks labour supply. *Financial Times*, 16 August, p. 4.

Human Rights in China (2002) Chinese government policy shuts out poorest migrant children from urban schools, new study shows. Human Rights in China press release, 7 May. <http://www.hrichina.org/content/2498> (accessed 10 December 2012).

Jacobs, A. (2010) China editorials assail a government system. *New York Times*, 2 March, p. A11.

Johnson, T. (2004) Labor unrest: migrant workers shun factory region in China. *Detroit Free Press*, 13 September.

Kuhn, A. (2004) A high price to pay for a job. *Far Eastern Economic Review*, 22 January, pp. 30, 32.

Kwan, D. (2003) Powers of police to detain migrants will be scrapped. *South China Morning Post*, 19 June. <http://www.scmp.com/article/419094/powers-police-detain-migrants-will-be-scrapped> (accessed 30 August 2013).

Kynge, J. (2001) China to allow more peasants to move. *Financial Times*, 30 August, p. 9.

Kynge, J. (2004) China's urban workforce fuels rural economy. *Financial Times*, 25 February, p. 11.

Lee, D. (2009) China's migrant workers face uncertain new year: with the economy sagging and many factories that fed the export boom closing, millions have no job to return to after the holiday. *Los Angeles Times*, 24 January, C1.

Li, L. M. and Li, S. M. (2010) The impact of variations in urban registration within cities, in M. K. Whyte (ed.) *One Country, Two Societies* (Cambridge, MA: Harvard University Press), pp. 188–215.

Li, M. and Hu, X. (eds) (1991) *Liudong renkou dui da chengshi fazhan di yingxiang ji duice* (The influence of the floating population on big cities' development and countermeasures). (Beijing: Jingji ribao chubanshe: Economic Daily Publishing House).

Liu, C. B. (1990) Er shehui jiegou yu chengshihua (xu) (Dual social structure and urbanization (continued)). *Shehui*, 4, pp. 34–35.

Liu, Weijun (2002) Local authorities ordered to return migrant worker fees. China News Digest, 28 April. <http://www.cnd.org/Global/02/04/28/020428-1.html> (accessed 10 December 2012).

NBS (National Bureau of Statistics) (2010) National survey of peasant migrant workers in 2009, August. <http://wenku.baidu.com/view/065bc38a6529647d27285255.html> (accessed 10 December 2012).

Ng, Tze-wei (2010) End *hukou* system call earns rebuke. *South China Morning Post*, 6 March, p. 4. <http://www.scmp.com/article/707824/end-hukou-system-call-earns-rebuke> (accessed 10 December 2012).

Nongyebu 'Mingongchao' di genzong diaocha yu yanjiu' ketizu (Monitoring and Research Group of the Ministry of Agriculture on the wave of Peasant Migration) (1995) Jingji fazhanzhong di nongcun laodongli liudong—dui dangqian nongcun laodongli waichu qingkuang di diaocha yu sikao (Rural labour migration in economic development—investigation and thinking on the current situation of rural labour migration) *Zhongguo nongcun jingji (Chinese rural labour)*, 1, pp. 43–50.

Orlik, T. and Rozelle, S. (2009) Averting crisis in the countryside. *Far Eastern Economic Review*, 10 October, pp. 19–23.

Ostrom, E. (1990) *Governing the Commons: The Evolution of Institutions for Collective Action* (Cambridge: Cambridge University Press).

Pan, P. P. (2003) Getting paid in China: matter of life and death, *Washington Post*, 12 February, A 16.

Park, A., Cai, F., and Du, Y. (2008) Can China meet her employment challenge? Manuscript.

Pilling, D. (2010) Mismanaging China's rural exodus, *Financial Times*, 10 March. <http://www.ft.com/cms/s/0/c6ed2e24-2c78-11df-be45-00144feabdc0.html#axzz2aumLns9Z> (accessed 30 August 2013).

Potter, S. H. and Potter, J. M. (1990) *China's Peasants: The Anthropology of a Revolution* (Cambridge: Cambridge University Press).

Ransom, I. (2008) Beijing recyclers discarded in games security sweep. Reuter, 9 July. <http://www.reuters.com/article/2008/07/09/us-olympics-rubbish-idUSPEK15185520080709> (accessed 30 August 2013).

Saich, T. (2008) *Providing Public Goods in Transitional China* (New York: Palgrave Macmillan).

Solinger, D. J. (1985) Commercial reform and state control: structural changes in Chinese trade, 1981–1983. *Pacific Affairs*, summer, pp. 197–215.

Solinger, D. J. (1999) *Contesting Citizenship in Urban China* (Berkeley: University of California Press).

Solinger, D. J. (2004) Policy consistency in the midst of crisis: managing the furloughed and the farmers in three cities, in B. Naughton and D. Yang (eds) *Holding China Together: Diversity and National Integration in the Post-Deng Era* (Cambridge: Cambridge University Press), pp. 149–192.

Tam, F. (2010) Migrant workers get chance for urban residency. *South China Morning Post*, 9 June. <http://www.scmp.com/article/716615/migrant-workers-get-chance-urban-residency> (accessed 10 December 2012).

Tao, R. (2010) Achieving real progress in China's *hukou* East Asia Forum, 8 February. reform. <www. Eastasiaforum.org/2010/02/08/achieving-real-progress-in-chinas-hukou-reform> (accessed 10 December 2012).

Wang, Dewen (2008) Rural–urban migration and policy responses in China: challenges and options. ILO Asian Regional Programme on Governance of Labour Migration.

Wang, F. L. (2005) Brewing tensions while maintaining stabilities: the dual role of the *hukou* system in contemporary China. *Asian Perspectives*, 29(4), pp. 85–124.

Wang, T. (2009) Asian economic perspectives: how will China grow? Part 2. *UBS Securities*, 7 January.

Watson, A. (2009) Social security for China's migrant workers—providing for old age. *Journal of Current Chinese Affairs*, 38(4), pp. 86–116.

Wong, C. (1991) Central–local relations in an era of fiscal decline: the paradox of fiscal decentralization in post-Mao China. *The China Quarterly*, 128, pp. 691–715.

Wong, C. (2009) Rebuilding government for the 21st century: can China incrementally reform the public sector? *The China Quarterly*, 200, pp. 1–24.

Wu, R. (1990) Guanyu liudong renkou hanyi di tansuo (Defining the floating population). *Renkou yu jingji (Population and Economy)*, 3, pp. 53–55, 27. Working Paper No. 15.

Yin, S. C. (2010) New breed of migrant workers have higher expectations. *Straits Times*, 20 March, reprinted in *China Post*, 22 March. <http://www.chinapost.com.tw/china/national-news/2010/03/22/249389/New-breed.htm> (accessed 30 August 2013).

Zhang, X. H., Zhao, C. B., and Chen, L. B. (1995) Nongcun laodongli kuaquyu liudong di shizheng miaoda 1994. (A real description of rural labour's cross-regional flow 1994). *Zhanlue yu guanli (Strategy and Management)*, 6, pp. 26–34.

Zhang, Y. L. and Zhang T. (2010) Chongqing's call to urban conversion. *Caixin*, 25 August. <http://english.caing.com/2010/2010-08-25/100173950.html> and <http://www.21cbh.com/HTML/2010-8-2/wMMDAwMDE4OTgwMg.html>, 4 September (accessed 10 December 2010).

Zuo, M. (2010) Residence permits to replace *hukou*. *South China Morning Post*, 2 June. <http://www.scmp.com/article/715931/residence-permits-replace-hukou> (accessed 30 August 2013).

8

'Lopsided', 'Failed', or 'Tortuous': India's Problematic Transition and its Implications for Labour

STUART CORBRIDGE, JOHN HARRISS, & CRAIG JEFFREY

THE THREE ADJECTIVES of our title are the different ways in which different authors (the National Commission for Enterprises in the Unorganized Sector, Partha Chatterjee, and Pranab Bardhan respectively) refer to a cardinal fact about India's economy (Chatterjee, 2008: 55; NCEUS, 2008; refers to the failure of 'the narrative of transition'). This is that the structural transformation of the economy has not been completed, in spite of years of high rates of economic growth, and India's 'transition to an enlarged and dominating sphere of capital in the economy' (Bardhan, 2009: 31) is correspondingly problematic. In India, the declining share of income from the agricultural sector has not been accompanied by an equivalent decline in employment in that sector. In 1950–51 agriculture accounted for 61 per cent of GDP and for 76 per cent of employment, while it now contributes less than 20 per cent of GDP (16 per cent in 2007–08). Agriculture, however, still employs around 60 per cent of the labour force, according to census data from 2001, or 54 per cent in 2004–05, according to data from the National Sample Survey (NSS) that shows the daily employment status of individuals by activity (see Table 8.1).[1] The lowest share of agriculture in GDP across states is 9.5 per cent in Maharashtra, where the level of agricultural employment, however, remains at more than 53 per cent (Mahendra Dev, 2008: table 7.11).

The shift of labour from agriculture in India has been less than in some comparator countries (Table 8.2), though there is less sharp a contrast with China than Bardhan suggests (2009: 33 and see Riskin, Chapter 1, this volume). An important point of difference between India and China is that in

---

[1] But note that NSS data for 2007–08 show the share of farm employment as 55.4 per cent (Himanshu, 2011: 47).

Proceedings of the British Academy, **193**, 157–172, © The British Academy 2014

Table 8.1. Employment Structure in India—Daily Status (%)

Year	Agr	Mfg	CTT	G&P	Total
2004–2005	53.9	12.8	21.8	09.00	97.5
1999–2000	58.0	12.1	18.9	08.90	97.9
1993–1994	61.1	11.4	14.8	10.80	98.1
1983	63.4	11.8	13.3	09.90	98.4

Source: After Eswaran et al. (2009: table 6).
Note: Agr = Agriculture; Mfg = Manufacturing; CTT = Construction, Trade, and Hotels, Transport, Storage, and Communications; G&P = Government Services, Education, Health, Community Services, Personal Services. Total is less than 100 per cent because employment shares of mining and of real estate and finance are not included.

China 55 per cent of the cumulative increase in GDP between 1990 and 2005 was accounted for by manufacturing, which has generated, relatively, a great deal more employment than the services sector, which accounts for 60 per cent of the increase in GDP over the same period in India.

The dispossession of small-scale producers has gone on, and continues to go on, for industrial, mining, and infrastructural projects across the country, and has increasingly encountered resistance from them in actions that often involve the Maoists, who are now active in about a third of the districts of the country. The Indian agricultural economy, however, is still characterized by extensive small-scale, household-based production. The distribution both of ownership and of operational holdings is very distinctly pear-shaped, and what are described as 'marginal' operated holdings (of 1 hectare, or less, in extent) now account for 70 per cent of the total. Estimations made by Vikas Rawal (2008), using data from the 59th round of the National Sample Survey (NSS) for 2003–04, show that 31 per cent of rural households across the country as a whole own no land at all, and another 30 per cent own less than 0.4 hectare (or about 1 acre of land), while only a little over 5 per cent of households own more than 3 hectares (and just 0.52 per cent own more than 10). The absolute numbers and the relative share in the rural population of households without land—which have, for a long time, been considerable— have been increasing. The data from 2003–04 are not strictly comparable with those from an earlier round of the NSS, for 1992, but Rawal suggests that they show an increase of as much as 6 percentage points in landlessness, while inequality in land ownership also increased. Still, over most of the country, 'landlordism', where small producers depend for access to land and other assets upon the owners of large estates, has declined. The share of leased-in land in the total operated area, according to the NSS, declined from

Table 8.2. Distribution of GDP and of Employment across Sectors in India and Comparator Countries

Country	GDP (2007)			Employment	(2005/2006)	
	agriculture	industry	services	agriculture	industry	services
India	**17.7**	**29.4**	**52.8**	**53.9**	**12.8**	**30.8**
China	11.3	48.6	40.1	42.6	23.8	32.2
Brazil	5.5	28.7	65.8	19.3	21.4	57.9
Indonesia	13.8	46.7	39.4	42.0	18.7	37.2
Pakistan	20.6	26.6	52.8	43.4	20.3	36.6
Bangladesh	19.0	28.7	52.3	48.1	14.5	37.4

Source: World Bank Data (accessed at <www.worldbank.org/data>, September 2011).
Note: 'Employment' refers to distribution of the labour force by occupation/sector.

10.7 per cent in 1960–61 to just 6.5 per cent in the *kharif* (summer) season of 2002–03. Traces of classic 'landlordism' remain, however, and inequality in land ownership still gives considerable power locally—economic, social, and political—to the relatively small numbers of larger landowners and the increasing numbers of capitalist farmers.

At the same time, those depending upon wage employment have not, generally, been able to find what we might label as 'good jobs' in the organized or formal sector, or the most dynamic and productive sectors of the economy, so they take up activities in the unorganized or informal economy, which are often not very productive, and which are outside the purview of most employment legislation. Sinha estimates that the difference in productivity between those formally and those informally employed is as great as a factor of 1:19 (Sinha, 2010: 20, table 1). Workers who are informally employed have no protection—against the loss of their jobs, or in event of illness— and receive no benefits from employers. They are usually low-paid, and their work and their incomes are commonly irregular, though they may also work very long hours and in hazardous workplaces. It is reliably estimated that about two-thirds of India's GDP comes from such unregistered, informal activity, and that it accounts for more than 90 per cent of livelihoods—more than half of them being generated from self-employment (see Lerche, 2010, for a discussion of the informal economy and classes of labour). Meanwhile, according to data presented by the National Commission on Enterprises in the Unorganized Sector, the absolute numbers of protected 'formal sector' jobs actually *declined* marginally from 33.7 million to 33.4 million between 1999–2000 and 2004–05 (Table 8.3).

Table 8.3. Employment by Type and Sector (millions)

1999–2000, 2004–05

Sector	Informal workers	Formal workers	Total workers	Informal workers	Formal workers	Total workers
Informal	341.3	1.4	342.6	393.5	1.4	394.9
Formal	20.5	33.7	54.1	29.1	33.4	62.6
Total	361.7	35	396.8	422.6	34.9	457.5

Source: Sanyal and Bhattacharyya (2009), citing NCEUS.

While a classic theory holds that those employed (often self-employed) in informal activities constitute a 'reserve army of labour' (Altvater, 1993) necessary for the development of industrial capitalism over the longer run, it has been suggested (in an argument that will be considered further below) that, in India now, a large share of the labour force as a whole is better described as 'excluded', being unnecessary for the growth of the economy as a whole, and surviving in a wide range of activities that are of only marginal significance for the dynamic, corporate sector (Sanyal and Bhattacharyya, 2009). Whatever one makes of this argument, it is clear that the narrative of structural transformation and societal transition breaks down in regard to modern India.

Employment trends, 'jobless growth', and workers' responses

One significant indicator of employment trends in India in the period of economic liberalization is that the highly successful, widely celebrated IT industry, which now contributes an important share of GDP and of export earnings, generates so little employment. According to NSS data, the IT sector accounted for just 0.7 per cent of the non-agricultural labour force in 2004–05. The sector's revenues by that time accounted for 4.5 per cent of GDP (and 6.4 per cent by 2010–11), while contributing only 0.21 per cent of aggregate employment (Chandrasekhar, 2007). The major part of the services sector that contributes more than 50 per cent of GDP is still overwhelmingly constituted by traditional service industries, such as retail trade and personal services. In the following discussion, it should be noted that entrants to the Indian workforce grow at the moment by 10 million or more persons per year, a figure greatly exceeding that for *all* employment in 'private sector establishments' (8.8 million in 2006—of which the IT sector makes up only a small part).

It has been widely argued that India is experiencing 'jobless growth'—a view supported by National Sample Survey (NSS) data, showing that the rate of growth of the workforce as a whole fell below the rate of growth of

Table 8.4. Annual Rates of Employment Growth for Usual Status Workers (%)

Period	Rural	Urban
1983 to 1987–98	1.36	2.77
1987–98 to 1993–94	2.03	3.39
1993–94 to 1999–2000	0.66	2.27
1999–2000 to 2004–05	1.97	3.22
2004–2005 to 2009–10	-0.34	1.36

Source: National Sample Survey, various rounds (1983 to 2004–05 calculated by Chandrasekhar, 2007).

population in the later 1990s, and well below its rate of growth in the 1980s and early 1990s (see also Sen, Chapter 2). We will consider these trends, starting with rural labour.

Agriculture and rural labour

The NSS data (as reported by Chandrasekhar, 2007) show that the rate of rural employment growth has been consistently lower than that of the urban economy, as the share of all employment accounted for by agriculture has slowly declined. And, as Bardhan puts it, 'the agriculture sector is in bad shape' (2009: 31), after a decade—1994–95 to 2004–05—of the lowest growth rates in the sector since independence (0.6 per cent a year). This is the result of the very high incidence now of marginal holdings, of the rising costs of inputs, the degradation of the natural resource base, declining public investment, and decreased access to public sector credit (GOI, 2007). Agrarian distress is reflected in the apparently higher rates of suicide among farmers than among the general population (Nagaraj, 2008), and in Patnaik's calculation that over the period from 1994–95 to 2003–04 the real per capita incomes of India's agriculturally dependent population remained stagnant, when per capita incomes for the country as a whole increased by more than 4 per cent (cited by Jha, 2007). The point is brought home even more forcefully in findings of the Foundation for Agrarian Studies from village surveys in Andhra Pradesh, Uttar Pradesh, and Maharashtra: that it was virtually impossible in 2005–06 for households with operational holdings of 2 hectares of land or less (who account for all but a small share of all the cultivators in the country, remember), to earn an income sufficient for family survival. The net annual incomes from crop production of very many households were actually negative (Ramachandran and Rawal, 2010).

The rural poor include large numbers of cultivating households, therefore, but an even greater share of agricultural labour households, as we see in

Table 8.5. They might be expected to have been even more badly affected by the agricultural crisis than cultivating households.

The NSS data suggest that agricultural wage employment increased at the rate—at most—of 1 per cent a year between 1993–94 and 1999–2000 (a lower rate than in the 1980s), even while total agricultural employment stagnated; but subsequently it has declined. In line with these trends, the NSS data show that the annualized rate of growth of weekly wage earnings in agriculture declined from 3.27 per cent in 1983 to 1993–94, to 1.82 per cent in 1993–94 to 1999–2000, and to 1.11 per cent in the period from 2000 to 2004–05. The series *Agricultural Wages in India* shows a similar path of declining wage increases, and also that real wage rates in most operations actually fell in many districts across the country in the 1990s. This trend may have accompanied changes in the organization of agricultural labouring operations, certainly in some parts of the country, where there has been a shift to more piece-rated teamworking. In line with these trends, there is evidence of increasing indebtedness among agricultural labourers, especially to informal lenders, and of a weakening of school attendance among children from agricultural labour households.

Where real agricultural wages have increased, as in some parts of rural Tamil Nadu, it is in circumstances in which there has been an increase in non-agricultural employment opportunities (see Harriss, Jeyaranjan, and Nagaraj, 2010). Agricultural labour itself has become increasingly feminized, and— most likely—increasingly 'dailitized', as those from the Scheduled Castes confront particular barriers in entering even many casual labouring jobs outside agriculture (Harriss-White, 2003; Heyer, 2010). The rate of growth of rural non-agricultural employment in India over the period 1993–94 to 1999–2000, at 2.26 per cent a year, was more than twice the rate of growth of agricultural employment (1.06 per cent), and was higher still in the period to 2004–05, at 5.27 per cent a year, according to NSS data (Himanshu, 2007, table 8)—though it has fallen subsequently, as is reported below. Such increases in agricultural wages as have taken place have probably followed

Table 8.5. Classification of Rural Households According to Major Earnings Source, 2004–05

Income source	Non-poor households	Poor households
Self-employed in non-agriculture	16.5	12.9
Agricultural labour	22.1	41.8
Other labour	10.3	12.1
Self-employed in agriculture	38.4	26.7
Others	12.7	6.5

Source: Calculated from NSS data by Eswaran et al. (2009).

from a tightening in rural labour markets where non-farm employment is available. Rural distress, following from the crisis in agriculture that is attested most tragically in farmer suicides, but also shown in the evidence on declining trends in the growth of agricultural output and productivity at least until the middle of the present decade, has been offset, no doubt, by the growth in non-farm employment opportunities.

This is often associated, however, with increased migration, both rural–rural and rural–urban, much of it circular (when people move to and fro between village homes and distant work-sites). One recent estimate is that the numbers of such circulating migrants may have reached 100 million, while the National Commission on Enterprises in the Unorganized Sector estimates that the number of seasonal migrants is of the order of 30 million (Bird and Deshingkar, 2009; Deshingkar and Farrington, 2009). What we know of the conditions of life and work of this mobile labour force is limited, but shows that though workers may earn more than in agriculture, their livelihoods are characterized by high levels of vulnerability (Rogaly et al., 2002)—exactly as are those of the comparably large, or even larger, numbers in the mobile labour force of China. Thus far, however, there has been less political mobilization in protest against rural distress in the major agricultural regions of India than there has been in China, where the widespread occurrence of violent incidents has led the government to elevate rural development as a national priority (Dong, Bowles, and Chang, 2010).

'Jobless growth'?

The notion of 'jobless growth' has been contested, however, in interpretations of NSS data that showed an acceleration of employment growth in 2000–05, within both urban and rural areas and among both men and women. Not only was the 'jobless growth' thesis refuted, but it was also argued by Sundaram (2007) that there had been a marked increase of 'good-quality employment'. The essential points in this case were that self-employment had grown markedly in urban non-agriculture, especially among women; casual employment generally had declined; and regular salaried non-agricultural employment had increased, especially for women—at over 5 per cent a year. This argument depended heavily upon the assumption that self-employment represents 'good-quality employment', because over the period in question there had actually been a decline in all wage employment and a very significant increase in self-employment among all categories of workers. All told, about half of all those in the workforce are now self-employed. The idea that this is 'good-quality employment' reflects the emphasis in current development thinking, internationally, about the virtues of self-employment, which is understood as 'enterprise' (a way of thinking that is reflected in the title of India's National Commission for Enterprises in the Unorganized Sector). But there are many reluctant entrepreneurs among the poor, and the NSS data show that just under half of all self-employed workers do not find their work remunerative, in spite of their usually low expectations of reasonable returns. Chandrasekhar concluded that a large part of the increase in self-employment had been distress-driven, and that 'the apparent increase in aggregate employment growth may be more an outcome of the search for survival strategies than a demand-led expansion of productive employment opportunities' (2007).

For Unni and Raveendran (2007), too, the apparently rosy picture painted by Sundaram had to be qualified by recognition that some of the increase of regular salaried jobs was in a subsidiary capacity, indicating part-time working; while the increase in female participation was of women mainly at lower levels of education, implying that their access to employment was either in self-employment or at the bottom of the wage/salaried employment hierarchy (see also Sen's comments, Chapter 2, on the growth of unskilled employment). There was evidence, too, from the NSS, that the extent of home-working had increased quite significantly, especially among women. The increased employment of women in particular in subsidiary, part-time occupations, some of them involving home-working, and large numbers of them being poorly remunerated, are developments that have been characteristic of economies that have participated in economic globalization (Castells, 1997). Most significant of all, however, for Unni and Raveendran, was the fact that the average daily real wages of regular workers declined in 2004–05, by comparison with 1999–2000 (particularly for females), indicating the growth in urban areas of poorly remunerated jobs in regular salaried employment (and see Sen, Chapter 2, on the failure of employment growth in organized manufacturing). It is altogether likely that the growth of employment in the first five years of the new millennium was driven by distress, at a time when the agricultural economy was in crisis — as Chandrasekhar (2007) argued and as Himanshu, more recently, has shown in an analysis of employment trends over the longer run (2011: 53–55).

The estimates contained in the report on the 64th round of the NSS for 2007–08, and then in those of the 66th round of 2009–10, confirm the misgivings of other scholars as against Sundaram's optimism about the creation of 'good-quality employment' (*Economic and Political Weekly*, 2010: 7). Total employment increased at a rate of only 0.17 per cent per year between 2004–05 and 2007–08 (the lowest rate of employment generation of the last three decades, and occurring in the context of very high rates of growth of GDP); and rural employment actually declined. The 66th round of the NSS shows that between 2005 and 2010 usual status employment increased by just 0.1 per cent a year. In this period, the deceleration in the growth of urban employment (from 4.22 per cent a year in 1999–2005 to 1.36 per cent in 2005–10) and the decline in rural areas (the rate was -0.34 per cent a year in 2005–10) was accounted for largely by the sharp fall in female labour force participation. 'What seems to have happened is that a large majority of women workers moved into the labour force during 1999–2005 and looked for work outside the home due to the agrarian crisis and distress in rural areas. And it is these women workers who have moved back into their homes as soon as the situation improved because of higher agricultural productivity …' ('Editorial', 2010: 7). At the same time, the data show almost no diversification into rural non-farm employment. The intersectoral productivity gap widened over the period, as did the wage gap between the skilled and unskilled labour force. There is evidence, as Himanshu points out (2011: 56), that there is an inverse relationship between output growth and employment growth.

'Informalization' of employment, is of course, greatly to be desired, according to the advocates of economic liberalization, since labour market regulation beyond an absolute minimum is held to give rise to inflexibility. Besley and Burgess have concluded from comparison across Indian states that those 'which amended the Industrial Disputes Act in a pro-worker direction experienced lowered output, employment, investment, and productivity in registered or formal manufacturing' (2004: 91). Their arguments have been subjected to significant criticism (Bhattacharjea, 2009), and neither theoretical nor empirical work, in relation to India and to other countries, leads to unequivocal conclusions regarding the impact of employment protection legislation. As Bardhan says, 'there is hardly any study on the labour absorption question that conclusively shows that any adverse effect of labour laws is particularly large compared to the effects of other constraints on labour-intensive industrialisation' (2009: 33. See also Kannan and Raveendran, 2010). There is also substantial evidence that 'employers have been able to find ways to reduce the workforce even with "restrictive" provisions in place' — such as that on the retrenchment of workers, by using the mechanism of the voluntary retirement scheme in the later 1990s, or in the indications of the increase in the numbers of contract workers in the total number of workers in manufacturing (from about 12 per cent in 1990 to over 20 per cent by 2004–05) (Sharma, 2006; see also Nagaraj, 2004; and Sen, Chapter 2, this volume).

Informalization/'flexibilization' has certainly been taking place, and its negative consequences for workers are attested in a number of case studies. These show that total household incomes do not necessarily decline, partly because of increased workforce participation on the part of women, and in some cases of children, but that livelihoods have become much more vulnerable. Jan Breman's analysis of the impact of informalization in Ahmedabad makes this point very forcefully (Breman, 2001); and it is shown up as well in Nandini Gooptu's studies of once permanently employed workers in Kolkata (Gooptu, 2007). In both cities, the decline of 'permanent' formal employment in cotton (in Ahmedabad) and jute mills (in Kolkata) has led to what Mike Davis (2006) has referred to—with reference to cities throughout the erstwhile 'third world'—as 'urban involution', meaning the crowding of workers into such activities as local petty trade, transport, and construction, and (generally in relatively smaller numbers) into small manufacturing workshops. Coping with their changed circumstances has meant, in many households, that women and children have entered the labour force in larger numbers (contributing to the phenomenon of increasing self-employment, especially among women, that we noted earlier). It is for this reason that household incomes have not necessarily declined but livelihoods have become more vulnerable and—according to Breman's observations in Ahmedabad—living standards have declined. Karin Kapadia, from fieldwork in low-income households in Chennai, also thinks that it is likely that in many of them women have become the main breadwinners—though this coincides with evidence of decline in the status of women in Tamil society (Kapadia, 2010). Among men there has developed a strong sense of their powerlessness and of loss of dignity. Some have responded to their material and identity crises through resort to criminality, and some to violence, in aggressive assertions of masculinity (Gooptu, 2007). But these are not the only or the dominant responses. Some men have turned rather to clubs, and some of these to social service activities. There are signs, too, of increasing religiosity, and of the influence of fundamentalist religious ideology (Breman, 2002).

Labour organization

Is there evidence of a counter movement among urban, industrial workers, faced either with the lack of or with the loss of 'good jobs', reduced protection, and with being pushed into greater dependence upon forms of employment— casual work or self-employment or low-paid regular wage work—that leave them more vulnerable? The weakness of organized labour in this period is reflected in data on the incidence of industrial disputes. This has shown sharp decline, falling consistently below 1,500 a year after 1992, whereas the number had remained well above that level over the previous 30 years, except in the period of The Emergency (Agarwala, 2008: figure 3). What seems to have happened, according to Supriya RoyChowdhury (2008: 34ff.), is that industrial disputes have become increasingly company specific. 'What is absent,' she says, drawing on her studies of industrial disputes in Bangalore, 'is both a movement-like character to the activities of trade unions, and a broad class-based character to workers' struggles.' The disputes 'appeared to occur in a relative vacuum, led by trade unions, which were only tenuously connected, and in some cases not connected, to the mainstream trade unions. The form of these protests was that of isolated events which evoked little or no response from the larger body of industrial workers.' The unions have failed, in her view, to articulate class politics, so that, it seems, 'people are increasingly looking after themselves'. And, as Nandini Gooptu has described their ideas and values, this is absolutely the outlook of those who have found employment in one of the burgeoning sectors of the 'new economy', the shopping malls (Gooptu, 2009).

The overwhelming majority of the labour force of India, as we have seen, is employed in informal activity, so what is happening in 'the informal sector' is extremely important. Sanyal and Bhattacharyya (2009) argue that a very large share of those in informal employment in India constitute a 'surplus' labour force, outside the circuit of capital (rather than being linked to capitalist enterprises in the formal economy through subcontracting or a distinct form of capital—petty commodity production—in themselves (Harriss-White, 2010)). As we noted earlier, Sanyal and Bhattacharyya describe it as 'excluded labour' (see also Li, 2010). The two authors have developed an intriguing argument, inspired by their observation of the opposition to massive redevelopment plans in the huge Dharavi slum in Mumbai—opposition that has come about because of the way in which these take no account of the need for space for informal, home-based activities. The plans take account of Dharavi people only as 'residents' and not as 'producers'. Sanyal and Bhattacharyya suggest that in so far as excluded labour has structural power, it derives 'from its ability to encroach on the domain of capital; "squatting" becomes the new form of resistance' (2009: 42). The dispossessed, they argue, 'fight back through silent encroachment on property' (p. 42), in resistance that implies the tacit recognition of the impossibility of the completion of the transition to capitalism. Such tacit recognition seems to be reflected in the aims of organizations of informal workers that have come into existence, as among construction workers and women employed in rolling bidis. Agarwala (2008) has shown that the politics of these organizations are taking on a distinctive character, with demands being targeted towards the state rather than being directed against employers, for welfare benefits as citizens rather than for workers' rights. They are struggling not against informality (the historical objective of the trade union organization) but for rights of recognition in this status (though see also RoyChowdhury, 2003, for a less optimistic view of the potential in the recent organization of informal workers). Lerche, similarly, describes the activities of major unions in regard to the organization of informal workers as being focused on 'establishing a regulatory framework for conditions of work and pay, and promoting welfare issues, rather than undertaking more classical grassroots union activities ... The struggle against employers has been replaced by a struggle to secure improvements from government' (2010: 74).

There are no indications, therefore, of any very strong collective response among the urban labouring classes that would constitute a counter movement to liberalization and its effects on workers. But the Indian state has not entirely ignored the claims of the mass of the working poor for welfare. Indian governments' record of social provisioning is very mixed, but—under considerable political pressure from within civil society as well as from the left parties—the present government has introduced the most massive public employment programme in the world, in the Mahatma Gandhi National Rural Employment Scheme (which guarantees 100 days of employment to every rural household), and is now under similar pressure to improve food security. These measures lend credence to Chatterjee's argument that there is now, very generally, an increasing sense that the basic conditions of life must be provided to people everywhere (Chatterjee, 2008. See also Li, 2010). But at the same time, as Chatterjee also argues, mass politics are increasingly concerned with staking claims to state benefits, and there is no longer a perspective of transition, such as characterized the labour movements of the earlier twentieth century. Interventions—such as through the Unorganized Sector Workers' Social Security Bill of 2008, as well—only 'provide a way of making informalisation and casualisation more palatable' (Lerche, 2010: 76).

Conclusion: 'excluded labour'?

The evidence and argument of this chapter have shown that India's 'lopsided transition', with the limited movement of labour out of marginal smallholding agriculture as the economy grew over the first four decades from independence, has continued through the more recent years of very high rates of growth and in the context of India's partial pursuit of economic liberalism. These years are fairly described as a period of 'jobless growth', in spite of the apparently contrary evidence for the period 1999–2005. Employment in 'good jobs' in the formal sector has stagnated. There has been little growth of manufacturing employment (Kannan and Raveendran, 2010), and most new jobs have been created in construction and in traditional services (as shown in Table 8.1). The incidence of casual employment may have declined between 1999 and 2005, but real wages in regular employment declined over the same period (certainly in the lower half of the income distribution of regular earners, according to the recent analysis of Sarkar and Mehta, 2010). The assumption that the expansion over the same period of self-employment—which accounts for at least half of all jobs—is an indication of a movement into 'good-quality employment' is heroic, to say the least. There are strong indications that a significant share of the new jobs that people have taken up over this period has reflected distress rather than 'entrepreneurial enterprise' (as we see clearly from ethnographic studies such as Breman's or Gooptu's). The poor are often 'reluctant entrepreneurs' (as Gooptu has it). The informal sector continues to account for more than 90 per cent of all employment. Perhaps the most critical question, therefore, about labour in India, is that of whether the argument proposed by Sanyal and Bhattacharyya—that a very large share of Indian labour is 'excluded' (or constitutes 'surplus population' in Tania Li's more tendentious terminology)—carries weight, or not. What are the prospects for incomes and welfare for those in informal employment?

Both Sanyal and Bhattacharyya, and Tania Li, warn against the easy assumption of the inevitability of the linear pathway of structural transformation—such as appears, for example, in the arguments of the *World Development Report* for 2008 on *Agriculture for Development*—and critique the residual functionalism (as Li puts it) in the idea of the 'reserve army of labour'. They refer to (and Li describes in some detail, from across Asia) the 'new round of enclosures that have dispossessed large numbers of rural people from the land, and the low absorption of their labour, which is "surplus" to the requirements of capital accumulation' (Li, 2010). Of course, there are informal activities that are integrated within the circuit of capital, as through subcontracting and outsourcing, but a great deal of informal activity, which— as we have seen—involves large numbers of 'own account workers' or the self-employed, constitutes a non-capitalist production space (in Sanyal and Bhattacharyya's view). This is the economy of surplus or 'excluded' labour, which does not contribute to capital accumulation.

As Bardhan has pointed out, the problem with this argument is that the authors suggest that the non-capitalist space accounts for the great majority of informal workers, when the evidence on the point is scanty. This is a fair criticism, but Bardhan's own further arguments certainly provide no convincing rebuttal of the idea that there is an extensive force of 'excluded labour'. He refers to data showing that 'the all-India average market value of fixed assets owned per enterprise was Rs 58 000 in 2005–06 [$1200+] in the informal manufacturing sector'—but the conclusion that he draws when he says 'so the average informal enterprise is not run by destitute people' (2009: 34) is perhaps misleading. The great majority of 'informal enterprises', after all, are *not* in the manufacturing sector. Those that *are* may well include units that have become more capital-intensive over time, as Dibyendu Maiti and Kunal Sen report. But these authors also say that '(w)hether the informal sector can be a source of robust and productivity driven employment growth in the future, in the face of weak employment growth in the formal manufacturing sector, is a question that remains to be answered' (2010: 8). The results, however, of the research that they brought together to test the alternative hypotheses of 'informality as exploitation' (a 'site for primitive capital accumulation, with underpaid workers in abysmal conditions') versus 'informality as accumulation' (a 'venue for economic dynamism and entrepreneurial creativity', as they put it) generally supported the former. The further question, of course—posed by Li, and Sanyal and Bhattacharyya—is that of just how much informal activity really can be considered to be the site of 'primitive capital accumulation'. Isn't much of it reasonably seen as lying altogether outside the sphere of capital accumulation?

We have no means for mapping the distribution of informal economic activity and employment between that which is firmly within circuits of capital accumulation and that which can be held to be outside them, and the notion of exclusion is, to say the least, tendentious when we know that garbage-pickers, say, often are linked in ultimately to circuits of capital (as when they supply scrap metal for industry). Rather than referring to a large share of the labour force as being outside the sphere of capital accumulation, therefore, it is more sensible to think in terms of its being 'excluded' from the dynamic sectors of the economy, and engaged in activities of such low productivity as barely to allow for survival. There is no question that India's transition is indeed 'tortuous'; and there remains a 'marginal mass' of labour which barely survives without welfare provisioning on the part of the state, now through the Mahatma Gandhi National Rural Employment Guarantee (NREGA), and (it is to be hoped) through enhanced support for food security and more adequate public health. The 'inclusive growth' that was the stated aim of India's 11th Five Year Plan has remained elusive—and it is in this context, and in part perhaps because of the failure of aspirations to inclusive growth, that the government of India has passed social welfare legislation such as NREGA. The persistence of mass poverty in India has become politically unacceptable, and given the failures of inclusive growth, the state has had little alternative but to resort to the provision of a social safety net. Schemes such as (notably) NREGA, may deliver important benefits to poor people, but they do little to address the problems of human capital formation in India that are the outcome of decades of underinvestment in education, and that have helped to limit the possibilities for inclusive growth.

References

Agarwala, R. (2008) Reshaping the social contract: emerging relations between the state and informal labour in India. *Theory and Society*, 37(4), pp. 375–408.
Altvater, E. (1993) *The Future of the Market* (London: Verso).
Bardhan, P. (2009) Notes on the political economy of India's tortuous transition. *Economic and Political Weekly*, 44(49), 5 December, pp. 31–36.

Besley, Timothy and Burgess, Robin (2004) Can regulation hinder economic performance? Evidence from India. *Quarterly Journal of Economics*, 119(1), pp. 91–134.

Bhattacharjea, A. (2009) The effects of employment legislation on Indian manufacturing. *Economic and Political Weekly*, 44(2), pp. 55–62.

Bird, K. and Deshingkar, P. (2009) Circular migration in India, ODI Policy Brief No. 4, Overseas Development Institute, London.

Breman, J. (2001) An informalised labour system. *Economic and Political Weekly*, 36(52), pp. 4804–4821.

Breman, J. (2002) Communal upheaval as resurgence of social Darwinism. *Economic and Political Weekly*, 37(16), pp. 1485–1488.

Castells, Manuel (1997) *The Rise of the Network Society* (Oxford: Blackwell).

Chandrasekhar, C. P. (2007) Progress of 'reform' and retrogression of agriculture, Macroscan. <http://www.macroscan.org/anl/apr07/anl250407Agriculture.htm> (accessed 21 June 2010).

Chatterjee, P. (2008) Democracy and economic transformation in India. *Economic and Political Weekly*, 43(16), pp. 53–62.

Davis, M. (2006) *Planet of Slums* (London: Verso).

Deshingkar, P. and Farrington, J. (eds) (2009) *Circular Migration and Multilocational Livelihood Strategies in Rural India* (Delhi: Oxford University Press).

Dong, X–Y., Bowles, P., and Chang, H. (2010) Managing liberalization and globalization in rural China: trends in rural labour allocation, income and inequality. *Global Labour Journal*, 1(1), pp. 31–55.

Economic and Political Weekly (2010) Editorial: jobless growth, 25 September, pp. 7–8.

Eswaran, M. et al. (2009) Sectoral labour flows and agricultural wages in India, 1983–2004: has growth trickled down? *Economic and Political Weekly*, 44(2), pp. 46–55.

GOI (Government of India) (2007) *Report of the Expert Group on Agricultural Indebtedness* (New Delhi: Ministry of Finance).

Gooptu, N. (2007) Economic liberalization, work and democracy: industrial decline and urban politics in Kolkata. *Economic and Political Weekly*, 42(21), pp. 1922–1933.

Gooptu, N. (2009) Neoliberal subjectivity, enterprise culture and new workplaces: organised retail and shopping malls in India. *Economic and Political Weekly*, 44(22), pp. 45–54.

Harriss, J., Jeyaranjan, J., and Nagaraj, K. (2010) Land, labour and caste politics in rural Tamil Nadu in the twentieth century, Iruvelpattu 1916–2008. *Economic and Political Weekly*, 45(31), pp. 47–61.

Harriss-White, B. (2003) *India Working: Essays on Economy and Society* (Cambridge: Cambridge University Press).

Harriss-White, B. (2010) Globalization, the financial crisis and petty production in India's socially regulated informal economy. *Global Labour Journal*, 1(1), pp. 152–177.

Heyer, J. (2010) The marginalisation of Dalits in a modernising economy, in B. Harriss-White and J. Heyer (eds) *The Comparative Political Economy of Development* (London and New York: Routledge), pp. 225–247.

Himanshu (2007) Recent trends in poverty and inequality: some preliminary results. *Economic and Political Weekly*, 48(9), pp. 497–508.

Himanshu (2011) Employment trends in India: a re-examination. *Economic and Political Weekly*, 46(37), pp. 43–59.

Jha, P. (2007) Some aspects of the well-being of India's agricultural labour in the context of the contemporary agrarian crisis, Macroscan. <http://www.macroscan.org/anl/feb07/anl220207Agrarian_Crisis.htm> (accessed 21 June 2010).

Kannan, K. P. and Raveendran, G. (2010) Growth sans employment: a quarter century of jobless growth in Indian manufacturing. *Economic and Political Weekly*, 44(10), pp. 80–91.

Kapadia, K. (2010) Liberalisation and transformations in India's informal economy: female breadwinners in working-class households in Chennai, in B. Harriss-White and J. Heyer (eds) *The Comparative Political Economy of Development* (London and New York: Routledge), pp. 267–290.

Lerche, J. (2010) From 'rural labour' to 'classes of labour': class fragmentation, caste and class struggle at the bottom of the Indian labour hierarchy, in B. Harriss-White and J. Heyer (eds) *The Comparative Political Economy of Development* (London and New York: Routledge).

Li, T. (2010) To make live or let die? Rural dispossession and the protection of surplus populations. *Antipode*, 41(1), pp. 66–93.

Mahendra Dev, S. (2008) *Inclusive Growth in India: Agriculture, Poverty, and Human Development* (Delhi: Oxford University Press).

Maiti, D. and Sen, K. (2010) The informal sector in India: a means of exploitation or accumulation? *Journal of South Asian Development*, 5(1), pp. 1–13.

Nagaraj, K. (2008) Farmers' suicides in India: magnitudes, trends and spatial patterns, Macroscan. <www.macroscan.org/anl/mar08/anl030308Farmers_Suicides.htm> (accessed 21 June 2010).

Nagaraj, R. (2004) Fall in manufacturing employment. *Economic and Political Weekly*, 39(30), pp. 3387–3390.

NCEUS (National Commission for Enterprises in the Informal Sector) (2008) *Report on the Conditions of Work and Promotion of Livelihoods in the Unorganised Sector* (Delhi: Academic Foundation).

Ramachandran, V. K. and Rawal, V. (2010) The impact of liberalisation and globalisation on India's agrarian economy. *Global Labour Journal*, 1(1), pp. 56–91.

Rawal, V. (2008), Ownership holdings of land in rural India: putting the record straight. *Economic and Political Weekly*, 43(10), pp. 43–47.

Rogaly, B., Coppard, D., Safique, A., Rana, K., Sengupta, A., and Biswas, J. (2002), Seasonal migration and welfare/ill-fare in eastern India: a social analysis. *Journal of Development Studies*, 38(5), pp. 89–114.

RoyChowdhury, S. (2003) Old classes and new spaces: urban poverty, unorganised labour and new unions. *Economic and Political Weekly*, 38(50), pp. 5277–5284.

RoyChowdhury, S. (2008) Class in industrial disputes: case studies from Bangalore. *Economic and Political Weekly* (Review of Labour), 43(22), pp. 28–36.

Sanyal, K. and Bhattacharyya, R. (2009) Beyond the factory: globalisation, informalisation of production and the new locations of labour. *Economic and Political Weekly*, 44(22), pp. 35–44.

Sarkar, S. and Mehta, B. S. (2010) Income inequality in India: pre- and post-reform periods. *Economic and Political Weekly*, 44(37), pp. 45–49.

Sharma, A. N. (2006) Flexibility, employment and labour market reforms in India. *Economic and Political Weekly*, 41(21), pp. 2078–2085.

Sinha, A. (2010) Productivity of India's informal workers: do global impulses matter? *Journal of South Asian Development*, 5(15), pp. 1485–1488.

Sundaram, K. (2007) Employment and poverty in India, 2000–2005. *Economic and Political Weekly*, 42(30), pp. 3121–3131.

Unni, J. and Raveendran, G. (2007) Growth of employment (1993–4 to 2004–5): illusion of inclusiveness. *Economic and Political Weekly*, 42(3), pp. 196–199.

Part V

The Environment: Crises and Responses

9

China: Energy, Environment, and Limits to Growth

MINQI LI

THE CHINESE ECONOMY has grown rapidly since the 1980s, and China now ranks as the world's second largest economy. However, China's current model of economic development rests upon massive exploitation of natural resources and environmental degradation. As China's domestic ecological system stands on the verge of collapse and it becomes a major contributor to the global ecological crisis, its current model of development is no longer sustainable.

This chapter examines the growing conflicts between China's current pattern of economic growth and various dimensions of ecological sustainability: energy, climate change, and food availability. It argues that, in the long run, the pursuit of infinite economic growth is fundamentally incompatible with the requirements of ecological sustainability.

In the short and medium run, China needs to meet the imminent ecological challenges by adapting to much slower economic growth rates. The slower economic growth will have major macroeconomic and social implications. In the long run, a new economic and social system that is capable of operating with 'steady state' or zero economic growth is likely to be required.

The next section examines the general relationship between economic growth and environmental impact. Section 3 gives an overview of China's environmental crisis. Sections 4, 5, 6, and 7 discuss the limits to China's economic growth imposed by food availability, energy availability, and the budget of CO_2 emissions. Section 8 evaluates the implications for China's economic model, and concludes the chapter.

Economic growth and ecological sustainability

All human societies depend on material exchanges with the natural environment for survival and development. Material resources (including both renewable

Proceedings of the British Academy, **193**, 175–192, © The British Academy 2014

and nonrenewable resources) are extracted from the environment and used for human material production and consumption. Human production and consumption generate material wastes that are released into the environment.

The total amounts of nonrenewable resources (such as mineral resources) are limited from the human point of view. Thus, a truly ecologically sustainable society needs to minimize the use of nonrenewable resources. As a society undergoes transition from an unsustainable structure to a sustainable structure, it needs to gradually reduce the rate of consumption of nonrenewable resources until the rate of consumption eventually approaches zero.

Over the long run, the amounts of renewable resources (such as fresh water, soil, biological resources, and solar energy) are unlimited. However, within a certain period of time, the natural rates of regeneration of various renewable resources are subject to definite limits. Thus, the human rates of consumption of renewable resources need to stay below the ecological systems' natural rates of regeneration.

Within certain limits, the material waste generated by human production and consumption may be absorbed by the ecological systems without undermining the systems' natural operations. However, if the human rates of pollution stayed consistently above the ecological systems' natural rates of absorption, the ecological systems would no longer function normally and eventually would collapse. The collapse of the ecological systems would undermine the very foundation of human civilization.

For much of early human history, human impact on the various ecological systems was limited. Since the beginning of human civilization, there have been notable examples of local ecological failures (Diamond, 2005). But it was not until the industrial revolution, or the beginning of modern capitalism, that the human impact on the earth's ecological systems started to expand exponentially.

According to Angus Maddison (2003), there was little growth in world economic output between AD 1 and 1000. World economic output approximately doubled between 1000 and 1500, tripled between 1500 and 1820, and expanded by 50 times between 1820 and 2000. The modern capitalist world system is distinguished from all previous historical systems by its tendency towards exponential and infinite economic growth.

The so-called IPAT formula is commonly used in the environmental literature to illustrate the relationship between economic growth and environmental impact (Ehrlich and Holdren, 1971):

$$I = P * A * T$$

Where 'I' stands for environmental impact, 'P' stands for population, 'A' stands for affluence, and 'T' stands for technology. 'Affluence' is usually represented by gross domestic product (GDP) per capita. Thus, $P * A = GDP$. 'Technology' is defined as environmental impact per unit of GDP.

As is argued above, to achieve ecological sustainability a society must gradually reduce its rates of consumption of nonrenewable resources, keep its rates of consumption of renewable resources below the natural rates of regeneration, and keep its rates of pollution below the natural rates of absorption (Huesemann, 2003). These requirements can be summarized as the requirement of a stable or falling environmental impact (I).

Under modern capitalism, P * A (or GDP) tends to grow exponentially. Thus, to achieve stable or falling 'I', 'T' (or environmental impact per unit of GDP) will have to fall at least as rapidly as economic growth rate. Can technological progress proceed sufficiently rapidly to deliver ecological sustainability while maintaining infinite economic growth?

In the short and medium run, the pace of technological progress is limited by a society's existing capital infrastructure. Most new technologies need to be embodied in new machines, equipment, and buildings. However, capital infrastructure (such as machines, equipment, and buildings) is, by nature, long-lasting. There are physical limits to how rapidly a society's capital infrastructure can be replaced and updated.

Suppose a society each year replaces 5 per cent of its capital infrastructure, and optimistically assume that the new capital is 100 per cent more efficient than the old capital (and therefore, for the new capital, the environmental impact per unit of GDP falls by 50 per cent). For the society as a whole, 'T' falls at a rate of 5% * 50% = 2.5%. Thus, despite the very optimistic assumption of technological progress, the economic growth rate cannot be more than 2.5 per cent if the society intends to achieve ecological sustainability.

In the long run, 'T' (or environmental impact per unit of GDP) cannot be reduced to zero. Moreover, in several important areas, the world has already overshot the earth's ecological limits by large margins (Rockström et al., 2009). In these areas, to restore ecological sustainability, global environmental impact needs to fall rapidly. Thus, it is likely to require a steady state economy or an economy with zero growth to achieve ecological sustainability.

China: economic growth and environmental crisis

Over the past three decades, China has undergone major institutional changes that have led to the rise of an economic model based on capitalist economic relations (Hart-Landsberg and Burkett, 2004; Li Minqi, 2009). The Chinese economy has evolved from a socialist planned economy into one that is based on capital accumulation and profit-making, where the domestic and foreign private enterprises dominate most of the economic sectors, and the distribution of income and wealth is characterized by a level of inequality comparable with that in many capitalist countries.

According to China's National Bureau of Statistics (NBS), state-owned and state-controlled enterprises accounted for 49.6 per cent of China's total industrial output value in 1998. By 2009, the share of state-owned and state-controlled enterprises in China's industrial output value declined to 26.7 per cent. Out of 39 industrial sectors, state-owned and state-controlled enterprises accounted for the largest share in nine, domestic private enterprises in 21, and foreign-owned enterprises (including those invested by Hong Kong, Macau, and Taiwan) in another nine.

By 2009, private enterprises accounted for the largest share of employment in construction, information, and computer services, wholesale and retail, hotels and catering services, financial services, real estate, and leasing and business services. The state continues to play a dominant role only in those sectors where the products are obviously public goods, such as public transportation, postal services, scientific research, water conservancy, education, health care, culture, and government (NBS, 2010).

China has been transformed from an egalitarian socialist country into one of the most unequal countries in the world. According to the World Bank, in 2005, the richest 20 per cent of the Chinese households held 47.8 per cent of the income, while the poorest 20 per cent held only 5.7 per cent. The richest 10 per cent held 31.4 per cent of the income, while the bottom 60 per cent combined held 30.2 per cent. Measured by the Gini index, China's income distribution was more unequal than that of India, Pakistan, Indonesia, Egypt, and the Russian Federation. More than one-third of the Chinese population lives on an income of less than $2 a day (World Bank, 2011).

Despite the dramatic rise of inequality, few would dispute that the Chinese model of development has been very effective in promoting economic growth. Measured by purchasing power parity, China's share of world GDP grew from 7 per cent in 2000 to 13 per cent in 2010. Under the current trend, China could overtake the USA to become the world's largest economy (measured by purchasing power parity) by 2015.

According to the official statistics, the Chinese economy grew at an average annual rate of 9.3 per cent in the 1980s, 10.4 per cent in the 1990s, and 10.4 per cent from 2001 to 2010 (NBS, 2011). As is discussed in the previous section, rapid economic growth is likely to result in massive depletion of resources and environmental degradation.

Indeed, since 1980, China's energy consumption and CO_2 emissions have both increased by about six times. China has overtaken the USA to become the world's largest energy consumer and greenhouse gas emitter.

China has 16 out of the 20 most polluted cities in the world; the aquifers in 90 per cent of the Chinese cities are polluted; 75 per cent of the river water flowing through China's urban areas is unsuitable for drinking or fishing; and about 30 per cent of the river water is unfit for agricultural or industrial use.

Desertification has engulfed about a quarter of China's land area; about 40 per cent of China's arable land has been degraded; and 10 per cent of China's arable land has been contaminated (Wen and Li, 2006; Economy, 2007).

The pervasive air, water, and land pollution have already become an urgent public health problem. Every year, between 400,000 and 800,000 Chinese people die prematurely owing to respiratory diseases related to air pollution. Near 200 million Chinese people are sick from drinking contaminated water (Economy, 2007).

According to *China Ecological Footprint Report 2010*, in 2007, China's per capita ecological footprint (the productive land and water area required to produce the resources consumed and to absorb the wastes generated) was 2.2 hectares, or about 81 per cent of the world average. However, China's ecological footprint is now more than twice as high as China's own biocapacity (the productive land and water area available). Thus, China is now running a huge ecological deficit against its own available resources, and the size of China's ecological deficit has steadily grown since the 1970s (WWF, 2010).

In other words, China's consumption of resources and generation of material wastes have already overwhelmed its own ecological system. Unless this pattern is reversed in the near future, China's current model of development will inevitably lead to the collapse of the country's internal ecological system.

The following three sections discuss the limits to China's economic growth imposed by food availability, energy availability, and the budget of CO_2 emissions.

Food: demand and supply

Agriculture is the basis of all civilizations. World food production increased rapidly over the second half of the twentieth century. This made possible the massive expansion of world population from 2.5 billion in 1950 to 6.1 billion in 2000.

The rapid growth of modern agriculture has been based on mechanization, chemical inputs (fertilizers, pesticides, and herbicides), irrigation, and high-yield seeds responsive to fertilizers and irrigation. Modern agriculture depends heavily on nonrenewable fossil fuels for the production of chemical inputs, operation of farm machines, packaging, and transportation. By some estimates, modern agriculture now takes about 10 calories of fossil fuels to produce 1 calorie of food (McCluney, 2005).

From the ecological perspective, modern agriculture is fundamentally unsustainable. Mechanized tillage, use of chemical fertilizers, and large-scale monoculture lead to soil erosion. Pests develop generic resistance to pesticides.

Perennial irrigation leads to waterlogging, salinization, and aquifer depletion. Thus, all elements of modern agriculture eventually suffer from diminishing returns (Goldsmith, 2005; Heinberg, 2006: 49–54; Pfeiffer, 2006).

Since the 1970s, Chinese food consumption has increased rapidly. From 1980 to 2010, as the Chinese population grew from 987 million to 1,341 million, China's per capita grain consumption increased from 325 kilograms to 454 kilograms (NBS, 2011).[1] The rapid growth of China's food consumption has been made possible by the large-scale application of modern agricultural technologies. Figure 9.1 shows the relationship between China's grain yields and the intensive use of modern agricultural inputs.

From 1980 to 1990, China's grain yields on average grew by 120 kilograms per hectare a year, irrigated area as a percentage of the total agricultural sown area grew by 0.13 per cent a year, fertilizer applications grew by 8.8 kilograms per hectare a year, and agricultural machinery power grew by 93 watts per hectare a year. An increase in grain yields by 100 kilograms was associated with an increase in irrigated area by 0.11 per cent, an increase in fertilizer applications by 7.3 kilograms per hectare, and an increase in agricultural machinery by 77 watts per hectare.

From 2000 to 2010, China's grain yields in average grew by 71 kilograms per hectare a year, irrigated area as a percentage of the total agricultural sown area grew by 0.31 per cent a year, fertilizer applications grew by 8.1 kilograms per hectare a year, and agricultural machinery power grew by 241 watts per hectare a year. An increase in grain yields by 100 kilograms was associated with an increase in irrigated area by 0.44 per cent a year, an increase in fertilizer applications by 11.4 kilograms per hectare, and an increase in agricultural machinery by 340 watts per hectare. Thus, in the context of Chinese agriculture, every form of modern agricultural technology has suffered from diminishing returns since the 1980s.

By 2030, China's population is expected to grow to 1.6 billion (Li, 2009). If the per capita grain consumption stays around 450 kilograms, China's total grain consumption is expected to grow to 720 million tons (this could be an underestimate if the Chinese population's food structure continues to change towards a more meat-intensive diet). If China could sustain an annual net import of cereals and other grains of 60 million tons (roughly comparable with the current level of food imports), China's domestic grain production needs to grow to 660 million tons to meet China's food demand in 2030.

From 1980 to 1990, China's sown area of grain crops declined by rate at an average of 380,000 hectares a year. From 1990 to 2000, the rate of decline

[1] For 1980, China's grain consumption is assumed to be the same as domestic grain production. For 2010, the food consumption is estimated as the sum of domestic grain production, net imports of cereals, and net imports of soybeans.

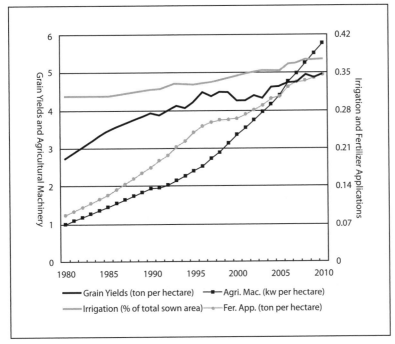

Figure 9.1. China's Agriculture, Inputs, and Grain Yields (1980–2010)
Source: NBS (2011).

accelerated to 500,000 hectares a year. From 2000 to 2010, the area sown to grain crops increased slightly, from 108.5 million hectares to 109.9 million hectares. In the future, owing to land degradation and urbanization, China's arable land is likely to keep declining. However, assuming optimistically that the area sown with grain crops could stabilize at around 110 million hectares, China's grain yields need to increase from the current level of about 5 tons per hectare to 6 tons per hectare.

Based on the observed input–output ratios in the early 2000s, an increase in grain yields by 1,000 kilograms per hectare would require an increase in irrigated areas as percentage of the total sown area of 4.4 per cent (or approximately 7 million hectares of additional irrigated area), an increase in fertilizer applications of 110 kilograms per hectare (or approximately 18 million tons of additional fertilizer applications), and an increase in agricultural machinery power of 3,400 watts per hectare (or approximately 540 million kilowatts of additional machinery power).

However, China's agricultural progress will have to overcome several major challenges in the coming decades. According to Li Yuanhua (2009), China's agricultural water demand is likely to increase from 418.6 billion cubic metres in 2010 to 463.4 billion cubic metres in 2030. On the other hand, the available water supply is expected to increase from 398 billion cubic metres in 2010 to 420 billion cubic metres in 2030 (reflecting efforts of water conservancy and recycling). Thus, there is likely to be a water deficit of 43 billion cubic metres in the agricultural sector, or about 10 per cent of the expected water demand in 2030.

Moreover, the intensive use of modern agricultural technologies (such as mechanized tilling, chemical fertilizers, and perennial irrigation) has led to widespread soil erosion. According to Ye et al. (2010), under 'business as usual', China's grain yields may decline by 11 per cent from 2005 to 2030 and by 15 per cent from 2005 to 2050, owing to soil erosion. As a result, China may face a food deficit of 14 per cent of the expected food demand by 2030 and a food deficit of 18 per cent by 2050.

Like modern agriculture in the rest of the world, contemporary Chinese agriculture is heavily dependent on fossil fuels for the powering of agricultural machines, the production of fertilizers, pesticides, and herbicides, and the operation of irrigation systems. Beyond the early twenty-first century, as the supplies of fossil fuels decline and the negative impacts of climate change become more visible, Chinese agriculture may have to confront more formidable and potentially insurmountable challenges.

Peak oil and the Chinese economy

World oil discoveries peaked in the 1960s (Heinberg, 2011: 100). Since oil is a nonrenewable resource, the peak of world oil production is likely to take place several decades after the peak of world oil discoveries.

Oil production in many individual countries has already peaked. An examination of the oil production historical data reported by the BP *Statistical Review of World Energy* suggests that out of the 48 significant oil producers listed by BP, 24 had a production level in 2010 that was at least 15 per cent below their respective historical peak. The 24 producers included some of the world's major oil producers such as the USA, Mexico, Venezuela, Norway, the UK, and Indonesia. Most of the 24 producers are likely to have permanently passed the oil production peak. In addition, 11 other producers had a production level in 2010 that was below their respective historical peak, though not by significant margins. Only 13 producers had oil production levels that had been on a clearly rising trend (BP, 2011).

Several recent studies find that world oil production may peak in the second decade of the twenty-first century. In 2009, after an extensive study that included 'a review of over 500 studies, analysis of industry databases and comparison of global supply forecasts', the government-sponsored UK Energy Research Centre published a report which concluded that there was a significant risk that world oil production could peak before 2020 (UKERC, 2009).

In 2010, the UK Industry Task Force on Peak Oil and Energy Security reported that world oil production capacity was likely to peak in 2015 (ITPOES, 2010). In an independent research report, the present author (Li, 2011) applied the 'Hubbert Linearization' technique to historical world oil production data, and concluded that world oil production could peak in 2016.[2]

Mainstream energy institutions, such as the US Energy Department and the International Energy Agency (IEA), have traditionally taken an optimistic view of the future oil supply potential. However, in the 2010 *World Energy Outlook*, the IEA admitted that the world conventional crude oil output might never regain its all-time peak of 2006 (IEA, 2010). According to the IEA, future increase in global supply of liquid fuels would have to rely upon the growth of natural gas liquids and unconventional oil (such as tar sands, oil shales, and biofuels). But independent experts point out that the growth of unconventional oil assumed by the IEA involves very high economic and environmental costs, and would require implausibly large investments in exploration and production (Heinberg, 2011: 106–113).

What has become clear is that the world's oil supply now struggles to meet the demand at a price that can support global economic growth. From 1994 to early 2004, on average, it took an increase in real oil price by $1 to bring about 1 million barrels of additional world oil supply. From late 2004 to 2011, on average, it took an increase in real oil price by $11.8 to bring about 1 million barrels of additional world oil supply. In other words, the observed relationship between the world oil supply and the world oil price has become highly 'inelastic'; that is, world oil production is no longer responsive to price changes.[3]

From 1981 to 2010, the Chinese economy grew at an average annual rate of 10.1 per cent and Chinese oil consumption grew at an average annual rate of 5.8 per cent. Thus for China, approximately each percentage point of economic growth was associated with about 0.6 per cent of oil consumption growth.[4]

For the period 2011–20, assume that the Chinese economy will grow at an average annual rate of 8 per cent. Given the observed historical relationships between economic growth and oil consumption, Chinese oil consumption needs to grow by 5 per cent a year. Assume that the real oil price rises by $11 a year from 2010 to 2020 (a rate similar to the recent historical trend), the real

[2] The 'Hubbert Linearization' technique refers to the regression technique used by Marion King Hubbert, who was the American geologist who corrected the peak of US oil production in 1970.

[3] These results are estimated using oil supply data from EIA (2012) and BP (2011).

[4] More formally, the results of simple linear regressions using data from 1981 to 2010 are as follows. Oil Consumption Growth Rate = 0.6 + 0.5 * Economic Growth Rate. Data are from BP (2011) and World Bank (2011).

oil price (measured in constant 2010 dollars) will rise from about $80 a barrel to about $190 a barrel.

Under these assumptions, China will have to spend a rising share of national income on oil imports. Spending on oil imports as a share of China's GDP is projected to rise from 2.5 per cent in 2010 to 5.2 per cent in 2020. By comparison, in 2010, US spending on oil imports amounted to 3.8 per cent of US GDP. In term of volume, Chinese oil imports may rise to 10 million barrels a day, comparable with current US oil imports. Given that China's exports growth is likely to slow down in the coming years, massive oil imports on such a level may become a major financial burden for the Chinese economy.[5]

Beyond 2020, if world oil production does pass the peak and start to decline, it is not clear how China's massive and rising demand for oil imports can be met. The competition between China and the rest of the world for the shrinking world oil supply could result in major international tensions, involving economic as well as geopolitical conflicts.

Climate stabilization and China's emission budget

Climate change is arguably the single most important global ecological crisis that could potentially threaten the survival of human civilization. The world average temperature is now about 1°C higher than pre-industrial times, and is rising at a rate of about 0.2°C per decade. If global warming rises to 2°C relative to pre-industrial times, dangerous carbon cycle feedbacks could be initiated, releasing more greenhouse gases into the atmosphere. If global warming rises to 3°C relative to pre-industrial times, the world will be warmer than any time over the past 3 million years. The sea level may eventually rise by 25 metres, Amazon rainforests may be destroyed, and billions of people may become environmental refugees. Under the scenario of a runaway global warming, most of the world's land area may cease to be inhabitable (Spratt and Sutton, 2008).

To preserve a liveable earth for future generations and to secure the long-term survival of human civilization, it is of paramount importance for the global economy to be restructured in accordance with principles consistent with a reasonable level of climate stabilization. However, because of the cumulative historical emissions of greenhouse gases, and given the constraints of the existing energy infrastructure, for all practical purposes it is no longer possible to limit global warming to no more than 2°C, despite the fact that

---

[5] China's oil imports are calculated as the difference between the projected oil consumption and the projected domestic oil production. China's domestic oil production was 4.1 million barrels a day in 2010, and is assumed to grow at a rate of 0.1 million barrels a year from 2010 to 2020.

most scientists consider this to be a threshold beyond which dangerous climate change may be unavoidable.

To limit global warming to no more than 2°C relative to the pre-industrial period, global cumulative CO_2 emissions over the twenty-first century have to be less than 1 trillion tons (IPCC, 2007). However, over the first decade of this century, global CO_2 emissions from fossil fuel consumption have already exceeded 300 billion tons (calculated using data from BP, 2011). When emissions from deforestation are included, the cumulative CO_2 emissions over the last decade are likely to have exceeded 350 billion tons. To keep the fossil fuel emissions over the rest of the century at no more than 700 billion tons (and make the obviously unrealistic assumption of zero emission from deforestation), global fossil fuel emissions will have to immediately start to decline, and decline at an annual rate of 4.5 per cent through the rest of the twenty-first century.

Even if one assumes zero global economic growth, the above rate of reduction would imply an annual reduction of emission intensity of world GDP by 4.5 per cent. There is no realistic possibility of the world economy achieving such a rapid pace of decarbonization.

If the goal is to limit global warming to no more than 3°C, then global cumulative CO_2 emissions over the twenty-first century have to be less than 2 trillion tons (IPCC, 2007). If global fossil fuels emissions immediately start to decline, the emissions need to fall at an annual rate of 1.5 per cent through the rest of the twenty-first century. If the world takes determined actions, this objective may be accomplished, but great difficulties will have to be overcome.

The global emissions budget needs to be distributed between countries by taking into account historical conditions and principles of global equity, as well as economic realities. This chapter assumes that China will be entitled to a share of 20 per cent of the global emissions budget: this roughly corresponds to China's share in the global population. If China demands a share greater than 20 per cent, the other developing countries can justifiably demand a share in the global emissions budget greater than their own population share. Given that the developing countries combined account for about 80 per cent of the world population, and the fact that Western developed countries have already emitted about 150 billion tons of CO_2 over the first decade of the century, any global emissions budget that assigns a share to the developing countries greater than their population share would leave the Western developed countries with practically no emissions allowances. Thus, the 20 per cent share may be regarded as the maximum politically acceptable limit for China's share in the global emissions budget.

Given the 20 per cent share, and assuming that the objective is to limit global warming to less than 3°C, then China's cumulative emissions budget over the twenty-first century would be 400 billion tons. However, over the first decade of the century, China has already emitted about 60 billion tons. To limit the cumulative emissions over the rest of the century to no more than 340 billion tons, China's CO_2 emissions from fossil fuels consumption need to start to decline immediately, and fall at an annual rate of 2 per cent through the rest of the twenty-first century.

Climate stabilization and economic growth

Can climate stabilization be made compatible with economic growth? The following formula explains the basic relationship between economic growth and CO_2 emissions. The formula is basically an application of the IPAT formula to the context of CO_2 emissions:

> Rate of reduction of CO_2 emissions = Rate of reduction of energy intensity of GDP + Rate of reduction of emission intensity of energy – Rate of economic growth

Thus, any reduction in energy intensity and emission intensity will contribute positively to emission reduction, but any increase in economic growth rate will subtract from the effort of emission reduction.

What would be the practical possibility of long-term improvement in energy efficiency? As is discussed in the section on economic growth and ecological sustainability, in the long run sustained energy efficiency improvement will have to be brought about through investment in new capital infrastructure and equipment. Thus, the pace of infrastructure change sets the practical limit to the pace of efficiency improvement. Supposing that, each year, an economy replaces 5 per cent of its infrastructure, and that the new infrastructure reduces energy intensity by 50 per cent relative to the old infrastructure (a heroically optimistic assumption), the energy intensity for the economy as a whole would only fall by 2.5 per cent (5% * 50% = 2.5%).

What about the reduction of emissions intensity of energy? The production of biofuels requires massive amounts of land and fresh water. China is already struggling to meet its population's rising demand for food and water, given the country's limited ecological resources (see above). Thus, biofuels are unlikely to play more than a minor role in China's future energy supply.

Other forms of decarbonized energy, such as nuclear, wind, and solar energy, can only be used to generate electricity (with the exception of limited uses of solar for direct heating). Supposing that by 2050 China achieves full decarbonization of its power generation sector (a highly optimistic scenario, given the various limitations of nuclear and renewable energies), it will then have reduced its emissions intensity of energy by about 40 per cent (emissions in the power sector currently account for about 40 per cent of the emissions from energy sources). This translates into an annual rate of reduction of emissions intensity of about 1 per cent.

Thus, using highly optimistic assumptions, China may be able to achieve a long-term energy intensity reduction rate of 2.5 per cent and a long-term emissions intensity reduction rate of 1 per cent. Since the required emissions reduction rate is 2 per cent, it follows that the maximum allowed long-term economic growth rate for the Chinese economy is only 1.5 per cent.

Figure 9.2 compares China's historical and projected CO_2 emissions from burning fossil fuels, assuming a twenty-first-century emissions budget of 400 billion tons.

The limits to growth: implications for the Chinese economy

China has achieved consistently high economic growth rates over the past three decades. However, it is widely recognized that China's existing economic model is extremely unbalanced and is economically, socially, and ecologically unsustainable. In particular, the Chinese economy has evolved to become

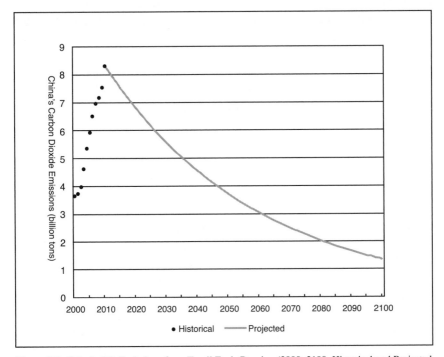

Figure 9.2. China's CO_2 Emissions from Fossil Fuels Burning (2000–2100, Historical and Projected, based on a Twenty-First-Century Emission Budget of 400 Billion Tons)
Source: BP (2011) and the author's calculations.

heavily dependent on investment. The excessive dependence on investment contributes to rapid growth in energy consumption and CO_2 emissions, which, as argued above, contribute to a global emissions trajectory leading to climate catastrophes. Moreover, excess investment leads to pervasive overcapacity that could end up causing a major economic crisis.

Currently, China's investment accounts for about 50 per cent of GDP. In the near future, if China's economic growth rate were to slow down to about 5 per cent (given the stagnation of the global economy and the constraints on the supply of key resources, such as oil and iron ore), then a reasonable investment–GDP ratio would be about 30 per cent (assume a long-term capital–output ratio of 3:1 and a depreciation rate of 5 per cent: 3 * (5% + 5%) = 30%).[6]

If China's economic growth rate were to slow down to 1.5 per cent (to be consistent with the requirement of climate stabilization), then the investment–GDP ratio needs to be adjusted to about 20 per cent (3 * (1.5% + 5%) = 19.5%).

Thus, in the medium term (or in about ten years' time), China's investment share of GDP needs to be lowered by about 20 percentage points. In the long run (or in about 20 years' time), China's investment share of GDP needs to be lowered by about 30 percentage points. However, for investment to be lowered by about 30 per cent of GDP, consumption needs to rise by about 30 per cent of GDP. Since the working class constitutes the great majority of the population, for consumption to rise by 30 per cent of GDP, the workers' total wages and social benefits need to rise by about 30 per cent of GDP. Thus, China will have to abandon its cheap labour model and manage a very large income redistribution from capital to labour by the 2030s. How could such a large income distribution be achieved? In a market-based economy, there are three possibilities. First, the government may use laws and regulations to strengthen working-class bargaining power, contributing to a higher share of wages in national income. Second, the government may raise taxes and use the taxes to increase social spending and employment. Third, if the rural surplus labour force becomes depleted, market forces may push for higher wages, bringing about a new pattern of income distribution.

Over the last few decades, the Chinese economy has already evolved into one that is dominated by capitalist private enterprises. Domestic and foreign capitalists have developed many de facto alliances with local and provincial governments. These alliances have favoured the cheap-labour regime of capital accumulation, and prevented effective labour and environmental

[6] The long-term capital–output ratio of the USA has been around 3:1. This may be considered the upper limit of China's capital–output ratio. According to basic economic growth theory, the relationship between capital–output ratio and the investment–GDP ratio is explained by the following formula: long-term capital–output ratio = (investment/GDP)/(long-term economic growth rate + depreciation rate).

regulations. There is no evidence suggesting that the general local and provincial conditions will become favourable for the implementation and enforcement of pro-labour laws and regulations in the near future.

The government could substantially increase its tax revenue as a share of GDP and use the revenue for social spending. Increased social spending could, in turn, contribute to stronger bargaining power for the working class. However, given the dominance of capitalist private enterprises and the pervasive tax evasion and corruption, there is little scope for the government to further expand its tax base.

Despite many recent media reports of wage rises in China, China's rural surplus labour force remains large, and there is no evidence suggesting that wages have started to grow more rapidly than productivity. Moreover, if in the future wages grow more rapidly than productivity for a prolonged period (given that the required redistribution is very large), this could lead to a general decline of the profit rate and precipitate a major economic crisis. So long as the Chinese economy continues to be dominated by capitalist private enterprises, it is difficult to see a smooth path for the Chinese economy to make the necessary adjustments to achieve the required rebalancing.

The above discussions suggest that the re-establishment of an economy based on public ownership of the means of production may be the precondition for the Chinese economy to evolve onto an economically, socially, and ecologically sustainable path, as well as meet its obligation of climate stabilization.

Conclusion

Over the past three decades, China has managed to achieve rapid economic growth so that it is now on the way to replace the USA as the world's largest economy. However, China's economic growth has been purchased with the heavy cost of environmental degradation and resource depletion. China's environmental impact has, by now, grown to a level that threatens to overwhelm its own ecological systems as well as contribute to global ecological catastrophes.

Using the requirements of climate stabilization and China's emission budget as the guideline, China's maximum long-run economic growth rate compatible with climate stabilization is about 1.5 per cent a year. Considering that the practically attainable rates of energy efficiency improvement and rates of energy decarbonization are likely to be less than what are assumed in the previous section, China eventually may have to adapt to a 'steady state' economy with zero economic growth to meet climate stabilization obligations and stabilize other forms of environmental impact.

However, a modern capitalist economy based on private ownership of the means of production inevitably leads to a tendency towards infinite economic growth. Unlike previous historical systems, capitalism is based on the pervasive dominance of market relations over both the economy and society. Under the pressure of market competition, private businesses are compelled to use most of their profits to pursue capital accumulation, leading to expansion of material production and consumption.

For an economy to operate stably with zero economic growth, it is necessary for the society's economic surplus to be used not for capital accumulation but for meeting the population's basic needs while maintaining ecological sustainability. This is likely to require social control over the society's economic surplus, which would only be possible with an economic system based on public ownership of the means of production.

References

BP (2011) *Statistical Review of World Energy*. http://www.bp.com/assets/bp_internet/ globalbp/globalbp_uk_english/reports_and_publications/statistical_energy_ review_2011/STAGING/local_assets/pdf/statistical_review_of_world_energy_full_ report_2011.pdf (accessed 28 November 2012).

Diamond, Jared (2005) *Collapse: How Societies Choose to Fail or Survive* (London: Penguin).

Economy, Elizabeth C. (2007) The great leap backward? *Foreign Affairs*, 86(5), September/ October, pp. 38–59.

Ehrlich, Paul R. and Holdren, John P. (1971) Impact of population growth. *Science*, 171, pp. 1212–1217.

EIA (US Energy Information Administration) (2011) International energy statistics. <http:// www.eia.gov/countries/data.cfm> (accessed 28 November 2012).

Goldsmith, Edward R. D. (2005) Farming and food production under regime of climate change, in Andrew McKillop with Sheila Newman (eds) *The Final Energy Crisis* (London: Pluto Press), pp. 56–73.

Hart-Landsberg, Martin, and Burkett, Paul (2004) China and socialism: market reform and class struggle. *Monthly Review*, 56(3), pp. 7–123.

Heinberg, Richard (2006) *The Oil Depletion Protocol: A Plan to Avert Oil Wars, Terrorism, and Economic Collapse* (Gabriola Island, BC: New Society Publishers).

Heinberg, Richard (2011) *The End of Growth: Adapting to Our New Economic Reality* (Gabriola Island, BC: New Society Publishers).

Huesemann, Michael H. (2003) The limits of technological solutions to sustainable development. *Clean Technology and Environmental Policy*, 5, pp. 21–34.

IEA (International Energy Agency) (2010) World Energy Outlook http://www.iea.org/ publications/freepublications/publication/name,27324,en.html (accessed 28 November 2012).

IPCC (Intergovernmental Panel on Climate Change) (2007) A report of Working Group III of the Intergovernmental Panel on Climate Change, ch. 3: Issues related to mitigation in the long-term context. <http://www.ipcc.ch> (accessed 28 November 2012).

ITPOES (UK Industry Task Force on Peak Oil and Energy Security) (2010) The oil crunch: a wake-up call for the UK economy. <http://peakoiltaskforce.net/wp-content/uploads/2010/02/final-report-uk-itpoes_report_the-oil-crunch_feb20101.pdf> (accessed 28 November 2012).

Li, Minqi (2009) *The Rise of China and the Demise of the Capitalist World Economy* (London: Pluto Press; New York: Monthly Review Press).

Li, Minqi (2011) Peak energy and the limits to global economic growth: annual report 2011. <http://www.econ.utah.edu/~mli/Annual%20Reports/Annual%20Report%202011.pdf> (accessed 28 November 2012).

Li, Yuanhua (2009) 21 Shiji chuqi Zhongguo shui ziyuan gongxu maodun yu duice (The dilemma of supply and demand for China's water resources in the early 21st century and the policy implications). Paper presented at the Third World Water Forum, Kyoto, Japan. <http://www.cws.net.cn/waterforum/news/3.pdf> (accessed 28 November 2012).

McCluney, Ross (2005) Renewable energy limits, in Andrew McKillop with Sheila Newman (eds) *The Final Energy Crisis* (London: Pluto Press), pp. 153–175.

Maddison, Angus (2003) *The World Economy: Historical Statistics* (Paris: Organisation for Economic Co-operation and Development).

NBS (National Bureau of Statistics of China) (2010) Statistical yearbook of China. <http://www.stats.gov.cn> (accessed 28 November 2012).

NBS (National Bureau of Statistics of China) (2011) Statistical yearbook of China. <http://www.stats.gov.cn> (accessed 28 November 2012).

Pfeiffer, Dale Allen (2006) *Eating Fossil Fuels: Oil, Food, and the Coming Crisis in Agriculture* (Gabriola Island, BC: New Society Publishers).

Rockström, Johan, Steffen, Will, Noone, Kevin, Persson, Åsa, Chapin III, F. S., Lambin, Eric, Lenton, Timothy M., Scheffer, Marten, Folke, Carl, Schellnhuber, Hans Joachim, Nykvist, Bjorn, De Wit, Cynthia A., Hughes, Terry, van der Leeuw, Sander, Rodhe, Henning, Sörlin, Sverker, Snyder, Peter K., Costanza, Robert, Svedin, Uno, Falkenmark, Malin, Karlberg, Louise, Corell, Robert W., Fabry, Victoria J., Hansen, James, Walker, Brian, Liverman, Diana, Richardson, Katherine, Crutzen, Paul, and Foley, Jonathan (2009) Planetary boundaries: exploring the safe operating space for humanity. *Ecology and Society*, 14(2), article 32. Web address: http://www.ecologyandsociety.org/vol14/iss2/art32/

Spratt, David and Sutton, Philip (2008) Climate code red: the case for a sustainability emergency. <http://www.climatecodered.net> (accessed 28 November 2012).

UKERC (UK Energy Research Centre) (2009) Global oil depletion: an assessment of the evidence for a near-term in global oil production. <http://www.ukerc.ac.uk/support/tiki-index.php?page=Global+Oil+Depletion> (accessed 28 November 2012).

Wen, Dale and Li, Minqi (2006) China: hyper-development and environmental crisis, in Leo Panitch and Colin Leys (eds), *Socialist Register 2007: Coming to Terms with Nature* (New York: Monthly Review Press), pp. 130–146.

World Bank (2011) World development indicators. <http://databank.worldbank.org> (accessed 1 October 2012).

WWF (World Wide Fund for Nature) (2010) China ecological footprint report 2010. <http://www.footprintnetwork.org/images/uploads/China_Ecological_Footprint_Report_2010.pdf> (accessed 28 November 2012).

Ye, Liming, Yang, Jun, Verdoodt, Ann, Moussadek, Rachit, and Van Ransk, Eric (2010) China's food security threatened by soil degradation and biofuels production. Paper presented at the 19th World Congress of Soil Science, Soil Solutions for A Changing World, Brisbane, Australia, 1–6 August 2010. <http://www.iuss.org/19th%20WCSS/Symposium/pdf/1237.pdf> (accessed 28 November 2012).

10

Environment and Development in India

S. RAVI RAJAN

THE PURPOSE OF THIS CHAPTER is to explore some of the key debates about environment and development in India. It begins by summarizing some of the country's key sustainability indicators. It then examines the natural resource management sector, focusing on forestry and irrigation. Finally, it explores the threats posed by environmental risks of technological origin—by considering five high-profile cases—the Bhopal gas disaster of 1984; the controversy over genetically modified organisms (GMOs); the seismicity concerns of the Tehri Dam; the handling of pollution and transportation policy in New Delhi; and the debate on nuclear safety.

Introduction

The environmental debate in India has, since independence, grappled with big questions, such as the relationship between the environment and human rights; the teleology of development; and the role of the environment in governance. The purpose of this chapter is to explore the two sectors—natural resource management and environmental risks—that have dominated the debate. After a brief context-setting section that defines some of the key trends pertaining to the country's ecological footprint, the chapter examines the natural resource management sector. The focus here is on forestry and irrigation, and the approach that of a historical overview, because many of the current conflicts and controversies are legacies of the colonial period. The rest of the chapter is devoted to some of the critical issues relating to technological risks, and adopts a case study approach, using iconic cases to illustrate particular issues. The cases are: a) the Bhopal gas disaster of 1984; b) the controversy over genetically modified organisms (GMOs); c) the seismicity concerns of the Tehri Dam; d) the handling of pollution and transportation policy in New Delhi; and e) the debate on nuclear safety.

The background

Despite being largely ignored in mainstream Indian economic and political discourse, the environment today poses one of the most potent threats to development and human well-being. The numbers and trends are clear and daunting. Consider the statistics on sustainability. Although the Indian economy, as well as its industrial sector, has grown at a lesser rate than China, and although its ecological footprint is less than that of its northern neighbour, it ranks third, after China and the USA, in its total demand on natural resources (CII, 2008). According to the Confederation of Indian Industry and the Global Footprint Network, 'India represents approximately 6 per cent of the world's Ecological Footprint, 4 per cent of the world's bio-capacity, and 17 per cent of the world's population' (CII, 2008). Moreover, the country's ostensibly low ecological footprint—India ranks 125th among 152 countries—is explicable by the fact that its population has doubled since 1961. With the country's headcount expected to be 1.7 billion by 2050, it does not take a diehard Malthusian to be concerned about the consequences of the fact that the country's domestic supply of life-sustaining resources is simply not adequate to meet the basic needs of its people.

According to the Government of India's own data, there are many other worrying trends (GOI, 2009). India faces a serious problem of species extinctions. It is a mega-diverse country, with 7–8 per cent of the recorded species of the world, and over 45,000 species of plants and 91,000 species of animals, in only 2.4 per cent of the planet's land area. Yet, no less than 172, or 2.9 per cent, of the International Union for Conservation of Nature (IUCN)—designated threatened species face extinction in India, with the numbers and percentages growing by the day. Further, erosion has other dark meanings. Approximately 130 million hectares of land, accounting for 45 per cent of the total geographical area, are afflicted with serious soil erosion. Erosion rates range from 5–20 tons per hectare, sometimes going up to 100 tons per hectare. Permanently degraded lands are growing at an annual rate of 6 million hectares. India also faces a severe and debilitating water supply crisis. If the assumption that the population will stabilize at around 1,640 million by the year 2050 is true, the country faces a significant gross per capita water availability decline—from 1,829 cubic metres per year in 2001 to as low as 1,140 cubic metres per year in 2050. Worse, estimates of total water availability by the year 2050 indicate that demand will be significantly less than projected potential supply (GOI, 2009).

The trends on pollution are equally damning. Per-hectare consumption of fertilisers has increased from 69.8 kilograms in 1991–92 to 113.3 kg in 2006–07, at an average rate of 3.3 per cent, with concomitant damage to the land because of overuse. Water sources across the country are increasingly poisoned (GOI, 2009). Groundwater contamination, for example, poses a huge problem, with geogenic (soil) contaminants, including salinity, iron, fluoride, and arsenic, widespread in over 200 districts spread across 19 states. Moreover, virtually all India's 14 major river systems are heavily polluted, on account of more than 50 million cubic metres of untreated sewage being discharged into them each year. Domestic waste by itself is a significant source of this pollution—the 22 largest cities produce over 7.267 million litres of domestic wastewater per day, of which almost 20 per cent is untreated. Nearly 15 per cent of the urban and 20 per cent of the rural population do not as yet have access to safe drinking water; and the numbers with access to adequate sanitation facilities is even lower. Air pollution presents a more positive trend, with fewer premature deaths in cities across the country as a result of the success of government measures. However, the estimated annual economic cost of damage to public health from increased air pollution, for 50 cities with a total population of 110 million, reached US \$3 billion in 2004 (GOI, 2009).

The unfolding reality of climate change presents a spectre of future shocks. Here are some long-term scenarios generated by the Ministry of Environment and Forests of the Government of India (GOI, 2009):

1. By the 2050s, India will experience a decline in summer rainfall, which accounts for almost 70 per cent of the total annual rainfall and is crucial to agriculture.
2. Some of the glaciers in the Himalayas are receding at an average rate of 10–15 metres per year. Himalayan glaciers could disappear within 50 years because of climate change, exposing an estimated 500 million people to the threat of a severe water scarcity.
3. Food production in India is still considerably dependent on rainfall. However, its quantity and distribution are highly variable, spatially and temporally. In the past 50 years, there have been about 15 major droughts, which adversely affected the productivity of rain-fed crops in drought years. There are few, if any, options of alternative livelihoods, and for millions of small and marginal farmers in the rain-fed agricultural region widespread poverty is both real and threatening.
4. Shifts in forest boundaries, changes in species assemblages or forest types, and changes in net primary productivity are possible, as is loss or change in biodiversity. Enhanced levels of CO_2 are projected to alter the primary productivity of ecosystems in more than 75 per cent of the forest area. About 70 per cent of the vegetation in India is likely to find itself less than optimally adapted to its existing location, some in a span as short as the next 50 years. About 15–40 per cent of species will face extinction, even if the warming amounts to barely 2°C above pre-industrial levels; and the most threatened flood plains in the world will be in South Asia.

5. Climate change could potentially engender a rise in sea level. An increase of 1 metre in sea level is projected to displace approximately 7.1 million people in India, and destroy about 5,764 square kilometres of land and 4,200 kilometres of roads.
6. Current government expenditure on adaptation to climate variability is already estimated to exceed 2 per cent of the GDP, with agriculture, water resources, health and sanitation, forests, coastal zone infrastructure, and extreme weather events being specific areas of concern.

As with virtually every other sector in India, environmental statistics and trends serve to indicate bigger and more fundamental problems. The lowest common denominator in environmental governance in India is, to adapt a phrase coined by Ernst Friedrich, the nineteenth-century German student of the expanding American frontier, *raubwirtschaft*, or the economy of plunder (Friedrich, 1904). Without doubt, the pillage of the Indian environment is a sad illustration of the kleptocratic tendencies in its economy and society, wherein opportunism and free enterprise in theft, and the capture of the state by self-serving interests at virtually every level—from a village headman to a large multinational corporation—is an unfortunate reality (Global Integrity, 2011). The fact that there is even a prospect of formulating and implementing public policy, and building institutions that run according to the rule of law, and are sensitive and accountable to the needs of the common Indian, is testimony to the untiring efforts of individuals, groups, and movements across the spectrum from the state to civil society (India Together, 2013).

The extent of corruption and the role of civil society in combating it, are subjects of chapters by other contributors to this volume. Rather than add an environmental dimension to these accounts, this chapter focuses on describing two of the most enduring of the many environmental problems in India. The first of these concerns the management of critical natural resources—forestry and irrigation. These two sectors have institutional origins and legacies that stem from the colonial era. They are examples of the fact that formal decolonization did not mark an end to what some scholars have described as environmental imperialism; and they also illustrate the tensions between nationalist development policies and the often divergent needs of citizens and subjects (Guha, 1988). They further serve to show how the most well-funded of government schemes can be hijacked to benefit a few. Moreover, they are examples of the persistence, in the post-colonial period, of colonial memes in agencies such as forestry, public works, and irrigation bureaucracies. Last but by no means least, they are also illustrative of the vibrancy of civil society, and the myriad attempts at forging alternatives in theory and practice.

Next, the chapter examines the issue of environmental risks of technological origin—a central issue as the Indian economy industrializes.

The problem of risk poses a number of fundamental questions relating to the capacity of the state to govern, and the efficacy of state expertise. Risk also raises questions about democracy; about how the state interacts with its citizens on basic decisions such as personal safety. Crucially, it also serves to explore how the state understands and calibrates the price of life of the average Indian, frames development choices, and chooses between competing priorities.

The state of nature

From the colonial period onward, governments in India have made significant investments in developing infrastructures to harness critical natural resources such as forests and water. However, the manner in which these investments were made engendered conflicts among various stakeholders, including industry, governments—from municipal to state and central (federal) levels—a wide range of community interests, and national and transnational environmentalists. Environmental politics in India has therefore been about conflicting resource-use priorities.

Given that the history of environmental conflicts dates back to the colonial period, it is instructive to start with a brief historical background. In the case of forestry, the British established a regime of forest management modelled on a system developed in Continental Europe during the eighteenth and nineteenth centuries. The aim of this regime was to serve the economic and infrastructural needs of the state. It therefore emphasized scientific management, but largely ignored the needs and, in many cases, abrogated the historic resource rights of local populations (Rajan, 2006). From the end of the nineteenth century, until well after independence, forest rights were redefined and landscapes transformed throughout the Indian subcontinent. Forest revenue yields rose and timber business elites developed, at the cost of livelihoods of local people denied rights to forest usufruct. Meanwhile, deforestation reduced topsoil quality, and changed water flow and local agro-ecologies (Gadgil, Prasad, and Ali, 1983).

Similarly, irrigation infrastructures such as canal building were established by the colonial state to increase agrarian productivity and widen the yield and reach of taxation. As a consequence of these investments, yields expanded, and, according to some estimates, per capita output of crops increased by nearly 45 per cent between 1891 and 1921 (Whitcombe, 2005). However, a vast authoritarian bureaucracy reaching down to village level used forced labour to maintain the canal network, and undertook ruthless water fee recovery on all lands deemed to be irrigated. It thereby encouraged farmers to grow cash crops to generate cash (Hardiman, 2002: 114), exacerbating economic inequities by privileging those who could afford the service payments—water rates for the use of canals. It also engendered widespread corruption. Moreover, the system caused a number of ecological problems such as salinity, and many areas of Punjab, once known for its good, well-watered soils, are today saline deserts, with alkaline and unproductive lands. The system also neglected, and in some cases destroyed, traditional water systems where they did not serve the revenue needs of the colonial state (D'Souza, 2006).

The dynamics of these biosocial processes did not change much until the late 1960s. Ignited by concerns for social justice, the new political era included the hitherto ignored politically neutral topics such as the environment, and fundamental issues of human rights and constitutionality (Hardiman, 2004). In the case of forestry, the first wave of change came with the Chipko movement in the Himalayas. Chipko was part of a wider critical interrogation of the fundamentals of development. A spate of experimentation followed, including attempts to build new management hybrids involving both the state forest departments and local communities (Khare et al., 2000). In a similar vein, there were important studies about the economic viability of devolving forest management to local communities and firms (Somanathan, Prabhakar, and Mehta, 2009). Many scholars and practitioners also focused their attention on inclusiveness. An important result of this emphasis was a burgeoning literature on gender, and in particular on the morbid interface between deforestation, increasing female workload and labour, and decreasing access for girls and women to education, nutrition, and community (Agarwal, 1992, 1997a, 1997b, 2001). Moreover, considerable attention was paid to understanding biodiversity in landscape terms, and building regimes that would preserve biological diversity, while at the same time creating productive agro-ecosystems (Negi, 1996). The result of these efforts has not been revolutionary. However, the national understanding and discourse on forests has shifted. In many states with forest lands, budgetary allocations indicate newer policies that emphasize inclusiveness as well as ecological integrity. There has also been an emergence of research institutions studying forest issues at the national as well as state and regional levels.

In the case of irrigation, a major rethink of state policy began soon after independence, with waterworks being seen as public goods (Shah, 2010). Irrigation charges were drastically reduced, and significant public funds were expended on irrigation. More than 400 large dams were built, making India the third largest dam builder in the world, after the USA and China. However, despite a progressive policy agenda, significant problems began to emerge. First, the canal systems built under the colonial regime were poorly maintained, necessitating large investments periodically to rebuild them (Shah, 2010). Second, unlike forestry, where the resource was managed by one central agency, irrigation water often existed in private or communal lands, with the result that a 'scavenging irrigation economy' was born, with a proliferation of wells (initially traditional and artisanal, but soon tube-wells, riding on subsidized electricity) displacing traditional lakes, and, indeed, medium and major systems (Shah, 2010). Third, the rapid spread of tube-wells meant the depletion of groundwater—and severe threats to hydrological systems (Dubash, 2002; Shah, 2010). The threat is particularly severe in peninsular India, which receives barely 100 hours of rainfall a year. Compounding these problems is the huge human cost of large dams, which, according to some estimates, resulted in at least 40 million people being displaced during the past 60 years (and of whom less than a quarter have been resettled) (Anon., 2005).

As with the case of forestry, there is also a vibrant debate, scholarly work, and policy experimentation. National water policy has been debated continuously over the past 30 years, and has raised a wide swathe of issues. These range from integrated river-basin-level approaches, to water planning and management, to debates about the efficacy of community-level organizations, and the best ways to build hybrid systems that meet the needs of various stakeholders while preserving long-term supply. There has also been vibrant debate about equity and rights in access to water resources; democracy and participation; inter-state conflict management; groundwater regulation; and pollution, among a host of issues (Iyer, 2003).

The state of risk

Like much of the world today, national security frames the public discourse on risk in India. However, like the rest of the world, the statistics on mortality and morbidity indicate a growing trend correlating human catastrophes with environmental changes. Some events, such as the 1984 gas tragedy in Bhopal, take thousands of lives, and seemingly occur without warning. Other, more chronic problems, such as air and water pollution, fester, causing havoc for health and the environment over prolonged periods of time. For example, according to the World Health Organization's Global Burden of Disease Report for 2010 (WHO, 2011), air pollution is the fifth leading cause of death in India, with 620,000 premature deaths in 2010, representing a sixfold increase since 2000 (CSE WHO, 2013). Yet other issues lurk in the background, dormant, waiting for a triggering event to vault them into headline news. They obviously include nuclear plants, which are slated to be a growing component of the energy sector. They also include large dams, which in some cases, such as when sited in seismic regions, threaten large populations; and emerging technologies, such as GMOs and nanotechnologies.

One productive way with which to analyse such trends has been offered by recent anthropological studies, which argue that hazardous agents or events in themselves do not inevitably result in disasters. Rather, 'a disaster becomes unavoidable in the context of a historically produced pattern of vulnerability' (Oliver-Smith, 1996). This section explores some of the iconic events related to risk and disaster in India's recent history by elaborating upon the histories of vulnerability that produced them. It begins with the Bhopal gas disaster. The gas spill continues, even three decades later, to be illustrative of how the Indian state and society at large value the life of an average Indian. It also serves as an example of the absence of expertise to govern complex environmental risks. Next, three events are explored that did not result in mass death and yet made significant news: a) the seismic risks posed by the Tehri Dam; b) the debate about how to mitigate vehicular air pollution in Delhi, leading to controversy over the adoption of compressed natural gas (CNG) in public transportation; and c) the continuing public controversy over GMOs. The reason for the choice of these three cases is that they serve well to understand the nature of environmental governance in India, especially in instances of scientific uncertainty about risk. Last, but by no means least, we look briefly at some of the issues underlying the nuclear safety debate.

The case of Bhopal

On the night of 2–3 December 1984, an explosion at gas tanks storing methyl isocyanate at the Union Carbide India Limited (UCIL) pesticide plant in Bhopal immediately killed between 2,259 and 3,787 people, and maimed about half a million others and their progeny (M.P. Government; Varma and Varma, 2005). The Bhopal gas disaster, as this iconic event has since been known, raised a host of issues about contemporary India's capacity to govern risks. This section will address two of these—political economy and accountability; and expertise and capacity.

By the time of the 1984 accident, Bhopal city had become a company town, with power and favour flowing from UCIL, the Indian subsidiary of Union Carbide Corporation (UCC), which took many of the key design decisions that precipitated the event (Chouhan, 2004). The Indian subsidiary, perhaps with the knowledge of the parent company, put in place an operational culture characterized by chronic lax maintenance, a low number of supervisory employees, and inadequate safety training, with the result that the plant was constantly plagued by accidents and mishaps (Jones, n.d.; Chouhan, 2005). Crucially, the corporate response after the disaster, by both UCIL and UCC, was to look after its own economic interests rather than adopt a strategy of corporate citizenship. The company hired top public relations firms, lobbied governments, and embarked upon strong divestment strategies, culminating first in record profits and then in the sale of the company to Dow Chemicals. However, the victims were neither rehabilitated nor adequately compensated

(Rajan, 1999). The perpetrators of the world's worst industrial accident got away with little penalty or consequence, while the victims received no favour or succour.

The Bhopal gas tragedy also raised a more fundamental question—of the capacity of the state to respond adequately to complex, multifaceted issues such as technological disasters. It has been widely reported that the Indian state, at both the central and state levels, failed to respond adequately (CSE, 1985). Elsewhere, I have argued at length that this inadequacy raises the broader problem of 'missing expertise' (Rajan, 2002). Three types of such absences can be identified. The first is 'contingent expertise'—the capacity to respond immediately and effectively to a potential hazard, including warning systems, and communication and evacuation procedures. Clearly, by most accounts, the state largely failed to demonstrate much by way of contingent expertise at Bhopal. The second type of missing expertise, 'conceptual expertise', addresses the innovation needed to respond adequately to unfolding novel situations. Most disasters manifest as sudden, catastrophic events. Although devastating by nature, their period of intensity is short. Bhopal, however, soon became a chronic event, affecting a large community over months, years, and decades. Rehabilitation in Bhopal therefore demanded a wide range of expertise, over and beyond the contingent. The state government did not, however, possess this kind of expertise, and approached social and economic rehabilitation as if it were a natural disaster, not a chronic and complex process. As the months rolled into years, and thence to decades, all that the victims received was a series of transplanted developmental schemes and poverty alleviation programmes. The capacity to conceptually plan a long-term recovery programme was missing. Last, but by no means least, the third kind of missing expertise is 'contextual'. This refers to the state's ability to observe how their policies and schemes play out in real societal and cultural contexts, and troubleshoot on that basis. For example, in Bhopal, eligibility for rehabilitation required the certification of victims, for which certain sets of documents were needed but were not always present. The result was the emergence of a parallel economy of false documents and bribery. State officials were presented with a trade-off—of tolerating, and thereby participating in, this parallel economy, or creating simpler rules that risked freeriders at the expense of making life easier for the majority of the victims (Rajan, 2002). The state machinery did not have the ability or the expertise to recognize or respond to such tragic choices (Calabresi and Bobbitt, 1978).

The state of risk governance in contemporary India

Even while Bhopal remains an iconic case study in its inability to govern a growing infrastructure that produces toxic chemicals, many new challenges concerning risk management have emerged. Crucial among them is the question of how to arbitrate between differing claims about risk, especially in contexts in which there is either inadequate conclusive scientific data or disagreement among experts, or indeed a political or institutional process that does not easily allow for such resolutions. The issues at stake can be understood by considering three cases. The first of these is that of the Tehri Dam—a massive multipurpose power project located in the state of Uttarakhand in India, the first phase of which was completed in 2006. Tehri is a component of a multipurpose river valley project, and the main dam at Tehri is the eighth tallest in the world. It is slated to generate 2,400 megawatts of electricity, besides irrigating 270,000 hectares of land, and supplying 270 million gallons of drinking water per year to industrialized cities in the surrounding states, including 500 cubic feet per second to the national capital, New Delhi. By mid-2006, when the dam was commissioned, more than US $1 billion had been spent on its construction. (Fink, 2000).

The Tehri Dam has been controversial for two broad reasons. First, like others, it submerged large areas of land and forced approximately 85,600 families to relocate against their will (Dogra, 1992). Second, it is sited in the Central Himalayan Seismic Gap, a major geologic fault zone, and barely 50 kilometres from the epicentre of a magnitude 6.8 earthquake in October 1991 (Brune, 1993). Third, the siltation rates used in calculating the long-term costs of the dam were disputed (Govardhan, 1993). Many stakeholders have been embroiled in these debates, ranging from the Indian central government to local NGOs (INTACH, 1987; Paranjpye, 1988; Bandyopadhyay, 1992). The result was that the authority of a sequence of expert committees, constituted by the central and state governments as well as courts, was questioned, and their scientific validity publicly disputed. The case in the Indian Supreme Court was therefore mired in controversy, and although the court ruled in favour of constructing the dam, the controversy was not closed by science, but furthered by it.

Another case illustrative of controversies over how to arbitrate between different claims of risk is that of the adoption of CNG in Delhi. Against the backdrop of rising vehicular air pollution, and the consequent public health epidemic, the Indian government constituted the Environmental Pollution (Prevention and Control) Authority for the National Capital Region of India in 1998. This was a statutory authority, in that its directions were binding on public policy. One of its key recommendations was the conversion of public transport vehicles to CNG, a recommendation that the Supreme Court of India accepted on 28 July 1998. However, after a couple of years, this ruling was contested by another committee of experts appointed by the Government of India, which refused to endorse the single fuel principle, and instead advocated a more complex system involving multiple fuel mixes and a range of other measures. A controversy soon erupted. However, despite the contradictions between the respective committees, the Supreme Court chose to endorse the first one, and in doing so questioned the motivations of the second. Notably, though, the Supreme Court cherrypicked and arbitrated between conflicting philosophical perspectives on the efficacy of particular technological interventions over others (Bell, Mathur, and Narain, 2004; Mathur and Narain, 2004; Mathur, 2005; Narain and Bell, 2006; Véron, 2006; Sahu, 2008; Gauri, 2009).

Yet another public controversy that has, among other things, raised questions about the institutional capacity within the Indian governing and regulatory apparatus to arbitrate amid scientific controversy concerns GMOs. The regulatory structure for GMOs adopted by the Government of India consists of: a) Rules (1989) under the Environment Protection Act (EPA) (1986) and b) the Seed Policy (2002). Together, they mandate a regulatory regime of safeguards that include prerelease testing following a US EPA precedent, and prescribe punitive action for any violation and noncompliance. Despite what appears, at first glance, to be a comprehensive regulatory structure, critics rejected governmental claims about environmental and health safety of GM crops and foods. They also raised a host of questions concerning biosafety, consequent to the import of GM foods into India. Further, they claimed that there was little transparency and participatory decision-making in the governance of GM technology in India. A particular focus in the Indian GM debate was Bt (Bacillus thuringiensis) cotton, which was formally released in 2002. The regulatory approval process for Bt cotton in India was highly contested, and the struggles were not just about science but encompassed values, world views, political economic gradients, and institutional processes and procedures. Critically, however, while many environmental activists stood opposed to Bt cotton, many farmers adopted it illicitly, thereby subverting the regulatory process and shortcircuiting public debate (Bharathan, 2000; Scoones, 2003, 2006; Lianchawii, 2005; Naik et al., 2005; Qaim et al., 2006; Raju, 2007; Gruère and Mehta-Bhatt, 2008; Laurie, 2008; Herring, 2009; Subramanian and Qaim, 2010).

Three conclusions can be drawn from the case studies described briefly above. First, the debate about the regulation of environmental risks in India reflects broader ideological arguments about development priorities. Second, the idea of a science-based policy process has, thus far, spluttered in India despite attempts, in a number of instances, to define clear procedures. Unable to parse through scientific evidence and build public policy on the basis of an understanding of the quality and quantity of data, especially in conditions of complexity and uncertainty, when scientific claims are contested, courts and other institutions in India appear to arbitrarily pick and choose. Third, there is, as yet, little by way of investment in analytics that might help address these crucial gaps. For example, the data infrastructure is good in patches, especially as it pertains to air pollution and, to a lesser degree, water pollution; but not very good in others, such as GMOs, on which risk-related data are barely collected, and where there is virtually nothing by way of a systematic monitoring of risks, either at the ecosystem and landscape level, or on human health. Crucially, there is no professional community of any significance specializing in serious risk management, and few research institutions of international renown that attempt systematic inter- and multidisciplinary scientific research, and have the analytical capacity to prioritize or resolve conflicting values.

The case of nuclear energy raises the stakes even further. Traditionally, the nuclear debate in India, as elsewhere, has revolved around three tectonic fault lines: safety, storage, and costs. Safety statistics are not easily forthcoming, but the consensus among those who study the Indian nuclear programme is that there have been too many safety lapses, including several instances of radiation leakage, to sustain the government's claim that it is safe and clean (Heritage, 1996; Ramana and Reddy, 2003; Raj, Prasad, and Bansal, 2006; Ramana, 2006; Mathai, 2013). India also faces a growing problem of how to store high-level radioactive waste, and, in the long run, of how to police the waste sites intergenerationally and ensure that they do not contaminate people and environments decades or centuries later (Makhijani, Hu, and Yih, 2000; Ramana, Thomas, and Varughese, 2001; Firm, 2008). Turning to costs, it is by no means obvious that nuclear power is either cheap or affordable in India. Moreover, most cost estimates exclude those of safety, storage, and decommissioning (Heritage, 1996; Grimston, 1997; Ramana and Reddy, 2003; Ramana, D'Sa, and Reddy, 2005; Ramana, 2007; Mathai, 2013). In recent times, the three traditional fault lines that shape the nuclear debate have been joined, in India, by movements for transparency and accountability. After five decades, in which India's atomic energy establishment took decisions without parliamentary or public scrutiny, a raft of public controversies in recent times has forced the debate into politics that pit central and state governments against each other, and thereby opened up many fissures that break the bubble of official consensus on nuclear energy policy. These controversies also raise serious questions about the capacity of the state, and especially of the atomic energy establishment, to respond adequately to the threat of nuclear accidents (Grimston, 1997; Gopalakrishnan, 1999; Anon., 2011; Bidwai, 2011; Ghate, Takwale, and Dhole, 2011; Abraham, 2012; Sovacool and Valentine, 2012).

The literature on risk in the context of complex systems elsewhere in the world highlights three issues to bear in mind while considering the question of the capacity of states to respond adequately to nuclear safety challenges (Smith and Wynne, 1989; Wynne, 1989, 2010, 2012; Irwin and Wynne, 2004; Leach, Scoones, and Wynne, 2005; Jasanoff, 2011). First, there is the question of the ability of a given state to initiate effective interdisciplinary and interagency research on risk—especially taking into consideration local cultural conditions about decision-making, behaviour, and authority. The second issue concerns the capacity of the institutions that constitute the nuclear regulatory establishment—with management structures based on established hierarchies and decision-making structures—to respond to rapidly changing scenarios far away from decision-making centres. Where there are high public and environmental safety stakes, the design of management systems that enable groups within organizations to interact and collaborate becomes crucial. More capable regimes on the world stage have the ability to incorporate recalcitrant information, incorporate intelligent crowdsourcing, and integrate whistleblowing and alternative ideas and analytical perspectives into their decision-making iterative churn.

Last but no means least, another critical facet in building regimes of safety concern the communications and interactions between atomic agencies and plants, and the communities in which they are located. Here, the manner in which nuclear establishments treat the people who live near nuclear plants (as partners or adversaries) becomes important, for it is crucial that communities near nuclear facilities understand warning alarms, and behave appropriately when, for example, evacuation procedures are necessitated. Prerequisites for this kind of behaviour, however, are trust, transparency, and consultation. Sadly, the history of interactions between atomic energy experts and laypeople worldwide is full of examples of mistrust and miscommunications. In the case of the Sellafield nuclear plant in the UK, there was a complete breakdown of trust on the part of farmers and shepherds, stemming from their perception that the atomic agency was not squaring up with the truth and not consulting them adequately (Wynne, 1989). Likewise, in Chernobyl, local residents openly flouted restrictions, and moved back to their old (and highly contaminated) residences within a year of the disaster, because of their distrust of the experts (Havenaar et al., 2003).

It is evident that India is challenged in each of these dimensions. To begin with, there are entrenched institutional structures in India with prejudices about the superiority of the so-called 'hard' sciences that are instilled from high school. Such memes challenge attempts at building institutions that bridge multiple disciplinary cultures. Moreover, the nuclear establishment is a closed door club, and often adopts a public posture that defies common sense about safety. For example, a report in the *Economic Times* (15 March 2011) quoted S. K. Jain, the Chairman and Managing Director of the Nuclear Power Corporation, as saying: 'There is no nuclear accident or incident in Japan's Fukushima plants. It is a well planned emergency preparedness programme which the nuclear operators of the Tokyo Electric Power Company are carrying out to contain the residual heat after the plants had an automatic shutdown following a major earthquake.' Equally incredible was a quote in the same news report, this time attributed to Dr Srikumar Banerjee, the Chairman of the Atomic Energy Commission, who was quoted as saying: 'Because of the unprecedented Tsunami, the external power was unavailable for the emergency diesel generators to take over ... during the process the pressure was building up in the reactor which had to be released in a phased manner, that resulted in the exothermic reaction due to hydrogen generation ... It was purely a chemical reaction and not a nuclear emergency as described by some section of media.' Such comments obviously do not encourage public trust. The claims in the first quote, for example, do not square with the rest of the information that was in the public domain at that time, and in the very newspaper that printed these statements. In contrast, the second quote indicates that the official does not fully grasp the fact that, in complex systems, it is precisely the unexpected breaching of the thin boundaries between chemical and nuclear systems that precipitate catastrophes.

Obviously, it is not responsible to generalize about the nuclear energy establishment on the basis of one or two such data points, especially given that they are based on newspaper sources. However, statements made in public attain the status of social facts, which can be the basis for either public trust or mistrust—for the simple reason that the public has very little third-party verification regarding the safety status of India's nuclear plants. Experts might argue that laypeople are wrong to distrust them, but they cannot deny that they are right to worry, given the record of safety in other industries, the lack of civic and political accountability, and the history of neglect by state and central governments when catastrophes have hit. Equally important, trust is not achieved when democratic expressions of fear and concern are dealt with in a heavyhanded manner, as was recently witnessed in demonstrations at sites such as Jaitapur (Bidwai et al., 2011). It is this kind of history that has spawned a culture of mistrust, and the lack of a route for public participation has only served to exacerbate this problem, and thereby an inability to foster critical conversations.

Conclusions

To summarize the argument, the debate about forestry and irrigation is about priorities—on how to deliver development to India's millions. It is also about the collateral damage—ranging from displacement to ecological degradation—brought about by the resource management regimes established by the state over a 100-year period. While the political process is sometimes up to the task of at least recognizing the rights and equity claims of sections of the citizenry, it has largely failed to grapple with ecological degradation—despite the ink, the protests, and the now mandatory platitudes. As for risk, the challenge is not just politics and political economy but expertise—especially the seeming lack of state capacity to regulate and manage the various challenges. In the case of Bhopal, the missing expertise involved the failure to respond to a contingency, the inability to conceive a long-term rehabilitation strategy, and the lack of any measure to troubleshoot in context and in situ. The cases of Tehri, Delhi air pollution, and GMOs indicate an inability, across institutional actors, to understand the scientific basis of complexity and uncertainty in risk assessments, and, in contexts where scientific claims are contested, to resolve disputes in a non-arbitrary manner. Last but not least, the nuclear case illustrates the huge schism that exists between official expertise and the democratic aspirations of local populations who fear that their lives are endangered. It also raises questions about the accountability of officials and publicly funded institutions.

Acknowledgements

I am extremely grateful to Professors Barbara Harriss-White and Delia Davin for inviting me to the conference; for their patience and encouragement; and for their careful and thoughtful editorial work. Any mistakes herein are entirely mine.

References

Abraham, I. (2012) Geopolitics and biopolitics in India's high natural background radiation zone. *Science, Technology and Society*, 17(1), pp. 105–122.

Agarwal, B. (1992) The gender and environment debate: lessons from India. *Feminist Studies*, 18(1), pp. 119–158.

Agarwal, B. (1997a) Environmental action, gender equity and women's participation. *Development and Change*, 28(1), pp. 1–44.

Agarwal, B. (1997b) Gender, environment, and poverty interlinks: regional variations and temporal shifts in rural India, 1971–1991. *World Development*, 25(1), pp. 23–52.

Agarwal, B. (2001) Participatory exclusions, community forestry, and gender: an analysis for South Asia and a conceptual framework. *World Development*, 29(10), pp. 1623–1648.

Anon. (2005) Large dam projects and displacement in India. <http://www.sandrp.in/dams/Displac_largedams.pdf> (accessed 18 February 2013).

Bandyopadhyay, J. (1992) Sustainability and survival in the mountain context. *Ambio*, 21(4), June, pp. 297–302.

Bell, R. G., Mathur, K., and Narain, U. (2004) Clearing the air: how Delhi broke the logjam on air quality reforms. *Environment*, 46(3), pp. 22–39.

Bharathan, G. (2000) Bt-cotton in India: anatomy of a controversy. *Current Science*, 79 (8), 25 October, pp. 1067–1075.

Bidwai, Praful (2011) People vs nuclear power in Jaitapur, Maharashtra. *Economic and Political Weekly*, 46(8), 19 February, pp. 10–14.

Bidwai, Praful, Singh, Bhasha, Shukla, S. P., Patil, Vaishali, and Ellias, Rafeeq (2011) Courting nuclear disaster in Maharashtra: why the Jaitapur project must be scrapped, Coalition for Nuclear Disarmament and Peace (CNDP). <http://www.sacw.net/article1914.html> (accessed 13 February 2013).

Brune, J. N. (1993) The seismic hazard at Tehri Dam. *Tectonophysics*, 218, pp. 218–286.

Calabresi, G. and Bobbitt, P. (1978) *Tragic Choices* (New York: Norton).

Chouhan, T. R. (2004) *Bhopal—The Inside Story*, 2nd edn (Goa, India: Other India Press; New York: The Apex Press).

Chouhan, T. R. (2005) The unfolding of Bhopal disaster. *Journal of Loss Prevention in the Process Industries*, 18(4–6), pp. 205–208.

CII (Confederation of Indian Industry) (2008) India's ecological footprint: a business perspective, Global Footprint Network and Confederation of Indian Industry. <http://www.footprintnetwork.org/download.php?id=504> (accessed 13 February 2013).

CSE (Centre for Science and Environment) (1985) *The State of India's Environment, 1984–85* (New Delhi, Centre for Science and the Environment).

CSE WHO (Centre for Science and Environment; World Health Organization) (2013) Air pollution is now the fifth largest killer in India, says newly released findings of global burden of disease report. <http://www.cseindia.org/category/thesaurus/global-burden-disease-gbd> (accessed 13 February 2013).

D'Souza, R. (2006) Water in British India: the making of a 'colonial hydrology'. *History Compass*, 4(4), pp. 621–628.

Dogra, B. (1992) *Forests, Dams, and Survival in Tehri Garhwal* (New Delhi: Forest Publishing).

Dubash, N. K. (2002) *Tubewell Capitalism* (New York: Oxford University Press).

Fink, A. K. (2000) Tehri hydro power complex on the Bhagirathi river in India. *Hydrotechnical Construction*, 34(8/9), pp. 479–484.

Firm (Contemporary News and Features (Firm)) (2008) *India's Nuclear Debate: Indo–U.S. Civil Nuclear Co-operation Agreement*, vol. 1, World Focus series. (World Focus in association with Academic Excellence Publishers and Distributors).

Friedrich, E. (1904) Wesen und geographische Verbreitung der Raubwirtschaft. *Petermanns Geographische Mitteilungen*, 50, pp. 68–70, 92–95.

Gadgil, M., Prasad, S. N., and Ali, R. (1983) Forest management and forest policy in India. *Social Action*, 33(2), April–June, pp. 1–30.

Gauri, V. (2009) Public interest litigation in India: overreaching or underachieving? World Bank Policy Research Working Paper No. WPS 5109, Washington, DC.

Ghate, T. P., Takwale, M. G., and Dhole, S. (2011) Fukushima to Jaitapur: battling fear of unknown. *Radiation Protection and Environment*, 34(3), pp. 159–163.

Global Integrity (2011) Global Integrity report, India 2011, no. 48. <http://www.globalintegrity.org/report/India/2011/> (accessed 13 February 2013).

GOI (Government of India) (2009) State of the environment report: India 2009. Report by the Ministry of Environment and Forests, Government of India.

Gopalakrishnan, A. (1999) Issues of nuclear safety. *Frontline*, 16(06), March, pp. 13–26.

Govardhan, V. (1993) *Environmental Impact Assessment of Tehri Dam* (New Delhi, Ashish).

Grimston, M. C. (1996) Chernobyl and Bhopal ten years on: comparisons and contrasts, in J. Lewins and M. Becker (eds) *Advances in Nuclear Science and Technology*, vol. 24 (New York: Plenum Press), pp. 1–45.

Gruère, G. P., Mehta-Bhatt, P., and Sengupta, Debdatta (2008) Bt cotton and farmer suicides in India: reviewing the evidence. IFPRI Discussion Paper No. 00808, October.

Guha, R. (1988) Ideological trends in Indian environmentalism. *Economic and Political Weekly*, 23(49), pp. 2578–2581.

Hardiman, D. (2004) *Gandhi in His Time and Ours* (New York: Columbia University Press).

Havenaar, J. M., de Wilde, E. J., van den Bout, J., Drottz-Sjöberg, B. M., and van den Brink, W. (2003) Perception of risk and subjective health among victims of the Chernobyl disaster. *Social Science and Medicine,* 56(3), February, pp. 569–572.

Herring, R. (2009) Persistent narratives: why is the 'failure of Bt cotton in India' story still with us? *AgBioForum*, 12(1), Article 2.

India Together (2013) <http://www.indiatogether.org> (accessed 13 February 2013).

INTACH (Indian National Trust for Art and Cultural Heritage) (1987) *The Tehri Dam* (New Delhi: Indian National Trust for Art and Cultural Heritage).

INTACH (Indian National Trust for Art and Cultural Heritage) (1996) *Nuclear Energy and Public Safety* (New Delhi: Indian National Trust for Art and Cultural Heritage).

Irwin, A. and Wynne, B. (2004) *Misunderstanding Science? The Public Reconstruction of Science and Technology* (New York: Cambridge University Press).

Iyer, R. R. (2003) *Water: Perspectives, Issues, Concerns* (New Delhi: SAGE Publications).

Jasanoff, S. (2011) *Reframing Rights*: Bioconstitutionalism *in the Genetic Age* (Cambridge, MA: MIT Press).

Jones, T. (n.d.) Engineers' role at Bhopal. <http://apps.engr.utexas.edu/ethics/profresp/lesson2/engineers.cfm> (accessed 13 February 2013).

Khare, A., Sarin, M., Saxena, N. C., Palit, S., Bathla, S., Vania, F., and Satyanarayana, M. (2000) *Joint Forest Management* (New Delhi: World Wide Fund for Nature—India; London: International Institute for Environment and Development).

Laurie, V. (2008) *Effect of Bt Cotton on Small and Medium Scale Farmers' Income in the Telegana Region, Andhra Pradesh, India 2002–2005* (Halifax, NS: Saint Mary's University).

Leach, M., Scoones, I., and Wynne, B. (2005) *Science and Citizens: Globalization and the Challenge of Engagement* (London: Zed Books).

Lianchawii (2005) Biosafety in India: rethinking GMO regulation. *Economic and Political Weekly*, 40(39), 24 September, pp. 4284–4289.

Makhijani, A., Hu, H., and Yih, K., (2000). *Nuclear Wastelands* (Cambridge, MA: MIT Press).

Mathai, M. V. (2013) *Nuclear Power, Economic Development Discourse and the Environment: The Case of India* (Abingdon and New York: Routledge).

Mathur, K. (2005) Battling for clean environment: technocrats and populist politics in Delhi, in Amita Singh (ed.) *Administrative Reforms: Towards Sustainable Practices* (New Delhi: Sage Publications), pp. 189–215.

M.P. (Madhya Pradesh) Government, Bhopal Gas Tragedy Relief and Rehabilitation Department, Bhopal facts and figures. <http://www.mp.gov.in/bgtrrdmp/relief.htm> (accessed 16 March 2013).

Naik, G., Qaim, M., Subramanian, A., and Zilberman, D. (2005) Bt cotton controversy: some paradoxes explained. *Economic and Political Weekly*, 40(15), pp. 1514–1517.

Narain, U. and Bell, R. G. (2006) Who changed Delhi's air? *Economic and Political Weekly*, 41(16), pp. 1584–1588.

Negi, S. S. (1996) *Biosphere Reserves in India* (New Delhi: Indus Publishing Company).

Oliver-Smith, A. (1996) Anthropological research on hazards and disasters. *Annual Review of Anthropology*, 25, pp. 303–328. <http://www.jstor.org/stable/2155829> (accessed 19 February 2013).

Paranjpye, V. (1988) *Evaluating the Tehri Dam: An Extended Cost Benefit Appraisal* (New Delhi: Studies in Ecology and Sustainable Development, Indian National Trust for Art and Cultural Heritage).

Qaim, M., Subramanian, A., Naik, G., and Zilberman, D. (2006) Adoption of Bt cotton and impact variability: insights from India. *Review of Agricultural Economics*, 28(1), pp. 48–58.

Raj, K., Prasad, K. K., and Bansal, N. K. (2006) Radioactive waste management practices in India. *Nuclear Engineering and Design*, 7–8, April, pp. 914–930.

Rajan, S. R. (1999) Bhopal: vulnerability, routinization, and the chronic disaster, in Anthony Oliver-Smith and Susanna Hoffman (eds) *The Angry Earth: Disaster in Anthropological Perspective* (New York: Routledge), pp. 257–277.

Rajan, S. R. (2002) Missing expertise, categorical politics, and chronic disasters' in Susanna M. Hoffman and A. Oliver-Smith (eds) *Culture and Catastrophe: The Anthropology of Disaster* (Oxford: James Currey), pp. 237–262.

Rajan, S. R. (2006) *Modernizing Nature* (Oxford: Oxford University Press).

Raju, K. D. (ed.) (2007) *Genetically Modified Organisms: Emerging Law and Policy in India* (New Delhi: TERI Press).

Ramana, M. V. (2006) Nehru, science and secrecy. <http://www.geocities.ws/m_v_ramana/nucleararticles/Nehru.pdf> (accessed 13 February 2013).

Ramana, M. V. (2007) Nuclear power in India: failed past, dubious future, ISN. <http://www.isn.ethz.ch/Digital-Library/Publications/Detail/?ots591=cab359a3-9328-19cc-a1d2-8023e646b22c&lng=en&id=47566> (accessed 5 August 2013).

Ramana, M. V. and Reddy, C. R. (2003) *Prisoners of the Nuclear Dream* (Hyderabad: Orient Longman).

Ramana, M. V., D'Sa, A., and Reddy, A. (2005) Economics of nuclear power from heavy water reactors. *Economic and Political Weekly*, 40(17), 23 April.

Ramana, M. V., Thomas, D. G. and Varughese, S. (2001) Estimating nuclear waste production in India. *Current Science*, 81(11), 10 December, pp. 1458–1462.

Sahu, G. (2008) Implications of Indian Supreme Court's innovations for environmental jurisprudence. *4/1 Law, Environment and Development Journal*, 4(1) (2008), p. 1. <http://www.lead-journal.org/content/08001.pdf> (accessed 13 February 2013).

Scoones, I. (2003) *Regulatory Manoeuvres: The Bt Cotton Controversy in India,* Working Paper No. 197, Institute of Development Studies, University of Sussex.

Scoones, I. (2006) *Science, Agriculture and the Politics of Policy* (Hyderabad: Orient Blackswan).

Shah, T. (2010) Past, present and the future of canal irrigation in India (Colombo: International Water Management Institute). <http://www.rimisp.org/FCKeditor/UserFiles/File/documentos/docs/sitioindia/documentos/Paper_Tushaar_Shah.pdf> (accessed 13 February 2013).

Smith, R. and Wynne, B. (1989) *Expert Evidence: Interpreting Science in the Law* (Abingdon: Routledge).

Somanathan, E., Prabhakar, R., and Mehta, B. S. (2009) Decentralization for cost-effective conservation. *Proceedings of the National Academy of Sciences of the United States of America*, 106(11), pp. 4143–4147.

Sovacool, B. and Valentine, S. V. V. (2012) *The International Politics of Nuclear Power* (Abingdon: Routledge).

Subramanian, Arjunan and Qaim, Matin (2010) The impact of Bt cotton on poor households in rural India. *Journal of Development Studies*, 46(2), pp. 295–311.

Varma, Roli, and Varma, Daya R. (2005) The Bhopal disaster of 1984. *Bulletin of Science,*

Technology and Science. <www.indiaenvironmentportal.org.in/files/Bhopal%20 Disaster.pdf> (accessed 13 February 2013).

Véron, R. (2006) Remaking urban environments: the political ecology of air pollution in Delhi. *Environment and Planning A*, 38(11), pp. 2093–2109.

WHO (World Health Organization) (2011) Global burden of disease report, 2010. <http://www.who.int/topics/global_burden_of_disease/en/> (accessed 13 February 2013).

Wynne, B. (1989) Sheepfarming after Chernobyl — a case study in communicating scientific information. *Environment*, 31(2), pp. 10–15 and 33–39.

Wynne, B. (2012) *Risk Management and Hazardous Waste: Implementation and the Dialectics of Credibility* (Heidelberg: Springer-Verlag).

Wynne, P. B. (2010) *Rationality and Ritual: Participation and Exclusion in Nuclear Decision-making* (Abingdon: Routledge).

Index

Africa, trade links with 3, 4, 10, 72, 83, 86, 89, 90
ageing population 28, 35, 73, 95–111, 115–130
agriculture 4, 6, 8, 10, 12–13, 17, 29, 32–33, 35, 47–54, 59, 78–79, 108, 157–163, 168–169, 179–182, 195–197
  crisis in 162–165
  employment in 32–33, 35, 108, 120, 157, 161–163, 165
  productivity in 4–5, 13, 19, 35, 52–54, 157, 161, 163, 165, 180–182, 189, 195, 197–198
  research 53
  technology of 180–182
aid 4, 80, 88–89
arranged marriage 12, 102, 121–124
autarkic policies 77, 80

bachelors 102–103, 106–108, 122
balance of payments 78–82, 85–87, 90
bank nationalization (India) 1969 57–58
Bhopal gas disaster (1984) 193, 199–202, 207
brideprice 103, 119, 123

Cai Fang 36–37, 41
capital account 9, 79–83, 85
capital accumulation 49–50, 57–59, 169–170, 177, 188, 190
capital inflows and outflows 79

capital market 39, 67, 72
carbon emissions 16–17, 91, 175, 179, 184–188, 195
casualization of employment 12, 102, 120, 163, 166–168
child and infant mortality 7, 11, 96, 98, 115–116, 118, 121
child labour 162, 165–166
childcare 34, 108–109, 128, 130
children 7, 11, 13, 15, 34, 96–102, 107–110, 116–120, 125–126, 128, 148, 162, 165–166
Chinese Communist Party (CCP) 1–2, 37, 102
Chipko movement 198
city policy 138–139, 141–142, 148, 152
climate change 16, 17, 88, 91, 175, 182, 184–185, 188, 195–196
climate stabilization 184–189
competitive society 101–102, 121, 125
construction 8, 32, 34, 36, 41, 51, 56, 143, 146, 166–168
consumption as proportion of GDP 5–6, 8, 10, 27–28, 30–31, 33, 36–39, 42–43, 66–67, 87–88, 188
contraception 115–116
corruption 1, 18, 127, 189, 196, 198

daughter aversion 115, 118, 124, 127, 130
debt as percentage of GDP 5
debt inflows 83, 85
decarbonization 17–18, 185–186, 189

deforestation 185, 197–198

democracy 197–199, 206–207

demography

　change 2, 10–12, 35, 65, 73, 88, 95–111, 115–130, 145–146, 161

　　dividend 12, 101, 119–120, 127, 130

　　of migrants 145–146

dependency ratio 12, 28, 100–101, 120

diaspora 86–87

dibao (Minimum Livelihood Guarantee) 36, 38–40

discrimination against rural migrants to cities 15, 139–149

disease 7, 10, 17, 95, 115, 129, 179, 199

dispossession 158, 169

domestic economy 3, 8, 27–43, 47–59

dowry 103, 118–119, 121–124, 126–127, 130

dualism 4, 8, 51, 59

ecology

　deficit 179

　footprint 17, 178–179, 193–194

　sustainability 16–19, 175–190, 193–207

economy

　crisis of 1991 (India) 1, 78, 81, 87

　domestic 3, 8, 27–43, 47–59

　growth 2–9, 13–19, 27–28, 30, 32–38, 41–43, 47–59, 65–66, 68, 70, 73–74, 77–81, 84–88, 90, 95, 120, 150, 157, 160, 162–165, 168, 170, 175–179, 181, 183–190, 194

　growth limits 175–190

　informal 1, 3–4, 13–15, 29, 51–52, 120, 159–160, 163, 165, 167–170

　policy 8, 29–30, 33, 35–36, 38, 41–42, 54, 57–58, 68–70, 72, 78–83

　protection 5, 53, 69, 77–78

　reforms 1, 47, 53, 55, 57–59, 157

　reforms 1991 78, 80

　stimulus package (1990s) 37; (2008) 8, 15, 34, 36–38, 41, 150

　structural change in 48, 50, 52

education 7–8, 13, 15, 27, 36, 38, 42, 73, 86, 89, 96, 101–104, 108, 116–118, 120, 122, 124–125, 127–128, 140, 142, 146, 148, 151, 164, 170, 198

elderly people 12–13, 100, 109–111, 124, 127–130

emergency of 1970s (India) 11, 166

emissions reduction 184–187

employment 3–4, 8, 12–14, 29, 32–39, 41–42, 49, 51–52, 56, 59, 65–66, 74, 85, 102, 108–109, 119–125, 127, 130, 157–170, 178, 188

　good quality 163–164, 168

　laws 14, 85, 159, 165, 188–189

　security 102, 120–121, 124, 146, 159, 166–168

energy

　efficiency 18, 186, 189

　use 10, 18, 36, 175, 178–181, 188, 199

environment 2, 4, 16–18, 33, 37–38, 56, 65, 73, 91, 175–190, 193–212

　crisis 16–17, 175–179

　degradation 175, 178, 181, 189, 194, 206

　governance 196–203

　impact 73, 175–177, 183, 189

　protection 37, 56, 73, 203

　regulation 188–189

　risks 193, 196–197, 199–206

exchange rate 6, 66, 70, 85, 88, 90–91

exports 3–4, 6, 8–9, 27, 30, 33–34, 37, 39, 41–42, 47, 52, 55, 58–59, 65–67, 69–70, 73–74, 77, 79–80, 88–90, 160, 184

　proportion of GDP 77, 79

family planning 11, 97, 107

family size 10–11, 95–99, 116

famine 18, 95–96

female child mortality 118, 121

fertility 10–11, 95–101, 107–109, 115–121, 124

　decline 11, 95–101, 107–109, 115–121, 123–130

　decline, regional variation 115–117, 120, 123–125, 130

financial deregulation 81, 86–87

floating population 140–144

food availability 15–17, 27, 33, 86, 95, 98, 115, 141, 146, 168, 175, 179–180, 182, 186, 195

foreign acquisitions by Indian companies 81–84

foreign companies 3, 29, 55, 65, 67–70

foreign currency reserves 4, 70

foreign direct investment (FDI) 3, 9, 29, 55, 65–74, 78–85, 143–144

   inward FDI 65–70, 74, 80–84, 143–144

   outward FDI 65–67, 70–72, 74, 81–84, 86

foreign exchange 1, 4, 66, 79

foreign portfolio investment 80–81, 83

forestry 14, 193, 195–198, 206

fossil fuel 10, 16–17, 179, 182, 185–187

Gandhi, Indira 57

gender bias 12, 117, 119, 123

gender imbalance 28, 96–110, 121

genetically modified organisms (GMOs) 193, 199–200, 203–204, 207

geographical mobility 109, 139–152

girls, discrimination against 11, 28, 97–98, 107–108, 117–118

global engagement 77–88

global impact 88, 90

global warming 91, 184–186

government

   economic policy 8, 29–30, 33, 35–36, 38, 41–42, 54, 57–58, 68–70, 72, 78–83

   social policy 87, 96–97, 188–189, 196–197, 199, 203

great growth debate 57–58

Great Leap Forward 35, 97

Green Revolution 52–53

greenhouse gases 16–18, 178, 180, 184–185

growth and employment, relationship between 13–14, 85–86, 158–171

growth model 9, 33, 35–37, 41–43, 58, 78, 178–179, 187

health care 5, 7, 8, 12–15, 17, 36, 38, 43, 67, 73, 83, 86, 95–96, 108–109, 120, 127, 129, 142, 149, 170, 178–179, 195–196, 199, 202

home-working 164

household

   consumption 5, 28, 30, 43, 66–67, 86–87, 123

   income 28–31, 33, 37, 40, 43, 66, 161, 165–166, 178

   registration system (*hukou*) 14–15, 27, 33, 140–141, 144, 150–151

housing 8, 36, 38, 141, 146, 148, 151

human rights 148, 151, 193, 198, 206

import restrictions 77–78

imports, proportion of GDP 79–80, 184

income

   inequality 2, 6, 27–28, 32–33, 36, 39–40, 43, 66, 86–87, 96, 99, 101, 120, 123, 142, 165, 177–178

   maintenance transfers (*dibao*) 38–40

   per capita 6, 29, 31, 33, 39, 48–50

   redistribution 37, 85–86, 188–189

industry

   industrial relations 15–16, 166–167

   industrial restructuring 68–69

   industrialization 3, 18, 47, 77, 85, 99, 141, 165, 197, 202

inequality, urban and rural 6, 27–28, 31–32, 99

infanticide 11, 98

informal economy 1, 3–4, 13–15, 29, 51–52, 120, 159–160, 163, 165, 167–170

information technology (IT) services 9, 55, 65, 79–80, 84, 87, 160

infrastructure investment 34, 36–38, 43, 58–59, 66, 68–69, 73, 150, 177, 186

innovation 3, 19, 38, 54, 65–70, 72–74

intellectual property rights 68, 70

interest rates 5, 28, 30, 43, 66, 85

intergenerational contract 12, 101, 109–111, 115, 119, 121, 127–130

international economy 65–74, 77–91
internationalization of companies 65, 72–73
IPAT formula 178, 186
irrigation 36, 53, 179–182, 193, 196–199, 202, 206

job creation 8, 13, 29, 37, 39, 55, 59, 85, 120, 125, 130, 164
jobless growth 13–14, 36–37, 120, 160–161, 163, 168

knowledge sector 3, 59, 70

labour
    excluded 14, 160, 167, 169–170
    labour/land ratio 53
    market 6, 15, 34–35, 39, 41, 85, 99, 101, 108, 163, 165, 188–189
    shortages 34–35, 37, 41, 150
    skilled 9–10, 19, 53, 55–56, 58–59, 70, 86, 90–91, 165
    surplus 28–29, 33–35, 42, 99
    unions 15–16, 29, 166–168
    unskilled 85–86, 164
land
    degradation 179, 194–195
    landlordism 158–159
    ownership 129, 158–159
Lewis model 34–35, 41–42
liberalization 3, 6, 9, 29, 54, 78, 81, 83–86, 123, 160, 165, 168
Licence Raj 9, 54, 59, 78
life expectancy 10, 73, 95–96, 109, 127
low-skilled workers 86–87, 143

malnutrition 7, 10, 18
manufacturing 3, 8, 36–37, 47–52, 54–56, 59, 80, 143, 147, 158, 165–166, 168
Maoists (India) 158
market
    market-based economy 29, 101, 188
    market-oriented economic reforms 57, 95–96, 143–144
marriage 101–108, 118–124

marriage age 12, 102–104, 107–108, 115, 120, 124
marriage market 28, 101–108, 118–126, 130
marriage migration 12, 101, 103, 105–106, 125–126
    patrilocal 118–119, 124–126
    squeeze 119, 121–123
medical services 95, 98, 151
migrants' workers 35–36, 39–41, 102, 139–152
    living conditions 148–152
    remittances 10, 80, 86–87, 110, 140, 149–150
    rights, campaign for 150
    working conditions 146–147, 151
migration
    consequences 149–150
    extent of 144
    external 9–10, 331, 83, 86–87
    internal 14–15, 33, 99–100, 139–150, 163
    seasonal 163
military expenditure 6–7
mineral resources 176, 188
Minimum Livelihood Guarantee (*dibao*) 36, 38–40
mortality 95–96, 115
multinational companies 4, 71, 80–81, 83–84, 86

natural resources 27, 29, 175–177, 179, 182–183, 185–186
New Delhi pollution and transport policy 193, 200, 203–204
non-agricultural rural employment 33–35, 51–52, 162–163
non-renewable resources 175–177, 179, 182–183, 185
nuclear power 186, 193, 199–200, 204–206

obesity 10
oil 182–184
one child family policy 11, 73, 97–99, 107, 109

organization of informal workers 167–168
outsourcing to India 80

Panchayati Raj system of local
    government 1
patrilocal marriage 118–119, 124–126
pensions 38–39, 109, 127, 149
planned economy 141–142, 177
political protest 15, 158, 163, 167–168
pollution 17, 176–179, 193–195, 199–200,
    202–203
population 97, 161, 176–177, 179, 185,
    193
poverty 6, 53, 162, 170, 195
poverty reduction 8, 51, 85
private enterprise 188–189
private investment 3
private ownership 3, 178
productivity 4, 41–42, 49–54, 57–59, 70,
    84, 165, 195
prostitution 12, 108
public investment 57–58
public ownership 189
public sector 3, 54
public services 142–143, 178
public spending 196, 198
public transport 36, 43, 202–203

rationing 141–143
rebalancing 3, 27, 35, 37, 41–43, 189
recession of 2008, effects of 35–36
regional inequality 27, 39–40, 66
residence permits 151
resources
    constraints 87
    consumption of 176–177, 182
    management 193–194, 196–199, 206
    renewable 175–177, 186
restructure of 1990s 30
restructuring 65–69
retail sector 167
retirement age 109
risk management 201–207
rural distress 163–165
rural employment programmes 8, 168

rural infrastructure 36, 38
rural migrant labour (*nongmingong*)
    141–142
rural–urban migration 33, 99, 139–150,
    163

sanitation 7
savings 5–6, 27–28, 30, 33, 58, 66–67, 78,
    110
schools for migrant children 148
self-employment 14, 147, 159–160,
    163–164, 166, 168
self-reliance 77
service sector 3–4, 47–52, 55, 59, 67, 147,
    158, 160, 168
sex bias 123–125
sex ratios 97–100, 102, 106–107, 117,
    119
sex-selective abortion 11, 98–99, 117–118,
    121, 127
slums 15
small and medium enterprises (SMEs) 5,
    29, 57, 67
small-scale producers 158
social security 51, 148–149
son preference 124–127
species extinction 193, 195
state
    monopolies 5, 54, 57
    support for capitalism 1, 57
    state-owned corporations 86
    state-owned enterprises (SOEs) 3, 5, 29,
        30, 32, 42, 54–55, 67, 70, 72, 178
statist model of development 78
supply-side structures 4–5

tariffs 77–78
tax
    income 33, 68
    taxation 2, 29, 188–189, 197
    taxsharing 2
technological innovation 3
technological progress 176–177, 182, 197
Tehri Dam 193, 200, 202, 207
telecommunications 3, 67, 55, 83

trade
  between India and China 86
  hotel and restaurants sector 55
  liberalization 3, 59, 78, 84–85
trafficking of women 12, 108, 123

unemployment 15, 29, 35–36, 74, 102, 120, 122, 149
unions 15–16, 29, 166–168
unskilled labour 85–86, 164
urban management 142–143
urbanization 14–15, 48, 56, 96, 99, 126, 181

wage arrears 147, 151
wages 8, 15–16, 18, 29, 33–35, 41–42, 51, 66, 70, 86, 143, 146–147, 150–151, 159, 162–165, 168, 188–189
  agricultural 162–163

water 16, 18, 29, 36, 87, 141, 176, 178–179, 181–182, 194–199, 202
welfare 7, 14–15, 38–40, 42–43, 86, 109–110, 142, 148, 150–151, 167–168, 170, 188
Wen Jiabao 36, 68, 147
widows 127–128
women
  autonomy 116, 118–119, 121
  trafficking of 12, 108, 123
  violence against 120, 124, 126
  workforce participation 5, 12–13, 96, 108, 120, 124, 130, 163–166, 198
working conditions 140, 146–147
World Economic Forum 36
World Trade Organization 9, 42, 67

Xi Jinping 68